Jesus Amplified

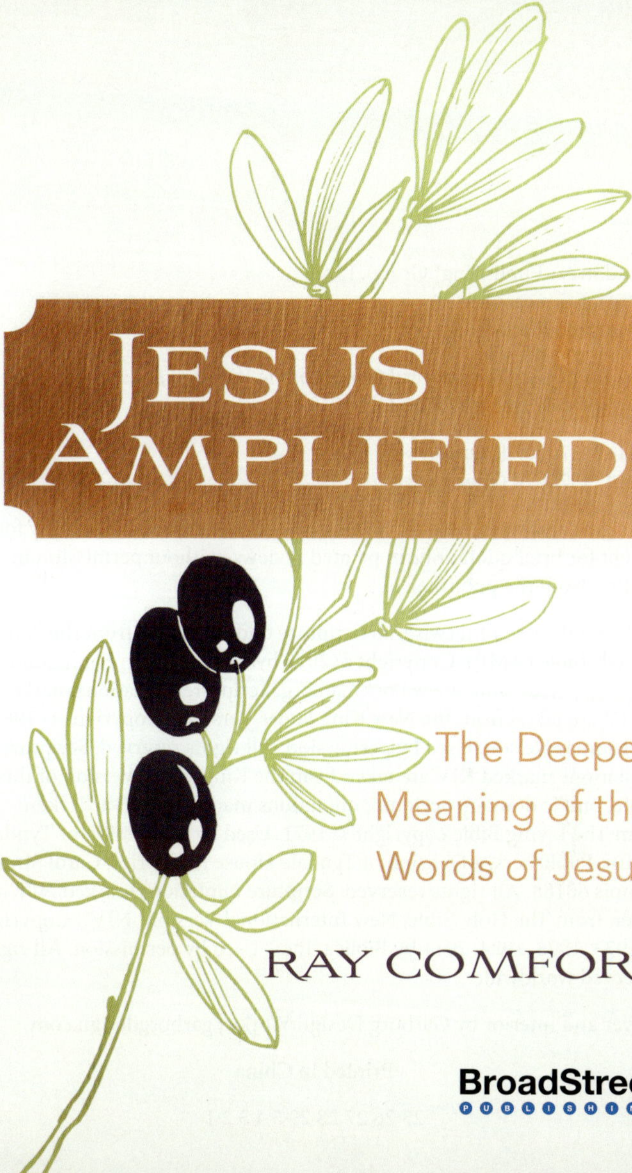

The Deeper Meaning of the Words of Jesus

Ray Comfort

BroadStreet Publishing

BroadStreet Publishing® Group, LLC
Savage, Minnesota, USA
BroadStreetPublishing.com

9781424570607 (faux)
9781424570614 (ebook)

Cover and interior by Garborg Design Works | garborgdesign.com

Printed in China

25 26 27 28 29 5 4 3 2 1

To Julia Zwayne

Introduction

I have always loved the Amplified Bible. It gives me a different perspective on Scripture passages with which I had become very familiar.

For that different perspective, take the English word "love." When texting first started using the "love heart" emoji, it took some time for me to feel comfortable sending it to men. This is because there is only one word for "love" in English. But the Greek language has an amazing eight different words.[1] Let's look at three.

Eros is the type of love that involves passion, lust, or romance. *Philia* is an affectionate love. *Philia* is the type of love that involves friendship. It is *philia* that I'm expressing to men when texting the love heart. Then there is *agape*. *Agape* is often defined as an unconditional, sacrificial love, and that word expresses the love that God has for us.

It's because of the richness of the Greek language and my love for Jesus that I have thoroughly enjoyed combining the two in *Jesus Amplified.* I hope you enjoy it as well.

Also, I would like to express my special thanks to Brad Snow for his work in generating the amazing pictures in this devotional.

May God bless and keep all of you.

Ray Comfort

September 2024

---

1 "8 Greek Words for Love That Will Make Your Heart Soar," Dictionary.com, March 28, 2024, https://www.dictionary.com/e/greek-words-for-love.

January

The temptation of Jesus in the wilderness (Matthew 4:1–11)

Permitting Things in Life

Jesus replied to him, "Permit it just now; for this is the fitting way for us to fulfill all righteousness." Then John permitted it [and baptized Him].

MATTHEW 3:15

The event in today's Scripture passage happened when Jesus met John the Baptist at the River Jordan. John had been preaching a baptism of repentance for the forgiveness of sins. When Jesus approached him to be baptized, John was initially reluctant. He recognized that Jesus was without sin and felt unworthy to baptize him. By submitting to baptism, Jesus was identifying with the sinful humanity he came to save. This prefigured his sacrificial death on the cross, where he fully identified with human sin and took it upon himself.

Sometimes we have to permit things to happen in life even when they make no sense. John had been baptizing sinners who came to him confessing their sins. It made sense for him to do that. But Jesus said, "Permit it just now." When logic and reason leave us, faith fills in the vacuum. And that's fitting. All is well. There's peace in the storm because God is in control. He has a plan, and we submit to his infinite wisdom because we are his.

Father, when I can't see the future, I gladly take hold of your faithful hand.

It Was Written Forever

Jesus replied, "It is written and forever remains written, 'Man shall not live by bread alone, but by every word that comes out of the mouth of God.'"

MATTHEW

The devil had tempted Jesus to turn stones into fresh bread. But Jesus resisted the temptation and quoted the Scriptures. All Scripture is written by the inspiration of God and is profitable (2 Timothy 3:16), and when God writes something, as Jesus said, "Scripture cannot be broken" (John 10:35 KJV). And that's what Jesus was saying here.

In other words, if it was divinely inspired it is utterly reliable because, like God, Scripture doesn't change. He is as good as his Word. How wonderful it is that in such a changing world—where we can't trust that what is said to be true today will still be considered true tomorrow—the Bible is true forever. The eternal Bread of Life was broken for us. He fully became a human being and dwelled among us so we could eat of the bread of heaven both now and forevermore.

Father, my heart beats with never-ending gratitude for Jesus and the cross.

On the Other Hand

Jesus said to him, "On the other hand, it is written and forever remains written, 'You shall not test the Lord your God.'"

MATTHEW 4:7, QUOTING DEUTERONOMY 6:16

Jesus had been led by the Holy Spirit into the wilderness to be tempted by the devil. This temptation occurred after Jesus had been fasting for forty days and nights. The Bible tells us that he was hungry. If we went for forty days and nights without food, most of us would be more than hungry. We would be close to death, depending on our state of health. And it was at that low point for Jesus that the Enemy came to him and said, "If You are the Son of God, command that these stones become bread" (Matthew 4:3 NKJV).

It is when we are at our lowest point that the Enemy will whisper to us to do something we know that would cause God to frown. Perhaps it's a temptation to allow bitterness, revenge, anger, hatred, greed, or lust have its way. Don't do it! Instead, "submit to God. Resist the devil and he will flee from you" (James 4:7 NKJV). Always look beyond the Father of Lies to your Father in heaven.

Father, help me always submit to your will first and resist the will of the devil.

It Forever Remains

Jesus said to him, "Go away, Satan! For it is written and forever remains written, 'You shall worship the Lord *your God, and serve Him only.'"*

Matthew 4:10, quoting Deuteronomy 6:13

The temptation in the wilderness was intense for forty days and forty nights. Satan had tempted Jesus in the area of his appetite by suggesting that he turn stones to bread. Then he tempted Jesus to take his own life, and finally the devil offered Jesus the world—if he would become a Satan worshipper. But you should never listen to the Father of Lies. Rather, listen to Scripture:

> Do not love the world or the things in the world. If anyone loves the world, the love of the Father is not in him. For all that *is* in the world—the lust of the flesh, the lust of the eyes, and the pride of life—is not of the Father but is of the world. (1 John 2:15–16 NKJV)

Whatever you do in this life, don't be tempted to listen to the whispering of the devil. If we love this evil world, we are bowing to the god of this world—Satan.

Father, never let me be tempted to love this sinful world. Deliver me from evil.

Regret Past Sins

From that time Jesus began to preach and say, "Repent [change your inner self—your old way of thinking, regret past sins, live your life in a way that proves repentance; seek God's purpose for your life], for the kingdom of heaven is at hand."

MATTHEW 4:17

Some wrongly believe that repentance isn't a turning from sin but a turning from unbelief to believing in Jesus. In other words, they think repentance has nothing to do with the sins of lying, stealing, greed, hatred, blasphemy, fornication, adultery, and idolatry. But the Scriptures make it clear that repentance is turning from sins (plural):

- "Repent ye therefore, and be converted, that your sins may be blotted out" (Acts 3:19 KJV; this refers to "sins," not to the "sin" of unbelief).
- "Unto you first God, having raised up his Son Jesus, sent him to bless you, in turning away every one of you from his iniquities" (Acts 3:26 KJV; "iniquities" is plural, not the singular sin of unbelief).
- "It behooved Christ to suffer, and to rise from the dead the third day: and that repentance and remission of sins [plural] should be preached in his name among all nations" (Luke 24:46–47 KJV).

Father, help me always to follow the example of Jesus by preaching that sinners must turn from their sin.

He Didn't Say That

He said to them, "Follow Me [as My disciples, accepting Me as your Master and Teacher and walking the same path of life that I walk], and I will make you fishers of men."

MATTHEW

Jesus could have said, "Follow me and you will see people miraculously healed. You will be eyewitnesses of the blind seeing and the deaf hearing. You will also see people raised from the dead—as well as seeing me walk on water and have the stormy wind and the sea obey me." But he didn't say that.

Instead he chose to state the ultimate reason for him being born. He had come to seek and save that which was lost. He came to fish for men, and if we are following him, that should be our number one priority. We mustn't forget the reason that God gave his Holy Spirit to the church: to give us power to reach the lost. "You shall receive power when the Holy Spirit has come upon you; and you shall be witnesses to Me in Jerusalem, and in all Judea and Samaria, and to the end of the earth" (Acts 1:8 NKJV).

Father, never let fear or wrong priorities cause me to neglect the Great Commission.

I Am Rich

"Blessed [spiritually prosperous, happy, to be admired] are the poor in spirit [those devoid of spiritual arrogance, those who regard themselves as insignificant], for theirs is the kingdom of heaven [both now and forever]."

MATTHEW 5:3

We are highly favored when we see ourselves in truth—that we are poor in spirit. We know that we can do nothing and are nothing without God. He gave us the very breath we breathe. But those are to be pitied who claim to be rich and in need of nothing, not knowing that they are "wretched, miserable, poor, blind, and naked" (Revelation 3:17 NKJV). But that is the delusion of self-righteousness. Like the rich young ruler, who in essence proclaimed his own goodness, we need the law to humble us and expose our shame.

Such understanding causes us to thirst after the righteousness of God in Christ. Blessed are those who have the light of that understanding because that is our first step toward the cross. The law acts as a schoolmaster to bring us to Christ (Galatians 3:24).

Father, it is the revelation of my sinful state that causes me to trust in grace alone and not in my works.

Sins Forgiven and Forgotten

"Blessed [forgiven, refreshed by God's grace] are those who mourn [over their sins and repent], for they will be comforted [when the burden of sin is lifted]."

MATTHEW 5:4

Listen to Scripture address the careless sinner as he enjoys the pleasures of sin for a season:

> Draw near to God and He will draw near to you. Cleanse your hands, you sinners; and purify your hearts, you double-minded. Lament and mourn and weep! Let your laughter be turned to mourning and your joy to gloom. (James 4:8–9 NKJV)

The prodigal son had his season of laughter, but famine left him miserable as he sat alone in the pigsty. God's law puts the careless, sin-embracing sinner alone in the pigsty, helping him to see that his appetites are unclean.

What a paradox that we mourn over sin but at the same time rejoice with joy unspeakable because God no longer sees those sins. The prodigal son no doubt never forgot the pigsty after he returned to enjoy his father's kindness. He had a robe over his shoulders, a ring on his finger, and a fatted calf as evidence that all was forgiven and forgotten.

Father, I am ever thankful that my sins are forgiven and forgotten by you.

They Are Strong

"Blessed [inwardly peaceful, spiritually secure, worthy of respect] are the gentle [the kind-hearted, the sweet-spirited, the self-controlled], for they will inherit the earth."

MATTHEW 5:5

The world considers the meek to be weak, like a tiny trembling mouse trapped helplessly in the corner of a large room. But the meek are strong because they trust in God (2 Corinthians 12:9–11). Their feet are fixed firmly upon the immutable promises of the God who cannot lie (Hebrews 6:18). Their meekness also rests in the knowledge that God is for them. Nothing makes them panic because they are spiritually secure on the Rock of Ages. And in that strength, they manifest the fruit of the Spirit. "The fruit of the Spirit is love, joy, peace, longsuffering, kindness, goodness, faithfulness, gentleness, self-control. Against such there is no law" (Galatians 5:22–23 NKJV).

Jesus said that he was both meek and lowly of heart (Matthew 11:29). That state was his strength, and it is our strength as we trust solely in him. "What then shall we say to these things? If God is for us, who can be against us?" (Romans 8:31 NKJV).

Father, weak though I am, in you I am strong because you favor me in Christ.

The Water That Satisfies

"Blessed [joyful, nourished by God's goodness] are those who hunger and thirst for righteousness [those who actively seek right standing with God], for they will be [completely] satisfied."

MATTHEW 5:6

In John 4, the woman at the well came to draw water, not knowing who would be waiting for her. When she met Jesus, she was mystified that he, as a Jew, would talk to her, an outcast Samaritan, and ask her for a drink. It was then when Jesus spoke of the water that completely satisfies—the Water of Life.

The burning sun often causes human beings to thirst for water. And it is the heat of God's law showing sinners their desperate state before a holy God that causes us to thirst for righteousness. Until we are confronted by our sin, we do not thirst for God or for righteousness. The Scriptures tell us that there is none who seek after God and that the only thing we thirst for is iniquity, which we drink in like water. That's why the moral law is so important. That brings us the knowledge of sin and shows us that we desperately need God's mercy.

Father, thank you so much for the law, which was a schoolmaster to bring me to Christ.

The Stealer of Contentment

"Blessed [content, sheltered by God's promises] are the merciful, for they will receive mercy."
MATTHEW 5:7

Nothing steals contentment like an unmerciful attitude. It's the hidden eggshell in our omelet, and it shouldn't be there for any Christian. If somebody sins against us and we don't have a merciful attitude, what should be a molehill suddenly becomes a mountain that will cast a shadow over everything we do.

This world's quest for happiness often ends in disillusionment because people miss the riches of contentment. They are in the continual pursuit of happiness, but we can be content with what we have because we have the promises of God today. There's no need for any pursuit. These promises are more to be desired than gold—they are both precious and exceedingly great (1 Peter 1:4).

We are nothing more than forgiven wretched sinners, and because we know what we are, we should never allow an unmerciful attitude into our hearts. That's why the merciful person is (as the original Greek language tells us) "blessed [content, sheltered by God's promises]."

Father, I will be content with what I have because you said you'll never leave nor forsake me.

Comfort in the Beatitudes

"Blessed [anticipating God's presence, spiritually mature] are the pure in heart [those with integrity, moral courage, and godly character], for they will see God."

Matthew 5:8

While the Christian (because of God's grace) can take comfort from the Beatitudes, when we look at them outside of God's mercy in Christ, they condemn us. The Scriptures ask:

> Who may ascend into the hill of the Lord?
> Or who may stand in His holy place?
> He who has clean hands and a pure heart,
> Who has not lifted up his soul to an idol,
> Nor sworn deceitfully. (Psalm 24:3–4 NKJV)

Those who think they are going to heaven and will see God *because* they have a pure heart will be sorely disappointed. Even the best person among us isn't pure of heart. "The heart is deceitful above all things, and desperately wicked; who can know it?" (Jeremiah 17:9 NKJV).

A person who believes he is pure in heart is one who has lifted up his soul to an idol. The popular image the world has of God is one of a bearded man in the sky—just one of many idolatrous conceptions of the infinite, almighty God. We can control and manipulate our idols. After all, we created them! But if we want to know the true God, we must move beyond our false beliefs about him and embrace what his Word teaches us about the great "I AM" (Exodus 3:14).

Father, help me to always see you as Holy Scripture portrays you.

Beautiful Feet

"Blessed [spiritually calm with life-joy in God's favor] are the makers and maintainers of peace, for they will [express His character and] be called the sons of God."

MATTHEW 5:9

The Bible speaks of different types of peace. It tells us about a peace that passes all understanding. This is the peace that is one of the fruits of the Holy Spirit. There is a peace that is the absence of noise, and there's the type of peace that is the absence of war.

Christians are called to be peacemakers, and our aim is to bring about peace between man and God. "How shall they preach unless they are sent? As it is written: 'How beautiful are the feet of those who preach the gospel of peace, who bring glad tidings of good things!'" (Romans 10:15 NKJV). While we would commend those who want to stop noise or bring a halt to the tragedy of wars, heaven commends those who preach the gospel of peace. It even says that the lowliest (and arguably ugliest) parts of our body, our feet, are beautiful if we preach the gospel of peace.

Father, help me to be faithful to proclaim the good news of the gospel.

All Who Live Godly Shall Suffer

"Blessed [comforted by inner peace and God's love] are those who are persecuted for doing that which is morally right, for theirs is the kingdom of heaven [both now and forever]."

MATTHEW 5:10

The sinful world resists God for the same reason darkness resists light—it exposes what is hidden and calls for change. Yet standing for God and his righteousness brings immense blessing.

The Bible assures us that "all who desire to live godly in Christ Jesus will suffer persecution" (2 Timothy 3:12 NKJV). But this is not a cause for despair; it is a badge of honor. When you side with God, you are his ambassador, shining his love and truth. The world may reject you, but heaven celebrates your faithfulness, and you are blessed because of it.

The apostles in Acts rejoiced in suffering for Christ. Stephen, as he was stoned, saw the heavens open. James, though struck down by the king's sword, received his eternal reward. Paul endured beatings and trials but found joy in his mission, knowing his faithfulness glorified God.

To suffer for Christ is to be blessed, for it identifies you with his victory, his righteousness, and his eternal kingdom.

Father, help me always to rejoice in the midst of persecution.

Moral Courage

"Blessed [morally courageous and spiritually alive with life-joy in God's goodness] are you when people insult you and persecute you, and falsely say all kinds of evil things against you because of [your association with] Me."

MATTHEW 5:11

Do you remember what Peter did when he was accused of associating with Jesus? He denied knowing him an amazing three times, something he said he would never do. But that happened before the day of Pentecost—when he received the power to boldly proclaim the gospel (Acts 1:8).

Now you and I have no excuse to deny the Lord. We should never be ashamed to be associated with Jesus Christ, even if the whole world hates him. To be "blessed" in the original Greek means to be "morally courageous." As witnesses of Christ, we can and must boldly stand for the cause of righteousness, as Peter so often did in the face of very real persecution in the book of Acts. "Now when they saw the boldness of Peter and John, and perceived that they were uneducated and untrained men, they marveled. And they realized that they had been with Jesus" (Acts 4:13 NKJV).

Father, may I never forget the moral courage that drove Jesus to the cross.

Your Reward in Heaven Is Great

"Be glad and exceedingly joyful, for your reward in heaven is great [absolutely inexhaustible]; for in this same way they persecuted the prophets who were before you."

MATTHEW 5:12

As we often find with our Christian walk, the words of Jesus from today's Scripture passage seem to be contrary to common sense. He told us that when the world hates us and even tries to kill us, we should be glad and exceedingly joyful. For the world, it doesn't make sense, but to us, it does because Jesus gave us the reason we should rejoice in the face of terrible persecution. He said that the same thing had happened to the godly who suffered persecution for the sake of righteousness. When we suffer for the cause of the gospel, we are standing arm and arm with Isaiah and Jeremiah and so many of the prophets of the Old Testament. What a privilege we have!

Listen to Scripture speak of these men and women. "They were stoned, they were sawn in two, were tempted, were slain with the sword. They wandered about in sheepskins and goatskins, being destitute, afflicted, tormented—of whom the world was not worthy" (Hebrews 11:37–38 NKJV).

Father, thank you for the honor of standing with those whom you have honored in the past.

Good for Nothing

"You are the salt of the earth; but if the salt has lost its taste (purpose), how can it be made salty? It is no longer good for anything, but to be thrown out and walked on by people [when the walkways are wet and slippery]."

MATTHEW 5:13

At the time of Christ, salt was mainly used to preserve food. When Jesus referred to his disciples being the "salt of the earth," it suggests that he meant for them to be preservatives in the world, preserving goodness, truth, moral integrity, and particularly the proclamation of the gospel. But here, it seems, we also have reference to the contemporary church. The church is supposed to have a very real influence in the world, but it has lost its purpose.

Ask the average person for the purpose of the church and they will probably say it exists for weddings and funerals. But we as the church should be more than that. We should be a lighthouse in the stormy darkness of life, steering perishing sinners to the safety of the Savior. When we stop doing that, we are good for nothing but to be thrown out by this world and despised because we have become distasteful.

Father, this day I pray that I will be an influence for good in this evil world.

Light of the World

"You are the light of [Christ to] the world. A city set on a hill cannot be hidden; nor does anyone light a lamp and put it under a basket, but on a lampstand, and it gives light to all who are in the house."

MATTHEW 5:14–15

Nobody appreciates light like someone who has known it and then becomes blind. We tend to take light for granted because we have it during the day and have access to it during the night. But without it, we would truly be in darkness. Yet Jesus isn't speaking of physical light in Matthew 5 but rather the light that comes from him as the Light of the World. He told his disciples, "I am the light of the world. He who follows Me shall not walk in darkness, but have the light of life" (John 8:12 NKJV).

The moment we were born again and had Christ in our hearts, we had the light of life living within us. And Jesus said to let our light shine because that sort of light cannot be hidden. We can let our light shine through our good works or through the preaching of the gospel, which the Bible calls "the glorious light" (2 Corinthians 4:4 TLB).

Father, shine your glorious light through me today.

The Skeptic's Mouth-Stopper

"Let your light shine before men in such a way that they may see your good deeds and moral excellence, and [recognize and honor and] glorify your Father who is in heaven."
MATTHEW 5:16

When we drop money into the collection bag, we're not to blow a trumpet (Matthew 6:2). Instead, we shouldn't let our left hand know what our right hand is doing (v. 3). The gift is a secret between God and yourself. Jesus said that when you keep it a secret, he will reward you openly (v. 4). However, not so with our good works. Jesus said that we should let the world see these. Our good works show the lost that we genuinely love God and love people.

The Scriptures further tell us that by our doing good for others, we "put to silence the ignorance" of the foolish (1 Peter 2:15 NKJV). In other words, when they see that we're rich in good works, they are also seeing "moral excellence." The good Samaritan was displaying this moral excellence (Luke 10:25–37). One good deed can speak more to the heart of a skeptic than a thousand sermons. Therefore, we should keep our eyes peeled for opportunities to let that light shine.

Father, please give me opportunities to let my light shine before men.

A Satisfied Law

"Do not think that I came to do away with or undo the Law [of Moses] or the [writings of the] Prophets; I did not come to destroy but to fulfill."

MATTHEW 5:17

It's interesting that Jesus said that his hearers were not to think that he was doing away with the law of Moses or the Prophets. The Bible tells us that the natural (carnal) mind of men is in a state of hostility toward God and specifically his law (Romans 8:7). They would, therefore, like nothing better than for the divine law to be done away with. They would like a society where no one is responsible to God for his actions or his thoughts.

We may as well try to get rid of the law of gravity than to get rid of the law of God. It is eternal, written in stone, and a manifestation of the character of God, which never changes. It's always wrong to lie, steal, murder, commit adultery, and so on, and it is an understanding of the spiritual nature of the law that brings the knowledge of sin. This pushes us toward the mercy of God (Galatians 3:24).

Father, help me to warn the world of your unchanging and holy nature.

It Is Finished!

"For I assure you and most solemnly say to you, until heaven and earth pass away, not the smallest letter or stroke [of the pen] will pass from the Law until all things [which it foreshadows] are accomplished."

MATTHEW 5:18

When Jesus said from the cross, "It is finished," he was not only saying that our redemption was accomplished because the law was satisfied with a sacrifice, but he was also saying that the law's sacrificial system was no longer necessary. This was because the ultimate sacrifice had been provided by the perfect Lamb of God. All those sacrifices of the Old Testament were just a shadow of the reality of the cross.

The Bible puts it this way: "For the law, having a shadow of the good things to come, and not the very image of the things, can never with these same sacrifices, which they offer continually year by year, make those who approach perfect" (Hebrews 10:1 NKJV). The apostle Paul said that before we came to faith in Jesus, "we were kept under guard by the law" (Galatians 3:23 NKJV), awaiting the liberation of the gospel—when Jesus released us from its curse. Through him we are no longer condemned. We have been set free!

Father, thank you for the wonderful liberty that we have in the glorious gospel.

A Strange Verse

"Whoever breaks one of the least [important] of these commandments, and teaches others to do the same, will be called least [important] in the kingdom of heaven; but whoever practices and teaches them, he will be called great in the kingdom of heaven."

MATTHEW 5:19

Perhaps the greatest truth of the Christian faith is that we're saved by grace through faith, and that not of ourselves (Ephesians 2:8–9). Our salvation has nothing to do with keeping God's law. The law was rather a schoolmaster to bring us to Christ (Galatians 3:24). And even though the law remains—and it is greatly appreciated because it gave us the knowledge of sin—we're saved by grace alone. And so we strive to obey God, not to be justified but out of gratitude to God for his mercy in Christ.

What is important about this verse is that it tells us that we can use God's law to teach sinners. After David cried out for mercy for his transgressions, he said, "Then will I teach transgressors thy ways" (Psalm 51:13 KJV). And the way we teach sinners is by using the law as a schoolmaster. That's what schoolmasters do. They give us knowledge.

Father, teach me to teach sinners in the way.

Our Moral Essence

"I say to you that unless your righteousness (uprightness, moral essence) is more than that of the scribes and Pharisees, you will never enter the kingdom of heaven."

MATTHEW 5:20

Today's Scripture verse is a devastating statement to those who are trying to earn their way to heaven. The scribes and the Pharisees *displayed* a perfect righteousness. Jesus said that they were clean on the outside, but on the inside they were filthy. Most of us can give the impression that we are morally good—on the outside. However, God requires truth in the inward parts. "Behold, You desire truth in the inward parts" (Psalm 51:6 NKJV). He requires purity of thought. Anything short of that incurs his just wrath.

Jesus told his hearers that they would never enter the kingdom of heaven unless they obtained a *perfect* righteousness (Matthew 5:48). Self-righteousness is a dead end. It does not and cannot lead anywhere—except to hell. Thank God that Jesus intervened through the cross so that instead of trying to earn heaven by means of our own righteous deeds, it comes by the *gift* of perfect righteousness. Such is the kindness of God.

Father, may I never trust in my own righteousness, which is like filthy rags in your sight.

But I Say to You

"You have heard that it was said to the men of old, 'You shall not murder,' and 'Whoever murders shall be guilty before the court.' But I say to you that everyone who continues to be angry with his brother or harbors malice against him shall be guilty before the court; and whoever speaks [contemptuously and insultingly] to his brother, 'Raca (you empty-headed idiot)!' shall be guilty before the supreme court (Sanhedrin); and whoever says, 'You fool!' shall be in danger of the fiery hell."

MATTHEW 5:21–22

The Bible tells us that the Messiah would "magnify the law, and make it honourable" (Isaiah 42:21 KJV). And that's what we see happening in the Sermon on the Mount. Jesus said, "You have heard that it was said to the men of old…but I say to you," and then he gave us the spiritual nature of the law. In doing so, he showed us how it is impossible to reach heaven by our own works.

Just saying angry words to another person is deadly. Who of us has never felt murder in his heart on a freeway or when someone crosses us at our workplace? This is why we constantly need the mercy of the cross.

Father, may your love in me today keep my heart free from sin.

Then Present Your Offering

"If you are presenting your offering at the altar, and while there you remember that your brother has something [such as a grievance or legitimate complaint] against you, leave your offering there at the altar and go. First make peace with your brother, and then come and present your offering."

MATTHEW 5:23–24

In the Old Testament, the children of Israel would bring offerings to the Lord. We are reminded of these offerings when we see that Mary and Joseph only had two turtle doves (Luke 2:24), but as Christians, we were not told to bring an offering. God doesn't want what we have; he wants what we are. This is why the apostle Paul says, "I beseech you therefore, brethren, by the mercies of God, that you present your bodies a living sacrifice, holy, acceptable to God, which is your reasonable service" (Romans 12:1 NKJV).

And it is a reasonable service to give back to God what he's so graciously given to us—our very lives. It is vital to take the spirit of what Jesus is saying, making sure that we don't harbor any resentment or bitterness toward another person when we offer ourselves.

Father, I present myself this day as a living sacrifice to you.

Going to Court

"Come to terms quickly [at the earliest opportunity] with your opponent at law while you are with him on the way [to court], so that your opponent does not hand you over to the judge, and the judge to the guard, and you are thrown into prison."

MATTHEW 5:25

There are times when we should take people to court. Recently, a blind woman was sharing the gospel in a park when the local city had her arrested for violating their ordinances. While her arrest for evangelizing may be permitted or even expected in other countries, that's not so in the United States, where the First Amendment of the Constitution protects the right to freedom of speech. So the woman's lawyers took the city authorities to court, and she won her case.

However, as Christians, we should try to go to court only as a very last resort. This is because the only ones who really win in most cases are the lawyers. They usually make money no matter what the outcome. Therefore, it's best to take any grievances directly to the Judge of the universe and let him preside over the case. This is what Jesus did (1 Peter 2:23).

Father, I cast all my cares upon you because you judge righteously and you care for me.

Woe Is Me, I'm Undone

"You have heard that it was said, 'You shall not commit adultery'; but I say to you that everyone who [so much as] looks at a woman with lust for her has already committed adultery with her in his heart."

MATTHEW 5:27–28

Today's verses bring me very sweet memories. Way back on April 25, 1972, I read the words from Matthew in a friend's Bible and took consolation with the first verse. I thought to myself, *If there's a heaven, I'll probably make it there because I've never committed adultery*. But then I read the next verse, and my mind screamed, *Oh no, God sees my thought life!* And it was the knowledge that I had sinned against God in such a terrible way that made me not only hunger and thirst for a right standing with God but also appreciate what Jesus did on the cross.

Look at what Scripture says fills the wicked human heart: "Out of the heart proceed evil thoughts, murders, adulteries, fornications, thefts, false witness, blasphemies" (Matthew 15:19 NKJV). Such words should send us minute by minute to the shelter of the glorious cross where we find adequate grace and mercy.

Father, thank you for your everlasting mercy.

Pluck It Out

"If your right eye makes you stumble and leads you to sin, tear it out and throw it away [that is, remove yourself from the source of temptation]; for it is better for you to lose one of the parts of your body, than for your whole body to be thrown into hell."

MATTHEW 5:29

Today's frightening and sobering verse shows us the deadly serious nature of sin. While a godless world mocks the thought of sin and makes jokes about it, death is a good reason to take seriously that God means what he says. The soul that sins shall die. It pays deadly wages: "For the wages of sin is death" (Romans 6:23 NKJV).

Jesus said that sin is so serious that if our eye causes us to sin, we should pluck it out and cast it from us. He wasn't saying to do that physically but rather to remove yourself from the source of temptation. Run from sin. That's what Joseph did when Potiphar's wife tempted him to sin (Genesis 39:12), and it's what King David should have done when sexual temptation presented itself to him.

Father, please help me to fear my own heart and its overwhelming propensity to sin.

The Sanctity of Marriage

"I say to you that whoever divorces his wife, except on grounds of sexual immorality, causes her to commit adultery; and whoever marries a woman who has been divorced commits adultery."

MATTHEW 5:32

No wonder the religious leaders hated Jesus so much. And after more than two thousand years, Jesus is still hated with a passion because of what he said. The world hates him because he testifies of their evil deeds (John 7:7). He is the only human being to ever have his name used as a cuss word. God gave him the name above every name; "Therefore God also has highly exalted Him and given Him the name which is above every name, that at the name of Jesus every knee should bow" (Philippians 2:9–10 NKJV). But wicked humanity uses his name to express filth.

Jesus didn't compromise. Tradition said that if a married man desired another woman, all he had to do was to write a bill of divorce and the marriage was nullified. "Not so," said Jesus. The bill of divorce meant nothing. They were still married. The only grounds given for divorce were if one of the spouses was unfaithful. Marriage vows, Jesus taught, were binding.

Father, may I be like Jesus today and refuse to compromise.

Just Say Yes

"Again, you have heard that it was said to the men of old, 'You shall not make false vows, but you shall fulfill your vows to the Lord [as a religious duty].'"

MATTHEW 5:33

Jesus went on to say not to swear at all: "neither by heaven, for it is God's throne; nor by the earth, for it is His footstool; nor by Jerusalem, for it is the city of the great King" (vv. 34–35). Then he said, "Nor shall you swear by your head, because you cannot make one hair white or black. But let your 'Yes' be 'Yes,' and your 'No,' 'No.' For whatever is more than these is from the evil one" (vv. 36–37 NKJV).

Be suspicious of a person who makes a promise. This is because the promise reveals that their word is not enough. They have to back it up with an oath. "Above all, my brethren, do not swear, either by heaven or by earth or with any other oath. But let your 'Yes' be 'Yes,' and your 'No,' 'No,' lest you fall into judgment" (James 5:12 NKJV). If we say we will do something, we need to just do it. Nothing more is required.

Father, help me to be someone who always keeps their word.

Maintain Your Dignity

"You have heard that it was said, 'An eye for an eye, and a tooth for a tooth [punishment that fits the offense].' But I say to you, do not resist an evil person [who insults you or violates your rights]."

MATTHEW 5:38–39

After today's words, Jesus then went on to say, "Whoever slaps you on your right cheek, turn the other to him also" (Matthew 5:39 NKJV). We are to turn the other cheek—simply ignore insignificant insults or trivial losses.

This verse is so often misquoted by the world. They think that when the Bible says "an eye for an eye, and a tooth for a tooth" (v. 38), it is saying we should take revenge ourselves. But Jesus was saying something different: he was saying that if somebody steals your car, they should give back your car or the equivalent, nothing more. It is restitution rather than retribution. And if somebody resorts to violence because they lack self-control, you and I shouldn't stoop to do the same. Look at the Greek meaning of what Jesus says we should do: "Simply ignore insignificant insults or trivial losses and do not bother to retaliate—maintain your dignity, your self-respect, your poise" (v. 39). It's not that we are weak and don't want to retaliate. It's that we live by a higher law. The law of love.

Father, this day, may I imitate Jesus and love my enemies.

February

Walk the extra mile—from the sermon on the mount (Matthew 5:41)

Let Your Love Be Seen

"Give to him who asks of you, and do not turn away from him who wants to borrow from you."
MATTHEW 5:42

In today's Scripture verse, Jesus gives us an open-ended commandment. Jesus didn't confine it to the Romans—those who occupied Israel. In the preceding verses, he said that if *anyone* wants to sue you and take your shirt, let him have your coat also. When doing this, we're not being just a doormat. There are two reasons why we should act this way.

The first is that we are witnesses for Christ. Christians act differently than this sinful world. We love our enemies, and when the world sees our love, it glorifies God. And the second reason is because we are no longer our own. We have been bought with the price of the cross. Everything we have belongs to God, and Scripture reminds us that he will take care of us. If someone does us an injustice, God will pay them back—and he will pay us back. This is the essence of trusting him to be our "Lord" (our supreme master) as well as our loving heavenly Father.

Father, my desire today is to glorify you in every way.

Love Your Enemy

"You have heard that it was said, 'You shall love your neighbor (fellow man) and hate your enemy'; but I say to you, love [that is, unselfishly seek the best or higher good for] your enemies and pray for those who persecute you."

MATTHEW 5:43–44

Today we consider perhaps the most radical of the teachings of Jesus. He didn't say to love just your neighbor as yourself but also to love your enemies, and the love of which he is speaking is not passive. This is not love in word only. The love of which Jesus is speaking is unselfish. It seeks the best or higher good for those who hate us—even if they wish to kill us. This was the love Stephen exhibited as he was being stoned to death. It was the love Jesus exhibited on the cross when he cried for God to forgive those who were so cruelly murdering him.

So if you have an enemy, you could send him or her a gift as an act of love. How they react to it isn't our business; it's our Father's business. We are doing this as to the Lord—to glorify him and not ourselves.

Father, please help me to love all people this day, no matter who they are or what they've done.

The Hypocrite

"So whenever you give to the poor and do acts of kindness, do not blow a trumpet before you [to advertise it], as the hypocrites do [like actors acting out a role] in the synagogues and in the streets, so that they may be honored and recognized and praised by men. I assure you and most solemnly say to you, they [already] have their reward in full."

MATTHEW 6:2

It's strange how the world seems to confine hypocrites to the church. In reality, hypocrites are everywhere. A hypocrite is someone who pretends to be something that they are not; and that kind of person appears within the church, within politics, at our workplace, and at our sporting events. The pretense is there because hypocrites are seeking the praise of men.

The religious hypocrite lives a lie. The political hypocrite says one thing and does another. The sporting hypocrite secretly takes drugs to enhance his performance, and the hypocrite in the workplace lies to the boss to get promoted. The most famous of hypocrites would be Judas Iscariot. He faked it for three years and suffered the terrible consequences. The antidote to hypocrisy is to cultivate a healthy fear of God.

Father, never let any hypocrisy into my heart.

When You Pray

"Also, when you pray, do not be like the hypocrites; for they love to pray [publicly] standing in the synagogues and on the corners of the streets so that they may be seen by men. I assure you and most solemnly say to you, they [already] have their reward in full."

MATTHEW 6:5

Jesus said, "*When* you pray…." Prayer should be as natural as our breathing. We should not only pray, but our prayer, like breathing, should be continuous. "Rejoice always, pray without ceasing" (1 Thessalonians 5:16–17 NKJV). Some wrongly believe that we have to go into a building we call a "church" to pray, and that's the only place where God hears. But the Scriptures teach us that God is omniscient, and he can hear us whether we are inside a building or outside.

Jesus told us not to be like hypocrites who deliberately stood outdoors and prayed to be seen and admired by men. Then he warned that those who do so already have their reward—they have the empty and meaningless admiration of other human beings. He said that if we want to be heard, we should go into a room and shut the door so that nobody else can hear us but God.

Father, may all my prayers always be sincere.

The Omniscience of God

"When you pray, do not use meaningless repetition as the Gentiles do, for they think they will be heard because of their many words."

Matthew 6:7

Jesus said not to be like the gentiles [praying as they do] because God knows what we need before we ask him. We therefore may be tempted to ask, "What's the point of praying, if God knows exactly what we are going to pray?" But that's the wrong question. Of course, God knows what we're going to pray. He is omniscient. He knows all things. He intimately knows the future. He's not bound by the present as we are. Rather, the questions we should be asking are "How is it that Almighty God would involve me in the miracle of prayer? Why would he be concerned with my desires and needs?"

We pray because we've been told to pray. We pray because that's the way God works. He moves the mountains through prayer. So we must do what the Bible says. We are to pray without ceasing. We share our hearts and needs with our heavenly Father. It's been well said that prayer is us talking to God, and the Bible is God speaking to us. It's a two-way conversation.

Father, thank you for hearing my every prayer.

The Power of Mercy

"If you forgive others their trespasses [their reckless and willful sins], your heavenly Father will also forgive you."

MATTHEW 6:14

Jesus went on to say, "If you do not forgive men their trespasses, neither will your Father forgive your trespasses" (Matthew 6:15 NKJV). These words should make every Christian tremble. This is because almost every day somebody says something or does something that's annoying. It may be a Christian brother or sister, your pastor, someone at work, or a family member. However, the great shield against resentment, bitterness, and unforgiveness is love.

As we read in 1 Corinthians 13, love is patient and kind. It's never selfish. It *always* cares about others. It sees other people's perspectives and, in so doing, has a merciful attitude toward others. If someone is rude or thoughtless, mercy considers, *He must be going through a really tough time. I will pray for him and ask if there's anything I can do to help make his day better*. Listen to Scripture: "Blessed are the merciful, for they shall obtain mercy" (Matthew 5:7 NKJV).

Father, I want to be blessed. Help me to exhibit mercy today.

Where Your Treasure Is

"Do not store up for yourselves [material] treasures on earth, where moth and rust destroy, and where thieves break in and steal."

MATTHEW 6:19

There's nothing wrong with having money in the bank or even a safe in our home. In financially hard times, it's good to be able to use savings to put food on the table and even better to use money to help those around you. The essence of what Jesus is saying in today's verse is not to put our trust in money. We mustn't let money take the place of God in our lives as our source of joy, our peace, and our sense of security for the future. God should be our joy and peace, and our faith should be in him to take care of us by supplying all of our basic needs.

To see where our treasure is, the big test is to ask ourselves, *What are my greatest wishes? What are my deepest desires? On what do I center my life?* If our answers are something other than God and his kingdom, we have a wrong order of affections, and that's a scary place to be.

Father, help me to keep you first and foremost in my affections and desires.

The Light of the Eye

"The eye is the lamp of the body; so if your eye is clear [spiritually perceptive], your whole body will be full of light [benefiting from God's precepts]."

MATTHEW 6:22

Jesus said what would happen if there were no light: "If your eye is bad, your whole body will be full of darkness. If therefore the light that is in you is darkness, how great is that darkness!" (v. 23 NKJV). In many ways, the eye is similar to a traditional camera. The camera has an aperture that expands or contracts to allow more or less light. The "eye" of the human heart is the conscience. It is the conscience that will allow light or darkness.

If our conscience is seared, it will hinder light from the soul, and the heart will become a vacuum for darkness. And when evil takes over, we become devoid of God's precepts. Jesus warned that "if the [very] light inside you [your inner self, your heart, your conscience] is darkness, how great and terrible is that darkness!" (v. 23). Such a thought should put the fear of God in us because when the vacuum pulls in sin, it automatically pulls in death and eventually the judgment of God.

Father, please guard my eyes today.

The Dichotomy

"No one can serve two masters; for either he will hate the one and love the other, or he will be devoted to the one and despise the other. You cannot serve God and mammon [money, possessions, fame, status, or whatever is valued more than the Lord]."

MATTHEW 6:24

It is because of the love of money that Hollywood is so devoid of godly people. And this is tragic because the entertainment industry is arguably the most powerful influence in modern society. What they produce can build or destroy the values of our culture. John Bunyan's 1678 book *The Pilgrim's Progress* called it "Vanity Fair," the town where "all that is there sold, or that comes thither is vanity." Hollywood glorifies the glitzy world, along with the flesh and the devil.

And while Hollywood loves this evil world and the things of the world, they cannot love God. The two don't mix: "Do not love the world or the things in the world. If anyone loves the world, the love of the Father is not in him" (1 John 2:15 NKJV). This is why the faith of so many celebrities is so often anemic and short on truth. And if by chance a celebrity does courageously speak of sin, righteousness, and judgment to come, they will almost certainly find themselves blacklisted.

Father, keep my heart from the subtlety of loving this world.

Look to the Birds

"Therefore I tell you, stop being worried or anxious (perpetually uneasy, distracted) about your life, as to what you will eat or what you will drink; nor about your body, as to what you will wear. Is life not more than food, and the body more than clothing?"

MATTHEW 6:25

Jesus pointed to the birds and described how they don't plant seeds or raise crops. They're not concerned about storing up food. He said, "Look at the birds of the air, for they neither sow nor reap nor gather into barns; yet your heavenly Father feeds them. Are you not of more value than they?" (Matthew 6:26 NKJV).

In another passage, Jesus is more specific, saying that God even cares for the common sparrow. That's why we should never at all be anxious or perpetually uneasy or distracted by fears about the future. "Are not two sparrows sold for a copper coin? And not one of them falls to the ground apart from your Father's will. But the very hairs of your head are all numbered. Do not fear therefore; you are of more value than many sparrows" (Matthew 10:29–31 NKJV).

Father, let every common sparrow I see always remind me of your love and care.

Look to the Flowers

"Why are you worried about clothes? See how the lilies and wildflowers of the field grow; they do not labor nor do they spin [wool to make clothing]."

MATTHEW 6:28

After Jesus pointed to the birds as a sign of God's love and care, he pointed to the flowers and said, "I say to you that even Solomon in all his glory was not arrayed like one of these. Now if God so clothes the grass of the field, which today is, and tomorrow is thrown into the oven, will He not much more clothe you, O you of little faith?" (Matthew 6:29–30 NKJV). The people had seen nothing as grand as Solomon's kingdom.

When Jesus compared a flower to Solomon, with all his wealth, riches, and glory, he said that the king didn't come anywhere near the beauty and intricacies of a common flower. When we think of beauty, majesty, color, and elegance, we perhaps think of a deep red rose and its marvelous fragrance. But modern electron microscopes now show us a greater beauty which is unseen to the naked eye. Now we can see amazing details of creation, making the words of Jesus make even more sense.

Father, forgive me for my little faith. I will trust you today.

God's Rightful Place

"First and most importantly seek (aim at, strive after) His kingdom and His righteousness [His way of doing and being right—the attitude and character of God], and all these things will be given to you also."

MATTHEW 6:33

This verse comes from Jesus' Sermon on the Mount and is foundational to Christian discipleship. It highlights two key pursuits for believers: seeking God's kingdom and his righteousness. They call for prioritizing God's reign and rule in our lives and the world, which involves aligning our values and decisions with his purposes.

God's kingdom is marked by love, justice, peace, and truth. Practically, Jesus' call to seek God's kingdom invites believers to focus on spiritual goals over worldly concerns, trusting God to provide for their needs as they pursue his will.

This kingdom focus also requires embodying God's character in our attitudes, actions, and relationships. We need to strive to live in a way that reflects God's holiness, love, and integrity. This takes not just changes in our external behavior but a transformation of our heart, aligning it with Jesus' teaching on inner purity and genuine faith.

Jesus assures us that when we prioritize God, our material needs will be met. This doesn't necessarily mean wealth but sufficiency—trusting that God, as a loving Father, knows and provides for what we need.

Father, today I put you first and foremost in my affections. Nothing else matters.

Judge Not

"Do not judge and criticize and condemn [others unfairly with an attitude of self-righteous superiority as though assuming the office of a judge], so that you will not be judged [unfairly]. For just as you [hypocritically] judge others [when you are sinful and unrepentant], so will you be judged; and in accordance with your standard of measure [used to pass out judgment], judgment will be measured to you."

Matthew 7:1–2

The Pharisees and the Sadducees were perfect examples of hypocrisy. They looked down their long, judgmental noses at Jesus and condescendingly accused him who was without sin. Their problem was that they couldn't make righteous judgments because of the log of sin in their self-righteous eyes (Matthew 7:3).

Judas Iscariot eventually gravitated to these hypocrites because he was like them. The Bible tells us he was stealing money when he openly judged a woman who broke an alabaster box of ointment in an act of worship toward Jesus (John 12:6). The subtlety of hypocrisy is that it is self-deceiving, and the Amplified Bible wonderfully gives us insight into the motive of those who judge others wrongfully. People often judge others harshly because of some secret sin in their own hearts.

Father, may I never be guilty of hypocrisy.

The Hard Heart

"Do not give that which is holy to dogs, and do not throw your pearls before pigs, for they will trample them under their feet, and turn and tear you to pieces."

MATTHEW 7:6

Some people use these verses as an excuse to not preach the gospel to someone who has a hard heart. However, we must understand that human beings in their unredeemed state do not have a heart toward God. There is none that seek after God, and there is none that understand (Romans 3:11). The Bible speaks of one hardhearted man who hated the name of Jesus and persecuted those who followed him. But Jesus arrested this Saul of Tarsus on the road to Damascus and gave him a new heart.

The biblical way to handle a hardened heart is to deal with it the same way that God dealt with Saul of Tarsus. According to Paul's own testimony, it was the law that showed him his sin (vv. 19–20; 7:7) and opened his eyes to the forgiveness that is in Christ. So if somebody has a hard heart, don't give up on them; instead, use the law, the Ten Commandments, to bring the knowledge of sin and allow it to be a schoolmaster to bring them to Christ.

Father, thank you for pursuing me when I had a hard heart.

Ask and It Shall Be Given

"Ask and keep on asking and it will be given to you; seek and keep on seeking and you will find; knock and keep on knocking and the door will be opened to you."

MATTHEW 7:7

In today's verse, Jesus tells us that if we seek, we will find, and if we knock, the door will be opened. This isn't an open invitation to the bank of heaven, as some prosperity preachers would have us believe. Before we came to Christ, most of us esteemed money and looked to it for our joy and sense of security. But when we were born again, we received a new heart that loves God and his righteousness.

No longer do we desire the sinful pleasures of this world. Our hearts now yearn for the lost (as Jesus did), and rather than being consumed by our own selfish desires, we're horrified to think of their terrifying fate.

Charles Spurgeon said, "Prayer is the natural outgushing of a soul in communion with Jesus. Just as the leaf and the fruit will come out of the vine-branch without any conscious effort on the part of the branch, but simply because of its living union with the stem, so prayer buds, and blossoms, and fruits out of souls abiding in Jesus."[2]

Father, help me to be pure in prayer.

---

2 Charles H. Spurgeon, "The Secret of Power in Prayer," January 8, 1888, https://www.spurgeon.org/resource-library/sermons/the-secret-of-power-in-prayer/#flipbook.

Our Father in Heaven

"If you then, evil (sinful by nature) as you are, know how to give good and advantageous gifts to your children, how much more will your Father who is in heaven [perfect as He is] give what is good and advantageous to those who keep on asking Him."

MATTHEW 7:11

Jesus' words remind us of the incredible generosity and goodness of God. Despite human imperfections, we naturally desire to provide good things for our children, acting out of love and care. If flawed human beings can do this, how much more will our perfect heavenly Father, who is wholly good and loving, bless his children?

This scripture encourages us to approach God with trust and confidence. It emphasizes the importance of prayer—continuously asking, seeking, and knocking. God's response is not random or reluctant; rather, it reflects his deep love and understanding of what is truly beneficial for us. He promises to give good gifts, not just material blessings but gifts that nurture our spiritual growth, peace, and joy.

The verse invites us to marvel at God's character: he is not distant or indifferent but actively attentive to our needs. It reassures us that we are loved by a perfect Father who delights in giving us what we truly need when we trust and turn to him.

Father, thank you for showing me this side of your character.

The Golden Rule

"In everything treat others the same way you want them to treat you, for this is [the essence of] the Law and the [writings of the] Prophets."

MATTHEW 7:12

Today's verse is what most call "the Golden Rule," and it's an ideal that many unsaved people claim will merit their entrance into heaven. It's common for them to say that they try to treat others as they would like to be treated and that this lifestyle is evidence that they are a good person. What they don't take into account is the serious nature of their sin. Even if they were able to continually treat others as they would like to be treated, who is going to forgive their past multitude of sins? What judge is going to dismiss a criminal for serious crimes because he maintains he treats others well?

In contrast, the Christian also strives to keep the Golden Rule—but not to merit his entrance into heaven. That's already assured through his faith in Jesus. Our love for others is merely an expression of our godly character in Christ. It's a manifestation of love and goodness—the natural fruit of the Spirit (Galatians 5:22).

Father, may I, with a pure motive, treat others today as I would like to be treated.

The Narrow Gate

"Enter through the narrow gate. For wide is the gate and broad and easy to travel is the path that leads the way to destruction and eternal loss, and there are many who enter through it."

MATTHEW 7:13

Jesus said that there are only two gates, and if we don't enter one, we will default to the other. These are gates that we *enter*. One is wide and easy and leads to eternal destruction. The other is narrow and difficult and leads to eternal life (as Jesus mentioned in the following verse). There are multitudes who enter the gate of false conversion. They profess faith in Jesus but live after the flesh. They don't battle daily with the world, the flesh, and the devil. They surrender to sin. They believe in Jesus but don't obey him.

Scripture says, "Though He was a Son, yet He learned obedience by the things which He suffered. And having been perfected, He became the author of eternal salvation *to all who obey Him*" (Hebrews 5:8–9 NKJV, emphasis added). The genuine convert is obedient not *to be* saved; he is obedient *because* he is saved. The difference is life and death.

Father, this day let your will be done in my life.

False Prophets

"Beware of the false prophets, [teachers] who come to you dressed as sheep [appearing gentle and innocent], but inwardly are ravenous wolves."

MATTHEW 7:15

Jesus warned us that we are to know these false brethren (including false teachers) by their fruit. How can we recognize these deceivers when they look and sound like genuine ministers of the gospel? They are "dressed" as sheep—appearing gentle and innocent. But that's only how they appear. We must listen closely to what they say. Are they deeply concerned for the lost—as Jesus was? Do they preach the cross and speak about sin, righteousness, and judgment—as Jesus did? Or are they preaching an unbiblical message of self-gain?

The Amplified Bible explains that the original Greek meaning of the *fruits* of these false prophets is "their contrived doctrine and self-focus" (v. 16). Scripture says, "Such are false apostles, deceitful workers, transforming themselves into apostles of Christ" (2 Corinthians 11:13 NKJV). Paul told Timothy not to follow these prosperity preachers, whose teachings he called "useless wranglings of men of corrupt minds and destitute of the truth, who suppose that godliness is a means of gain. From such withdraw yourself" (1 Timothy 6:5 NKJV).

Father, help me to beware—to discern the true from the false.

Evidence of Salvation

"Every healthy tree bears good fruit, but the unhealthy tree bears bad fruit."

MATTHEW 7:17

The word "every" is one of the most comprehensive words in the English language. It's like the tiny word "all." It leaves no wiggle room. There's no room for us to compromise. A healthy tree *will* produce good fruit, and you will see this evidence in the life of the true believer. By their fruits you will know them: "The fruit of the Spirit is love, joy, peace, longsuffering, kindness, goodness, faithfulness, gentleness, self-control" (Galatians 5:22–23 NKJV).

Scripture also speaks of the fruit of righteousness (always doing what is right), the fruit of praise and thanksgiving, and the fruit of repentance. Then in the next verse from Matthew, Jesus uses the word "every" once again. "*Every* tree that does not bear good fruit is cut down and thrown into the fire" (Matthew 7:18 NKJV, emphasis added). Such sober warnings should put a healthy fear of God in our hearts. This is why we must examine ourselves to see if we are in the faith. "Examine yourselves as to whether you are in the faith. Test yourselves" (2 Corinthians 13:5 NKJV).

Father, this day I examine myself for fruit of your presence in my life.

They Called Jesus "Lord"

"Not everyone who says to Me, 'Lord, Lord,' will enter the kingdom of heaven, but only he who does the will of My Father who is in heaven."

MATTHEW 7:21

Again in today's verse, Jesus stays with the vital theme of the true and false convert. He tells us that obedience is the fruit (or evidence) of a genuine conversion. The phrase "the will of My Father who is in heaven" is crucial. It points to the importance of aligning one's life with God's desires and commands. This isn't just about moral behavior but more importantly about a relationship with God that transforms and guides every aspect of our lives. It's not, as some believe, salvation by works but evidence of the new birth of John 3:1–5. Only those who do the will of God can be assured of their salvation.

This verse urges all believers to reflect on their lives and ask whether they are truly following God's will. Are their actions consistent with their profession of faith? It calls for a deeper introspection and a commitment to aligning one's life with the teachings of Jesus Christ. In a nutshell, are we playing the hypocrite?

Father, may I show my love for you by obedience to your will.

Who Are These People?

"Everyone who hears these words of Mine and acts on them, will be like a wise man [a far-sighted, practical, and sensible man] who built his house on the rock."

MATTHEW 7:24

Jesus said that when the rain came down and beat on that house built on the rock, it didn't fall because its foundation was solid. But then he spoke of those who ignored his sayings. He likened them to a foolish man who built his house on sand, and when the rain came down, the floods came, and the winds blew and beat on that house, and it fell. And great was its fall.

Once again, Jesus continued with a theme of true and false conversion. He said that whoever hears those sayings of his and does not do them is foolish (v. 26). This portion of Scripture is often attributed to people in the secular world who build their houses on sand. The world doesn't hear the sayings of Jesus. Likewise, many profess to be Christian but ignore his words. They are the ones who build their house on sand, and they are the ones who will fall when the storms come.

Father, today I will put the words of Jesus into practice.

Jesus Reached Out

Jesus reached out His hand and touched him, saying, "I am willing; be cleansed." Immediately his leprosy was cleansed.

MATTHEW 8:3

Jesus reached out his hand. This leper didn't reach out to Jesus with his hand. Jesus took the initiative. And so it is with our salvation. A holy God reaches out to touch leprous sinners with his hand, and we are cleansed because of God's grace and not because of anything we do (Ephesians 2:8–9). The Bible says that no one can come to Jesus unless the Father draws him (John 6:44), and it's God who gives repentance so we might know the truth (2 Timothy 2:25).

Nothing we do could ever play a part in our salvation. It's all of him, and he rightfully gets all the glory: "For of Him and through Him and to Him are all things, to whom be glory forever. Amen" (Romans 11:36 NKJV). Nor do we blink or breathe without his permission. He even owns our free will—and if you have a humble heart, such thoughts will make you rejoice. "My soul shall make her boast in the LORD; the humble shall hear thereof, and be glad" (Psalm 34:2 KJV).

Father, thank you for reaching out to me.

Don't Tell Anyone

Jesus said to him, "See that you tell no one [about this]; but go, show yourself to the priest [for inspection] and present the offering that Moses commanded, as a testimony (evidence) to them [of your healing]."

MATTHEW 8:4

Sometimes we can look at the words of Jesus and read into them something that's not there. But here, when he told the healed leper not to tell anyone about his healing, it was more than likely just common sense. There were times when Jesus could not move because the crowd pressed in on him, and he had to have a boat pushed out for him to sit in to speak to the crowd.

He therefore told the man he had healed not to tell anyone, but instead to go and show the priest that he was healed and get a certificate from him of his healing. This was what the law of Moses instructed lepers to do if their disease had disappeared. Charles Spurgeon said of this incident, "While the ceremonial law stood, Christ was very careful to pay it honor. He came not to destroy, but he came to build up and to fulfill."

Father, please give me insight into your Word.

Jesus Was Amazed

The centurion replied to Him, "Lord, I am not worthy to have You come under my roof, but only say the word, and my servant will be healed. For I also am a man subject to authority [of a higher rank], with soldiers subject to me; and I say to one, 'Go!' and he goes, and to another, 'Come!' and he comes, and to my slave, 'Do this!' and he does it."

MATTHEW 8:8-9

When he heard the centurion make his declaration of faith, Jesus was amazed, and he told those who were following him that he hadn't found such great faith with anyone in Israel like the faith this man had exhibited.

Here was the Creator of the sunrise and sunset, the Maker of all things, so how could anyone or anything impress him, let alone amaze him? The Scriptures don't say Jesus was amazed when he walked on water, when he calmed in the storm with his voice, or when he raised Lazarus from the dead. This was Almighty God in human form, so again, how could anything impress him? But we read that he was amazed by this man's faith. Without faith, it's impossible to please God (Hebrews 11:6); therefore, with great faith, we can make heaven smile.

Father, may I have great faith in you today.

Deliberate Thoughts

"I say to you that many [Gentiles] will come from east and west, and will sit down [to feast at the table, and enjoy God's promises] with Abraham, Isaac, and Jacob in the kingdom of heaven [because they accepted Me as Savior], while the sons and heirs of the kingdom [the descendants of Abraham who will not recognize Me as Messiah] will be thrown out into the outer darkness; in that place [which is farthest removed from the kingdom] there will be weeping [in sorrow and pain] and grinding of teeth [in distress and anger]."

MATTHEW 8:11–12

It's natural for the mind to want to stay on pleasant thoughts. Experts say that we forget much of what we find distasteful. However, we should force ourselves to think about the terrible fate of the ungodly even though such thoughts are most unpleasant.

Think of what Scripture says about it: "There will be weeping [in sorrow and pain] and grinding of teeth [in distress and anger]." It was thoughts of God's anger against sin that provoked the apostle Paul to seek the lost (2 Corinthians 5:11). And if we don't think on these things, we will become complacent in our concern for the unsaved.

Father, help me today not to be selfish in my thoughts.

Fiery Trials

Jesus replied to him, "Foxes have holes and the birds of the air have nests, but the Son of Man has nowhere to lay His head."
MATTHEW 8:20

I don't think that today's quote would be a prosperity preacher's favorite Bible verse. It doesn't say that Jesus lived in luxury in the finest of hotels as he itinerated. Rather, Jesus said that animals have better beds than he does. He had nowhere to lay his head at night. Such a thought is a great consolation for the Christian because sometimes the heavens seem as brass when God doesn't quickly supply that which we ask.

However, those folks who listen to prosperity preaching will become disillusioned with Christianity if God doesn't step up to the plate as an obedient divine butler. In reality, the Christian life is filled with lions' dens, Red Seas, temptations to sin, and fiery trials that leave us burned if we let them. The key to overcoming all these things is a simple childlike trust in the promises of God. No matter what comes our way, we have his immutable promise that he will work it out for good.

Father, no matter what life throws at me today, I will use it to draw closer to you.

Following Jesus

Jesus said to him, "Follow Me [believing in Me as Master and Teacher], and allow the [spiritually] dead to bury their own dead."

MATTHEW 8:22

In today's Scripture verse, when Jesus told this man to follow him and be his disciple, the man responded by saying that he would follow Jesus after his father had died and he buried him (v. 21). It is because unbelievers so love their sins that they will come up with all sorts of excuses (and scenarios) to keep from following Jesus. Many console a guilty conscience by putting off their eternal salvation until the future. This is very foolish because we don't know what the future will bring. Death could seize upon us at any time, and if we die in our sins, God will justly damn us to hell. That's why there is a sense of urgency when it comes to our eternal salvation.

Let those who are spiritually dead bury their own dead. Nothing should stop us from coming to Jesus because nothing is so important. Listen to his sobering words: "Whoever desires to save his life will lose it, but whoever loses his life for My sake and the gospel's will save it" (Mark 8:35 NKJV).

Father, never allow anything to come between me and your will.

Perfect Peace

He said to them, "Why are you afraid, you men of little faith?" Then He got up and rebuked the winds and the sea, and there was [at once] a great and wonderful calm [a perfect peacefulness].

MATTHEW 8:26

Our life can sometimes erupt like a violent storm. When we look at the turmoil around us, the inclination is to become fearful. And this inclination reveals that we have little faith. A lack of trust in God in a sudden storm comes without any effort. Instead, we have to make an effort to have faith. We should then resolve to always remember that our Creator cannot lie. Make sure you memorize this faith-exploding verse: "By two immutable things, in which it is impossible for God to lie, we might have strong consolation, who have fled for refuge to lay hold of the hope set before us" (Hebrews 6:18 NKJV).

The Bible speaks of a peace of God "which passeth all understanding" (Philippians 4:7 KJV). This is the peace we need when we cannot see the future. It seems dark and ominous. But faith in the promises of God helps us see beyond the storm.

Forgive me when I look at the storm rather than at your promises.

March

The healing of the paralyzed man (Luke 5:18–25)

Jesus Said to Go

He said to them, "Go!" So they came out [of the men] and went into the pigs, and the whole herd rushed down the steep bank into the sea and died in the water.

Matthew 8:32

The Bible is filled with strange stories. In the Old Testament, a man was swallowed by a large fish (Jonah 1:17), a donkey spoke with a man's voice (Numbers 22), and the walls of Jericho came tumbling down with just the shout of the children of Israel (Joshua 6:20). And here in the New Testament there is a very strange story about thousands of pigs who became possessed by demons and then killed themselves by running off a cliff.

Despite it being a ridiculously crazy story, we know that there is something deeper here than meets the eye. While the reason for the mass suicide isn't clear, there is one lesson that we can learn. Demons obey Jesus when he tells them to do something. He just said the word "Go," and they immediately obeyed the voice of the Son of God. We are also told to "Go" (Mark 16:15), and yet so many of us who call ourselves Christians stay. We can learn an important lesson from pigs.

Father, may my life continually fulfill the Great Commission.

Which Is Easier?

They brought to Him a man who was paralyzed, lying on a stretcher. Seeing their [active] faith [springing from confidence in Him], Jesus said to the paralytic, "Do not be afraid, son; your sins are forgiven [the penalty is paid, the guilt removed, and you are declared to be in right standing with God]."

MATTHEW 9:2

Despite his evident disease, Jesus first addressed the man's spiritual need by forgiving his sins before healing his paralysis. This reminds us of the difference between the temporal and the eternal. No doubt the healing of this man's disease was of primary importance to him, but in God's eyes, it was secondary to the forgiveness of his sins—because forgiveness opens the door to heaven.

By declaring the man's sins forgiven, Jesus made a profound statement about his divine authority. The Jews believed that only God could forgive sins, so his pronouncement was a clear indication of his divinity. It seems that the religious leaders were very slow thinkers. If Jesus could do miracles, that proved that he was the Son of God. The fact that he miraculously healed a paralyzed man showed that he had the authority to forgive sin.

Father, I thank you that my sins are forgiven because of what Jesus did on the cross.

Definition of a Disciple

As Jesus went on from there, He saw a man named Matthew (Levi) sitting in the tax collector's booth; and He said to him, "Follow Me [as My disciple, accepting Me as your Master and Teacher and walking the same path of life that I walk]." And Matthew got up and followed Him.

MATTHEW 9:9

When Jesus truly calls us, it is radical. Matthew was collecting taxes, and suddenly, he became a follower of Jesus—a fisher of men. But he didn't just have a change of vocation. He also had a change of heart that caused him to want to go in another direction. The Amplified Bible gives us insight into the meaning of the word *disciple*. It means to accept Jesus as our Master and Teacher and walk the same path he walked.

Before Jesus called us, we were busy pursuing our own agenda. But if anyone comes to Christ, they become a new creation; old things pass away, and all things become new (2 Corinthians 5:17). Like Matthew, we certainly have a changed heart, and that changes everything. Everything we now do is with the purpose of making God smile.

Father, may I always be a genuine disciple of Jesus Christ.

Our Sobering Task

When Jesus heard this, He said, "Those who are healthy have no need for a physician, but [only] those who are sick."

MATTHEW 9:12

A sick person who is convinced that he's healthy will never seek a cure. Why should he? It makes no sense. And why would any sinner seek a savior if he thinks he's morally well? It makes no sense. Our sobering task (with the help of God) is to convince those who believe they're healthy that they are deathly sick. It's only when they understand this truth that they will see their need of the great physician.

The way we do this is to do what Jesus did and use the moral law to bring the knowledge of sin (Mark 10:17–18). The apostle Paul said that he thought he was morally healthy until the law gave him a diagnosis. Sadly, almost every unsaved human being believes they have a healthy relationship with God. That's why they don't see their need to repent and put their trust in Jesus alone. May God help us to have courage to be like a good doctor and show sinners the symptoms of the disease that will be the death of them.

Father, help me to be a true and faithful witness today.

They Will Fast

Jesus replied to them, "Can the guests of the bridegroom mourn while the bridegroom is with them? The days will come when the bridegroom is taken away from them, and then they will fast."

MATTHEW 9:15

Do you ever fast a meal or two? There are a number of good reasons why we should. The first is that here Jesus implied that each of us will fast. This is just part of taking up our cross daily and denying ourselves. There are a number of other reasons we should fast. One is that fasting teaches us self-control. There are many who are digging their graves with their spoon simply because they haven't learned to control their own appetite.

Another good reason to fast is that we humble ourselves when we deny our appetites. "As for me, when they were sick, my clothing was sackcloth; I humbled myself with fasting" (Psalm 35:13 NKJV). Fasting shows us how weak we are and that we are often slaves to our appetites. Also, fasting makes us appreciate the fact that we can eat all the wonderful things that God has given us, and that appreciation produces a heart of thanksgiving.

Father, never let my appetite be my god.

They Laughed at Him

He said, "Go away; for the girl is not dead, but is sleeping." And they laughed and jeered at Him.

MATTHEW 9:24

We are told earlier in the chapter that while Jesus was speaking, a ruler approached him and worshiped him, saying that his daughter had just died. He pleaded with Jesus to come with him and lay his hand on her, and then he added, "and she shall live" (Matthew 9:18 KJV). Jesus got up and followed the man, and so did His disciples. When they arrived at the ruler's house and saw all the mourners and musicians, Jesus told them that the girl wasn't dead. She was sleeping. That's what upset the mourners—and rightly so. She was obviously dead. But Jesus cleared the room and took the girl by the hand, and her life miraculously came back to her.

Two thousand years later, this evil world is still laughing at and ridiculing Jesus and telling him to go away. They don't think there's any hope in the face of death. But we know better. He took us by the hand and pulled us out of death.

Father, thank you for pulling me out of the grave.

The Harvest Is Plentiful

He said to His disciples, "The harvest is [indeed] plentiful, but the workers are few."
MATTHEW 9:37

Jesus said to pray to the Lord of the harvest to send out laborers into his harvest. So don't believe it when people say that the world isn't open to the gospel. Jesus said the harvest is indeed plentiful: human beings are ripe for the harvest. The problem is twofold. First, the laborers are few, and second, most Christians don't know how to present the gospel so that it makes sense.

If I want you to appreciate the value of a parachute as we fly ten thousand feet up in a plane, the best way to do that is to hang you out of the plane by your ankles for a few seconds. If you have any sort of sense, the fear of you falling ten thousand feet will make you want to put on the parachute. Similarly, the way to interest sinners in the Savior is to hang them over eternity for a few minutes. Tell them that they have to face a law that is more harsh than unforgiving gravity. Make Felix tremble (Acts 24:25). Give the Philippian jailer an earthquake (Acts 16:26). And when he calls out to be saved, point him to Jesus.

Father, give me wisdom when I speak to the lost.

The Jew First

Jesus sent out these twelve, instructing them: "Do not go among the Gentiles, and do not go into a city of the Samaritans."
MATTHEW 10:5

After instructing the twelve to avoid the gentiles and Samaritans, Jesus told them to "go rather to the lost sheep of the house of Israel" (v. 6 KJV). And as they went, they were to preach, saying, "The kingdom of heaven is at hand" (v. 7 KJV). They were to confine the gospel to Jews. Some may think that Jesus wasn't being politically correct—that he was preferring Jew over gentile and Jew over the Samaritan.

The apostle Paul did a similar thing. He also went to the Jew first. And the reason was because God had given his law to the Jews first: "What advantage then has the Jew, or what is the profit of circumcision? Much in every way! Chiefly because to them were committed the oracles of God" (Romans 3:1–2 NKJV). They had the advantage of having the law to give them a knowledge of sin, and consequently, they should have been more likely to embrace the gospel.

God has his perfect timing for each of us to hear the gospel—as he had for the Samaritans (John 4:39–41).

Father, thank you that the gospel is universal.

When You're Rejected

"Whatever city or village you enter, ask who in it is worthy [who welcomes you and your message], and stay at his house until you leave [that city]."

MATTHEW 10:11

Jesus then told his disciples that as they traveled and went into a city or house, they were to give it their greeting of peace. Then he added that if they were rejected by that household or city, they were to leave and even "shake off the dust of [their] feet" (v. 14 KJV).

These verses remind us that we should be peacemakers and that we are to preach the gospel of peace. They also tell us what to look for when we are reaching out to the lost. We are like bees going from flower to flower, looking for the nectar of an open heart. If someone welcomes our message, we are to then cultivate the warmth of Christian fellowship. We are further told what to do if they don't welcome the message. If they refuse to listen, we shouldn't fret. We shouldn't take it personally. Instead, we should keep in mind that God is the one who opens hearts. We simply move on and find someone who is open to what we have to say.

Father, help me to exhibit peace, love, and kindness to all who listen.

Heavenly Wisdom

"Listen carefully: I am sending you out like sheep among wolves; so be wise as serpents, and innocent as doves [have no self-serving agenda]."

MATTHEW 10:16

The KJV uses the word *behold* to begin this verse. Someone once said that the word *behold* is like a trumpet, heralding a message to get the attention of the hearers. The Amplified Bible uses "Listen carefully." While we should listen carefully to everything Jesus said, this verse should get our undivided attention because it's easy to miss or forget what he was saying.

When we walk through this world, we are among those who want to devour us. They want to confound us, trip us, and cause us to stumble. These are demonic personalities that seek to invade our minds through ungodly thoughts, filthy billboards, magazines, TV, social media, and other sinful sights and sounds. Therefore, be on your guard. Be vigilant. And do this through the wisdom that God gives—the wisdom that is from above, the wisdom that is dove-like: "The wisdom that is from above is first pure, then peaceable, gentle, willing to yield, full of mercy and good fruits, without partiality and without hypocrisy" (James 3:17 NJKV).

Father, today give me the wisdom that is from above.

When God Speaks

"When they hand you over, do not worry about how or what you are to say; for what you are to say will be given you within that [very] hour."

MATTHEW 10:19

Jesus went on to tell them that they wouldn't be the one who would be speaking—the Spirit of God would be. After he told his disciples the sobering warning that he was sending them out as sheep among wolves, he gave them instructions for what to do when persecution came. The book of Acts begins with great cause for rejoicing with thousands coming to Christ on the day of Pentecost and on the following days.

But the day came when persecution raised its ugly head. Stephen was taken by evil men and tried like a criminal. The religious leaders set up false witnesses who accused him of blasphemy and even repeated the same lies they had said about Jesus (Acts 6:13–14). Then we are told, "All who sat in the council, looking steadfastly at him, saw his face as the face of an angel" (v. 15 NKJV). Stephen's face exhibited the dove-like gentleness of God, and the words that he then spoke were inspired by heaven (7:2–53).

Father, it is an honor to have you speak through human vessels.

The Name of Jesus

"You will be hated by everyone because of [your association with] My name, but it is the one who has patiently persevered and endured to the end who will be saved."

MATTHEW 10:22

Notice that Jesus pinpointed the hatred that would come because of his name. While the evil world hates the light of his words, the hatred is sparked by his name. It is Jesus' name that offends. And then Jesus added, "But it is the one who has patiently persevered and endured to the end who will be saved." We don't endure to the end *to be* saved but *because* we are saved (Ephesians 2:8–9).

Listen closely to how prayer is portrayed in movies or on TV, whether it's at a funeral or as a family bows in prayer before a meal. The prayer is never offered in the name of Jesus and is often said as a joke. Hollywood uses the name of Jesus or Jesus Christ as a cuss word with great zeal, but they rarely say it in truth. We should use these incidents as a reminder to exalt the name of Jesus in our daily lives and to come to God in prayer in the name that is above all names.

Father, help me to always exalt the name of Jesus in my thoughts and words.

Strength in Humility

"A disciple is not above his teacher, nor is a bond-servant above his master. It is enough for the disciple to be like his teacher, and the bond-servant like his master. If they have called the head of the house Beelzebul (Satan), how much more [will they speak evil of] the members of his household."

MATTHEW 10:24–25

There was an embarrassing dispute among the disciples about who among them was the greatest: "Now there was also a dispute among them, as to which of them should be considered the greatest" (Luke 22:24 NKJV). They were thinking like carnal men. This world is structured in such a way. The rich and powerful dominate the weak and vulnerable.

But not so in the kingdom of God, where everything is turned on its head. The last become first, and the weak become strong. In God's kingdom, there isn't room for carnal ambition. Then Jesus strangely connects that subtle form of pride with persecution. This is because even though Jesus was greatest of all, the world still hated him, and if they hated him, they will hate us. But our greatest defense is to speak in lowliness of heart and humility of mind. That's our greatest strength.

Father, may I be free this day from delusional or conceited thoughts.

Fear and Love

"Do not be afraid of those who kill the body but cannot kill the soul; but rather be afraid of Him who can destroy both soul and body in hell. Are not two little sparrows sold for a copper coin? And yet not one of them falls to the ground apart from your Father's will. But even the very hairs of your head are all numbered [for the Father is sovereign and has complete knowledge]. So do not fear; you are more valuable than many sparrows."

MATTHEW 10:28

Jesus often referred to nature in his living sermon illustrations because we are more likely to hold onto biblical truths by seeing and hearing. He spoke of the worth of the common sparrow, saying that God watches even the sparrow. He also said that even the very hairs of our heads are all numbered. We are more valuable than many sparrows. Then, staying with the theme of persecution, Jesus spoke about fear in an amazing way. He said not to fear someone who is about to murder you.

That fear is thoroughly natural. Fear makes us run for our lives. But once again, Jesus was using hyperbole. He was saying that a murderer can take our lives, but God is the one who can take our souls, and it's the soul that matters in the light of eternity. Then, right on the heels of talking about the fear of God, Jesus spoke of his great love, how the Father cares for us even more than he does the sparrows. For the child of God, fear and love should never be separated.

Father, I love you because of who you are, and I fear you because of what you can do.

The Rooster

"Therefore, the one who confesses and acknowledges Me before men [as Lord and Savior, affirming a state of oneness with Me], that one I will also confess and acknowledge before My Father who is in heaven."

MATTHEW 10:32

Jesus warned his followers what would happen to those who deny and reject him. He said that he will also deny and reject them when they stand before God. Peter denied Jesus. He was adamant that he wouldn't, but he did. And his fear blinded him to his foolishness until the rooster awakened him. But it had to crow twice to do that. He was deaf to the first time it crowed, but the second time, what he had done suddenly hit him like a burst dam.

That account was recorded in Scripture for our instruction. It is a lesson to never boast of what we will do in the future. We are to lay our hand over our mouth and stay close to Jesus, trusting in him and in his strength. This is because we deny him every time we choose our way above his. We can do it with a wandering eye, a sinful thought, or a thoughtless deed. That's why we should have an ear to hear the *first* crowing of our conscience.

Father, keep my conscience tender toward you.

The Sword of Division

"Do not think that I have come to bring peace on the earth; I have not come to bring peace, but a sword [of division between belief and unbelief]."

MATTHEW 10:34

The three words *Do not think* reveal a predictable but erroneous conclusion many make about why Jesus came to the earth. Even though he is called the Prince of Peace, he didn't come to bring peace. He came with a sharp sword in his mouth. His words brought a cutting division among the crowds. The Scriptures say that after he taught, "There was a division among the people because of Him. Now some of them wanted to take Him, but no one laid hands on Him" (John 7:43–44 NKJV).

As the original language reveals, the sharp sword brought about a division of belief and unbelief. If you believe that Jesus is the Christ, the Son of the living God, then you will believe his words—that without the mercy of Christ you will be justly damned. And your belief will produce repentance and trust in Jesus. But if you don't believe, you will stay in your sins and be condemned in a terrible place called hell.

Father, keep me from the damning sin of unbelief.

Not Worthy

"He who loves father or mother more than Me is not worthy of Me; and he who loves son or daughter more than Me is not worthy of Me."

MATTHEW 10:37

Following Jesus is the highest of callings, and nothing and no one should compete with it. He said that we are to take up our cross daily, warning that if we don't do that, we are not worthy of him. It is the revelation of our sinfulness (particularly the exaltation of our selfish desires) that can bring our priorities into the right order. And there is a sin that is most subtle and extremely deceiving. It's what the Bible calls "inordinate affection." It is so serious that it is listed with other more obvious transgressions that we are told to put to death: "Mortify therefore your members which are upon the earth; fornication, uncleanness, inordinate affection, evil concupiscence, and covetousness, which is idolatry" (Colossians 3:5 KJV).

What's wrong with loving your children more than anything in life and putting your family first in your affections? How could that be wrong? The answer is simple. It is loving the gift more than the Giver. And that is a wrong order of affections.

Father, may you always be first in everything.

An Ambassador for Christ

"He who receives and welcomes you receives Me, and he who receives Me receives Him who sent Me."

MATTHEW 10:40

We have the honor of being ambassadors for Christ: "Now then, we are ambassadors for Christ, as though God were pleading through us: we implore you on Christ's behalf, be reconciled to God" (2 Corinthians 5:20 NKJV). An ambassador has tremendous authority to speak on behalf of his president and his country. And as ambassadors for Christ, we must never forget that we represent Jesus Christ. Look at how he identifies with the believer: "He who receives and welcomes you receives Me."

What an honor and responsibility we have to make sure that we rightly represent our God, both in word and in deed. This is why we should be careful in everything we do—including even what we say and how we say it. We must be careful not to give any offense in anything, and that includes the mere appearance of evil (1 Thessalonians 5:22). This isn't a subtle legalism. It is rather an understanding of the freedom we have in Christ. We do not want anything we do to hinder a soul from coming to the Savior.

Father, may my every word and every deed bring you honor.

MARCH 19

The Blinder of Discouragement

Jesus answered, "Go and report to John what you hear and see: the blind receive [their] sight and the lame walk, the lepers are cleansed [by healing] and the deaf hear, the dead are raised, and the poor have the gospel preached to them."

MATTHEW 11:4–5

John the Baptist was discouraged as he sat in Herod's cold prison. There seem to be two mysteries here. The first one is how John could possibly forget that he had seen the Spirit of God descend upon Jesus like a dove when he baptized him in Matthew 3:16. Sadly, discouragement has a way of making us forget the blessings of the past, and those are things we should never forget. And second, if John was indeed the greatest man born of woman, as Jesus said in Matthew 11:11, why didn't God send an angel to release him from his prison?

There is a biblical explanation to the particular mystery: God's ways aren't our ways. The Scriptures tell us that "as heavens are higher than the Earth," so God's ways are above our ways (Isaiah 55:9 NKJV). Therefore, what we can't comprehend, we receive by faith. "Trust in the LORD with all your heart, and lean not on your own understanding" (Proverbs 3:5–6 NKJV).

Father, help me to trust you in times of discouragement.

He Is Trustworthy

"Blessed [joyful, favored by God] is he who does not take offense at Me [accepting Me as the Messiah and trusting confidently in My message of salvation]."

MATTHEW 11:6

It seems that the whole world is oiled by trust. Almost everything works by faith. There is contention among nations because of a lack of trust. There are conflicts in marriages and businesses because of a lack of trust. Conversely, a marriage or a business or countries that have relationships built on trust have a basis for success. We normally choose where to put our faith based on information we have about the other person. Are they trustworthy—worthy of our trust? We do this with doctors, lawyers, pilots, and particularly our spouses and friends.

However, no human being who has ever been born has near the integrity of Jesus Christ. He is utterly trustworthy and worthy of our faith in him. And better than anything any human person can give to another, Jesus forgives sin. So those who deem him worthy of trust and put their faith in him receive forgiveness of their sins and, consequently, receive everlasting life by the grace of God.

Father, I trust you this day with all of my heart.

The World's Empty Praise

"I assure you and most solemnly say to you, among those born of women there has not risen anyone greater than John the Baptist; yet the one who is least in the kingdom of heaven is greater [in privilege] than he."

MATTHEW 11:11

Scripture doesn't inform us too deeply about the virtues of John the Baptist. We do know that he was humble of heart: he said once that he wasn't worthy to loosen the sandals of Jesus. We also know that he was no respecter of persons. He called the Pharisees and Sadducees snakes and vipers, which they were (Matthew 3:7). We also know that he was a lover of righteousness in that he boldly reproved a king for committing adultery. This love of righteousness and faithfulness to God was eventually the reason why John was executed.

This world has praise for the rich and famous and for those who are proud. But all the collective praise of the entire world is nothing but empty, meaningless vapor when compared to praise from Jesus. And if you are faithful to your calling to be a humble servant of God, you, too, will hear praise from his lips: "Well done, good and faithful servant" (Matthew 25:21 NKJV).

Father, I seek your smile above all things.

The Accuser

"The Son of Man came eating and drinking [with others], and they say, 'Look! A glutton and a drunkard, a friend of tax collectors and sinners [including non-observant Jews]!' Yet wisdom is justified and vindicated by her deeds [in the lives of those who respond to Me]."

MATTHEW 11:19

Satan has been called "the accuser of our brethren" (Revelation 12:10 NKJV), and many in this world who hate God will gladly lend Satan their vicious lips. If you love the Lord, expect the world to accuse you of not caring about the poor. They will accuse you of being unloving in your approach and not representing Jesus correctly—because you boldly talk about sin, righteousness, and judgment. They will point the accusing finger at what they see as the slightest hypocrisy.

But this is nothing new. King David had the same problem: "They also opened their mouth wide against me, and said, "Aha, aha! Our eyes have seen it" (Psalm 35:21 NKJV). Instead of being discouraged, imitate David's prayer-filled reaction: "This You have seen, O LORD; do not keep silence. O Lord, do not be far from me. Stir up Yourself, and awake to my vindication, to my cause, my God and my Lord" (vv. 22–23 NKJV).

Father, if they accused Jesus, how much more will they accuse me (Matthew 10:25)?

Come to Jesus

"Come to Me, all who are weary and heavily burdened [by religious rituals that provide no peace], and I will give you rest [refreshing your souls with salvation]."

MATTHEW 11:28

While there is continual contention among Christians regarding the sovereignty of God and the free will of sinners in salvation, here Jesus told the ungodly to come to him. Without Jesus, there is no salvation. He is the only way to God and the only door to heaven (John 14:6). Religion cannot take the heavy burden of sin off the back of the laboring sinner. Paul wrote of the futility of religious works, saying, "These things indeed have an appearance of wisdom in self-imposed religion, false humility, and neglect of the body, but are of no value against the indulgence of the flesh" (Colossians 2:23 NKJV).

There is a scene in the wonderful allegory *The Pilgrim's Progress*, where the main character, Christian, is walking up a steep hill with a burden of sin upon his back. As he looks to the cross and understands what happened two thousand years ago, the burden automatically rolls off his back and down the hill. He stands tall and strong in Christ.

Father, may the essence of our message always be "Come to Jesus."

Guard Your Liberty

"The Son of Man is Lord of the Sabbath."
MATTHEW 12:8

Today's Scripture verse is so liberating. Jesus stands above the burden of seeking justification by the law. Yet there are many whose mission is to bring Christians back under the law. They won't say it openly. Instead, they will tell you that you don't *have* to keep the Sabbath; you keep it out of love for God. In other words, if you don't keep the law, you don't truly love God.

Here is my answer to those who try to put the yoke of the law on your shoulders: If there is even one verse in the New Testament telling Christians to keep the Jewish Sabbath, I will gladly keep it and tell others to keep it also. But there's not one. When the disciples met to find out what the attitude of the gentiles should be to the law of Moses (Acts 15), they didn't say that they should keep the Sabbath holy. So dear Christian, obey the admonition to keep your liberty: "Stand fast therefore in the liberty by which Christ has made us free, and do not be entangled again with a yoke of bondage" (Galatians 5:1 NKJV).

Father, thank you for the liberty we have in Jesus.

A Lost Sheep

He said to them, "What man is there among you who, if he has only one sheep and it falls into a pit on the Sabbath, will not take hold of it and lift it out?"

MATTHEW 12:11

Here, Jesus is addressing the Pharisees, who criticized him for healing on the Sabbath. In this statement, he uses a rhetorical question to challenge their rigid interpretation of Sabbath law. He points out that even they, if faced with a situation where one of their sheep fell into a pit on the Sabbath, would act compassionately to rescue it rather than allow it to suffer.

The point Jesus makes is twofold. First, he emphasizes the value of compassion and mercy over strict legalism. Second, he highlights the inconsistency in their reasoning: if it is permissible to save an animal on the Sabbath, how much more appropriate is it to help a person, who holds far greater value?

Jesus' statement reinforces that the Sabbath was made to serve humanity, not be an unyielding burden, and that acts of mercy align with God's intent for rest and holiness. Through this teaching, Jesus underscores the priority of love and goodness in following God's law.

Father, may your love help me to overcome my fears and reach out to the lost.

Knowing Their Thoughts

Knowing their thoughts Jesus said to them, "Any kingdom that is divided against itself is being laid waste; and no city or house divided against itself will [continue to] stand."

MATTHEW 12:25

Imagine a football team where half the players try to score while the other half work against them. Chaos ensues, and victory becomes impossible. The same principle applies to nations, communities, families, and even our own hearts.

Jesus spoke about a divided kingdom after being accused by the Pharisees of casting out demons by Satan's power. He exposed their flawed logic: How could Satan work against himself and still expect his kingdom to survive? A divided kingdom collapses; it's self-destructive. Jesus pointed out that their accusation made no sense, proving he operated under God's authority.

This truth also applies to us personally. If our hearts are divided—trying to serve God while clinging to sin—we face spiritual ruin. Just as a house cannot stand when it's split, our lives fall apart when we lack unity with Christ. That's why Jesus calls us to wholehearted devotion, aligning our thoughts, actions, and desires with his will. Unity with him brings strength, peace, and eternal life.

Father, help me to always unify with your will.

We Are Gathering or Scattering

"He who is not with Me [once and for all on My side] is against Me; and he who does not [unequivocally] gather with Me scatters."

MATTHEW 12:30

Today's Scripture verse is a frightening verse for the many professing Christians who believe in Jesus but don't have the "things that accompany salvation" (Hebrews 6:9 NKJV). They are a divided house. One foot is in the world, and the other (they believe) is in the kingdom of God. And Scripture says they are unfaithful. "Adulterers and adulteresses! Do you not know that friendship with the world is enmity with God? Whoever therefore wants to be a friend of the world makes himself an enemy of God" (James 4:4 NKJV).

Here is the dichotomy of salvation. We are either in or out, saved or lost, living in darkness or living in light, for Jesus or against him, gathering or scattering. No man can serve two masters. Those who try to serve two masters belong to the many that Jesus said called him "Lord" (Matthew 7:21) but were, in truth, workers of iniquity—meaning they had no regard for the moral law, the Ten Commandments.

Father, I turn from all sin. This day you have all of me.

Trees of Righteousness

"Either make the tree good and its fruit good, or make the tree bad and its fruit bad; for the tree is recognized and judged by its fruit."
MATTHEW 12:33

Not too many preachers can hold a crowd's undivided attention after calling them a brood of vipers and asking how they could speak good things when they were evil. But Jesus continued with the theme of the false convert, using the nature he created, trees, to illustrate spiritual truth. The Bible calls us "trees of righteousness" that are planted by the Lord. Isaiah says,

> To console those who mourn in Zion,
> To give them beauty for ashes,
> The oil of joy for mourning,
> The garment of praise for the spirit of heaviness;
> That they may be called trees of righteousness,
> The planting of the LORD, that He may be glorified.
> (Isaiah 61:3 NKJV)

And therein is the problem with the false convert. They weren't the planting of the Lord. They weren't born of God. They've never mourned over their sins and had a thirst for righteousness. They are a brood of vipers because they still follow that old serpent, the devil. May God awaken them before the day of wrath.

Father, keep me away from temptation. Deliver me from evil.

Fear God

"I tell you, on the day of judgment people will have to give an accounting for every careless or useless word they speak. For by your words [reflecting your spiritual condition] you will be justified and acquitted of the guilt of sin; and by your words [rejecting Me] you will be condemned and sentenced."

MATTHEW 12:36–37

Would to God that the world believed the words of Jesus! On the day of judgment, every human being will give an account of every idle word they have spoken. Instead of believing that and pleading with God for a new heart that thirsts for righteousness, many pour forth foolishness. "'Their throat is an open tomb; with their tongues they have practiced deceit'; 'The poison of asps is under their lips'; 'whose mouth is full of cursing and bitterness'" (Romans 3:13–14 NKJV).

Unbelief gives them comfort in their sin. How could God require an account? But a little thought could change what they believe about him. He's the maker of the hummingbird, the human eye, the seasons, the sun, and the universe.

But if Jesus has saved us, if our faith is in him, we will find the Judge of all the earth welcoming us, not condemning us.

Father, though you are a fearsome God, I'm deeply grateful that through your Son I no longer stand before you condemned.

If Any Be in Christ

Then some of the scribes and Pharisees said to Him, "Teacher, we want to see a sign (attesting miracle) from You [proving that You are what You claim to be]."

MATTHEW 12:38

Jesus told his listeners that they were "an evil and adulterous generation" who were seeking after a sign (v. 39). Then he said that no sign would be given to it except the sign of the prophet Jonah—who was three days and three nights in the belly of the great fish (vv. 39–40). After referencing Jonah, Jesus likened the prophet's experience to his own death and resurrection (v. 40). The sign that God gives us is the transforming power of the gospel—the death, burial, and resurrection of Jesus. And it is the most amazing sign that he is who he says he is.

And a skeptic who obeys the gospel will find that God makes him a brand-new creature (2 Corinthians 5:17). He will be born again with a new heart and new desires. Instead of drinking iniquity like water, they will thirst after righteousness. That will be our own undeniable and personal miracle—our own sign from heaven.

Father, thank you for making me a completely new creature in Christ.

Seeking a Home to Dwell

"When the unclean spirit has gone out of a man, it roams through waterless (dry, arid) places in search of rest, but it does not find it. Then it says, 'I will return to my house from which I came.' And when it arrives, it finds the place unoccupied, swept, and put in order. Then it goes and brings with it seven other spirits more wicked than itself, and they go in and make their home there. And the last condition of that man becomes worse than the first. So will it also be with this wicked generation."

MATTHEW 12:43–45

In these few verses, Jesus warns about the dangers of spiritual complacency. He describes an unclean spirit leaving a person but later returning with even worse spirits, leaving the individual in a worse state. This illustrates that merely removing evil without filling the void with God's presence leaves a person vulnerable to greater harm.

The "house" being empty, clean, and orderly symbolizes a life morally improved but spiritually vacant. Jesus uses this to address his generation, warning that without genuine repentance and commitment to God, its rejection of him would lead to deeper spiritual decline and judgment.

Father, I slam and lock the door of my life to sin.

April

Parable of the lost sheep (Luke 15:3–7)

The Mother of Jesus

Jesus replied to the one who told Him, "Who is My mother and who are My brothers?"

MATTHEW 12:48

Jesus then stretched out his hand toward his disciples and all his other followers, and said, "Here are My mother and My brothers!" (v. 49 NKJV). He then added that anyone who did the will of his Father in heaven by believing in Jesus and following him was his brother and sister and mother.

Mary, Jesus' biological mother, was a sinner who needed a savior, and she was there in the upper room, waiting to have her sins forgiven. After having at least another five children after she bore Jesus (Mark 6:3), she was obviously no longer a virgin. Nowhere in Scripture does it say that she ascended to heaven to be a mediator between God and man. Scripture is adamantly opposed to such a thought: "There is one God and one Mediator between God and men, the Man Christ Jesus" (1 Timothy 2:5 NKJV). If Mary should be honored as some sort of supernatural being above all others, Jesus didn't know about it. Here, Scripture makes the point that he didn't honor her above any other believer. He said that those who do the will of God are his brother, sister, and mother.

Father, help me to be gracious when expounding this biblical truth.

Neglected Instructions

Jesus replied to them, "To you it has been granted to know the mysteries of the kingdom of heaven, but to them it has not been granted."

MATTHEW 13:11

"For whoever has, to him more will be given, and he will have abundance; but whoever does not have, even what he has will be taken away from him. Therefore I speak to them in parables, because seeing they do not see, and hearing they do not hear, nor do they understand" (Matthew 13:12–13 NJKV). It never ceases to amaze me that some people reject the Bible without ever having opened its pages. They are willfully ignorant of the truth and even speak of it disparagingly in their ignorance.

Be careful to never devalue God's Word. Honor it with all your heart. It is humanity's precious instruction book. It should be a lamp to the feet of the ungodly and a light to their path (Psalm 119:105). But it's not. The world instead lives in darkness, and people mock and neglect the Bible. Because of this neglect, this sad world is predictably in such a terrible mess. Many people think they know better than the Maker, and therefore they ignore his instructions to their own peril.

Father, never let me neglect or devalue your Word.

The Life Source

"Blessed [spiritually aware, and favored by God] are your eyes, because they see; and your ears, because they hear. I assure you and most solemnly say to you, many prophets and righteous men [who were honorable and in right standing with God] longed to see what you see, and did not see it, and to hear what you hear, and did not hear it."

Matthew 13:16–17

In today's Scripture passage, Jesus was speaking of himself. There is good reason why the prophets of the Old Testament *longed* to see and hear what Jesus' disciples saw and heard. There is nothing more precious on this earth than life, and there's nothing more precious than the gift of life—than the very source of life. Jesus is that source of life in human form.

Listen to John speak of this wonder: "That which was from the beginning, which we have heard, which we have seen with our eyes, which we have looked upon, and our hands have handled, concerning the Word of life—the life was manifested, and we have seen, and bear witness, and declare to you that eternal life which was with the Father and was manifested to us" (1 John 1:1–2 NKJV).

Father, may the world come to know the identity of Jesus.

The Work of the Enemy

"When anyone hears the word of the kingdom [regarding salvation] and does not understand and grasp it, the evil one comes and snatches away what was sown in his heart. This is the one on whom seed was sown beside the road."

MATTHEW 13:19

Notice the criteria for someone receiving the word of God. It is that they understand it. These particular hearers—the ones Jesus refers to here—don't understand God's word, and that's why the Evil One is able to snatch the seed. They don't value it. It's similar to how a man on a plane won't value a parachute if no one tells him that he has to jump. However, if he knows he has to jump, there is no way anyone is going to get that parachute away from him because he knows his life depends on it.

That's why we need to preach that sinners have to face a holy God and be judged by his perfect law. When they receive Christ to escape the wrath to come, the Enemy will not be able to take away the gospel from their hearts because they value it.

Father, please give me the wisdom I need to share the biblical gospel.

Light to the Path

"The one on whom seed was sown on the good soil, this is the one who hears the word and understands and grasps it; he indeed bears fruit and yields, some a hundred times [as much as was sown], some sixty [times as much], and some thirty."

MATTHEW 13:23

Today's verse contains the words that the church must study if it is serious about reaching the lost world with the glorious gospel. As we've seen, the genuine convert hears and understands. The book of Romans, however, tells us that "there is none who understands; there is none who seeks after God" (Romans 3:11 NKJV).

So this understanding doesn't come from the human heart. Rather, it comes from an outward source. That source is the law of God. The reason the law brings understanding to the darkened human mind is that it brings the knowledge of sin. Charles Spurgeon said, "The law can do nothing else but reveal sin and pronounce condemnation upon the sinner."

If we want to see sinners embrace the gospel, we must do what Jesus did and first preach the law.

Father, help me to use the light of the law to show sinners the path to the gospel.

The Sleeping Church

Jesus gave them another parable [to consider], saying, "The kingdom of heaven is like a man who sowed good seed in his field. But while his men were sleeping, his enemy came and sowed weeds [resembling wheat] among the wheat, and went away."

MATTHEW 13:24–25

Jesus said that the Enemy sowed seeds "while his men were sleeping." That certainly sums up the church when it comes to the unbiblical gospel that teaches only that Jesus fills a God-shaped hole in the heart or that God has a wonderful plan for sinners. Those who allowed such unbiblical gospel proclamations gave the Enemy license to sow multitudes of false converts in the church and slept while he did so. These false converts look like genuine converts, but they secretly serve sin.

When David sinned against God, Nathan didn't speak of a wonderful plan or a hole in his sinful heart. He said, "Why have you despised the Commandment of the LORD?" (2 Samuel 12:9 NKJV). In the same way, sinners need to be confronted with their sin using the Ten Commandments—as Jesus confronted the rich young ruler (Mark 10:17–18). Thank God there has been an awakening to biblical evangelism in recent years.

Father, never let me sleep and give place to the devil.

Goats among the Sheep

He gave them another parable [to consider], saying, "The kingdom of heaven is like a mustard seed, which a man took and sowed in his field; and of all the seeds [planted in the region] it is the smallest, but when it has grown it is the largest of the garden herbs and becomes a tree, so that the birds of the air find shelter in its branches."

MATTHEW 13:31–32

The seed of the gospel entered the field of the world on the day of Pentecost, as the disciples received the Holy Spirit and the power to witness (Acts 1:8). Then throughout the book of Acts, the roots of the church began to spread across the earth. And two thousand years later, the church has grown into a massive multitude of believers, many of whom sleep and await the hope of the resurrection.

But note that Jesus warned that "the birds of the air find shelter in its branches." Birds are sometimes a type of the demonic realm in Scripture (Matthew 13:4; Revelation 18:2), and within the church, false brethren find shelter among genuine believers, as tares among the wheat, foolish virgins among the wise, goats among the sheep, and bad fish among the good.

Father, thank you for giving the Holy Spirit to give me the power to witness.

Hidden Treasure

"The kingdom of heaven is like a [very precious] treasure hidden in a field, which a man found and hid again; then in his joy he goes and sells all he has and buys that field [securing the treasure for himself]."

MATTHEW 13:44

The teachings of Jesus are filled with similes. These comparisons usually contain the words "like" or "as." Similes are most necessary when speaking of the things of God because we are seeking to relate spiritual things to natural men. It is like trying to speak of light and color to someone who was born blind: "The natural man does not receive the things of the Spirit of God, for they are foolishness to him; nor can he know them, because they are spiritually discerned" (1 Corinthians 2:14 NKJV).

In today's verse, Jesus likens what we have in Christ to hidden treasure that is so valuable that a man sells everything he has to get it. This could either mean we give up all to gain Christ (Philippians 3:8) or that Jesus gave his all to buy the church (1 Corinthians 6:20). On either view, it's clear that the treasure we have in Christ is immeasurably valuable—a priceless gift that we should hold onto no matter what comes our way.

Father, thank you for the unspeakable gift.

The Pearl

"Again, the kingdom of heaven is like a merchant in search of fine pearls, and upon finding a single pearl of great value, he went and sold all that he had and bought it."

MATTHEW 13:45–46

What Jesus taught is so important that he continually repeated the same truths from different perspectives. He did this so that his hearers wouldn't simply *hear* what he said but so that they would also *understand*. It is like telling a child that fire is hot. A loving parent will repeat the warning until the child understands.

Jesus had said that the kingdom of God is like a hidden treasure and that it is like a pearl of great value. Pearls, like treasure, are hidden. We must search to find hidden treasure and dive to find pearls. Again, this is why preaching future punishment using God's law is so important. Again, a parachute is of no value to a passenger until he understands that he must jump out of the plane. It is fear of the consequences of jumping without it that makes the passenger value what the parachute can do. We will not see Jesus as a priceless treasure until we understand what will happen to us if we die in our sins.

Father, thank you that I have the wonderful treasure of knowing Christ.

More Repetition

"Again, the kingdom of heaven is like a dragnet which was lowered into the sea, and gathered fish of every kind."
MATTHEW 13:47

After making the comparison in today's verse, Jesus then told his listeners that when the net was full, the fishermen dragged the net up onto the beach, sat down, and sorted out the good fish from the bad. The good they put into the baskets, and the bad ones they threw away. And then Jesus said that is what the angels are going to do with the church on the day of judgment—sort out the genuine from the false. Christ added that the wicked will be cast into a frightening and fiery hell.

Here's more reinforced teaching, and this time Jesus repeated the reality of true and false conversion. This teaching is worth repeating because so many within the body of Christ have no idea that there's such a thing as a spurious conversion. And Jesus spoke of this truth multiple times through the parable of the sower and in so many other teachings. When sinners make professions of faith, some are repentant and some are not. But both are gathered into the net of the church, and the true and the false will be sorted out on the day of judgment.

Father, make me wise to these great truths.

His Ways

Jesus said to them, "They do not need to go away; you give them something to eat!"

Matthew 14:16

The previous verses in Matthew's gospel tell us that Jesus had been ministering to a great multitude in a deserted place. It was evening, and it would soon be dark. So the disciples came to Jesus with a practical suggestion. They said it was a deserted place and that it was late in the evening. They suggested that he send the multitude away so the people could go to the villages and buy some food. That made sense. But if Jesus had taken up the suggestion, the multitude would've missed a miracle. Jesus invited them to stay, and then he told the disciples to get them food. All they had were five loaves and two fish. And with those five small loaves and two fish, Jesus fed five thousand men, plus women and children.

When we find ourselves in the deserted place with nowhere to go and no solution to a formidable problem, we tend to make suggestions to the Lord. However, it would be wiser for us to pray, *Lord, what would you have me do in this situation? I want your will rather than mine*. That's when we are more likely to see miracles.

Father, I want to trust you in all my circumstances.

Do Not Be Afraid

Immediately He spoke to them, saying, "Take courage, it is I! Do not be afraid!"

MATTHEW 14:27

Jesus made his disciples get into a boat and head to the other side of the sea. Then he went up into a mountain by himself to pray. A storm arose while the disciples were in the middle of the sea, and the boat was tossed by the waves and the winds. It was between 3:00 a.m. and 6:00 a.m. when Jesus walked by them on the water. When his disciples saw him walking on the sea, they were horrified, saying, "'It is a ghost!' And they cried out for fear" (v. 26 NKJV). That's when Jesus "immediately" spoke to them.

The Bible tells us that God is a very present help in time of need (Psalm 46:1). If we are in dire straits, we can be sure he's there immediately, and he consistently tells us in his Word to be of good courage. Why? Because "'It is I'" (v. 27 NKJV). We don't serve a dead religious philosopher but the living God, who is the lover of our souls. That's the reason we must never let fear have dominion.

Father, this day I take courage through trust in you.

Stepping out of the Boat

He said, "Come!" So Peter got out of the boat, and walked on the water and came toward Jesus.

MATTHEW 14:29

There is a huge lesson for us as Christians in today's one verse. The disciples were on a boat that was nearly sinking because of a storm. Suddenly Jesus appeared to them, walking on the water. We often look down on Peter because he is so impetuous. He said things without thinking very deeply. But what he suggested to Jesus in this passage of Scripture wasn't shallow. It was a wonderful example of initiative. Peter suggested to Jesus that he himself step out of the boat and supernaturally walk on water. This was Peter's idea, and Jesus put his blessing on Peter's desire both to be with Jesus and to walk supernaturally. And we know that Peter did indeed walk on water for a short time.

No other human being can boast of such an experience. But this is more than just walking on water. The lesson is that if we have an idea that glorifies the name of Jesus, we should step out in faith and trust him. And if by chance things don't work out and we begin to sink, we can be sure that he will take us by the hand and raise us up because he loves us.

Father, I always want to be where you are.

The Schoolmaster

"God said [through Moses], 'Honor your father and mother,' and, 'He who speaks evil of or insults or treats improperly father or mother is to be put to death.'"

MATTHEW 15:4

After reminding the scribes and Pharisees of God's law, Jesus wasn't finished. He added, "But you say, 'Whoever says to his father or mother, "Whatever profit you might have received from me is a gift to God"—then he need not honor his father or mother.' Thus you have made the commandment of God of no effect by your tradition" (Matthew 15:5–6 NKJV).

Jesus here rebuked the religious leaders for traditions that specifically watered down the Fifth Commandment so that they no longer believed that they had to honor their parents. However, that same law is still binding. It "worketh wrath" (Romans 4:15 KJV), and despite their tradition, it will fall upon its transgressors on judgment day.

In similar fashion, many contemporary churches prefer their own traditions to the Word of God and are therefore filled with those who are desensitized to the gospel. The gospel has been rendered useless because of their tradition.

Father, keep me from subtle and vain traditions.

From Death to Life

"'This people honors Me with their lips, but their heart is far away from Me. But in vain do they worship Me, for they teach as doctrines the precepts of men.'"

MATTHEW 15:8–9

There are millions (perhaps billions) in this category described in today's verse, who honor God with their lips but their hearts are far from him. This is because in their unregenerate state, they cannot please God, and all their prayers and traditions leave them under his wrath. They don't honor God's Word but instead embrace the traditions of men.

The apostle Paul was in this state until he was stopped in his tracks on the road to Damascus. He was *zealous* of the traditions of his fathers, and because of that, he was living contrary to the name of Jesus Christ. Every sinner who is walking contrary to the name of Jesus Christ needs a road to Damascus experience. Paul was radically converted, and every sinner can have an encounter that is just as radical. Upon their repentance and faith in Jesus, they receive light from heaven. God himself opens the eyes of their understanding, and they pass from death to life and become completely new (2 Corinthians 5:17).

Father, thank you for stopping me in my sinful tracks on the road to damnation.

Ignoring the Soul

"It is not what goes into the mouth of a man that defiles and dishonors him, but what comes out of the mouth, this defiles and dishonors him."

MATTHEW 15:11

An effective analogy we can use when speaking to the lost is to ask, "If you were going to receive $1 million at 8 a.m. (to spend as you wish) on the condition that you would be shot to death for a 'snuff' video at 8 p.m., would you do it?" Most are horrified at the thought and say that they wouldn't do that for all the money in the world. This is because their lives are so precious that they are without price.

Jesus asked what it is that we should give in exchange for our lives, and the unnecessary answer is that nothing is worth its exchange (Mark 8:37). And yet multitudes ignore their precious souls and worry themselves sick about what they put into their dying bodies. They pay for expensive health food but fail to give a thought to their own salvation. And that's why we should confront them with what they're doing so that they begin to take seriously the claims of Jesus.

Father, please make me creative and wise when I speak to the lost.

Faith and Persistence

Jesus answered her, "Woman, your faith [your personal trust and confidence in My power] is great; it will be done for you as you wish." And her daughter was healed from that moment.

MATTHEW 15:28

If you want to get in someone's favor, show that you trust them. Trust is a compliment both vertically and horizontally. In fact, without trusting in him, it's impossible to please God. In today's Scripture verse, Jesus not only acknowledges the gentile woman's faith, but he says that she has *great* faith. And that faith ushered in her personal miracle. Her precious daughter was healed, and that happened because of persistent, faith-filled prayer that wouldn't let go. Even though she was a gentile, the disciples implied that she was annoying them, and Jesus said that he was sent only to Israel, she didn't give up. The Bible says of her, "Then she came and worshiped Him, saying, 'Lord, help me!'" (Matthew 15:25 NKJV).

This loving and faithful mother shows us that we can intercede on behalf of others in need and move the hand of God. "Confess your trespasses to one another, and pray for one another, that you may be healed. The effective, fervent prayer of a righteous person avails much" (James 5:16 NKJV).

Father, help me to be a serious intercessor.

Beware of False Doctrine

Jesus said to them, "Watch out and be on your guard against the leaven of the Pharisees and Sadducees."

MATTHEW 16:6

When Jesus warned his disciples to guard themselves against the leaven of the Pharisees and Sadducees, he was telling them to beware of their hypocrisy. They *said*, but they didn't *do*. They outwardly appeared to be righteous, but they were corrupt inwardly. Jesus was also warning against their false teachings—the doctrinal errors of both the Pharisees and Sadducees. Leaven (or yeast) was used symbolically to represent something that spreads and influences for evil. The Pharisees were known for their strict adherence to the law as well as their own traditions while the Sadducees were more aristocratic, rejecting oral traditions in favor of the written law. They believed in unrestrained free will—meaning that God has no role in the lives of humanity. Every person is master of his or her own destiny.

Little has changed in two thousand years. Today, many embrace traditions over the Bible, while others erroneously think God has no influence over humanity nor requirements for us. We must be watchful of both errors by weighing everything against the Scriptures.

Father, help me to always be awake to and on guard against these things.

Who Do You Say I Am?

Simon Peter replied, "You are the Christ (the Messiah, the Anointed), the Son of the living God." Then Jesus answered him, "Blessed [happy, spiritually secure, favored by God] are you, Simon son of Jonah, because flesh and blood (mortal man) did not reveal this to you, but My Father who is in heaven."

MATTHEW 16:16–17

This passage highlights a pivotal moment in the New Testament when Simon Peter confesses his belief in Jesus as the Christ, the Messiah, and the Son of God. Peter's declaration reflects a deep spiritual insight that goes beyond human reasoning or perception ("flesh and blood did not reveal this to you"). Jesus affirms Peter's understanding as divinely inspired, recognizing it as a revelation from God the Father in heaven.

In calling Peter "blessed," Jesus emphasizes the spiritual security and favor that comes from receiving divine truth. This acknowledgment also underscores the unique relationship between God and humanity, where true understanding of Jesus' identity comes through divine revelation rather than human means. The passage invites reflection on the role of faith, revelation, and the recognition of Jesus as the cornerstone of Christian belief. It reminds believers of the importance of spiritual discernment and the profound blessings associated with acknowledging Christ as the Son of the living God.

Father, thank you for revealing the truth about Jesus to me.

The Rock of Ages

"I say to you that you are Peter, and on this rock I will build My church; and the gates of Hades (death) will not overpower it [by preventing the resurrection of the Christ]."
MATTHEW 16:18

While Peter's name does mean "a stone" and he was one of the pillars of the church, Scripture makes it clear that he is not the rock upon which the church is founded: "For no other foundation can anyone lay than that which is laid, which is Jesus Christ" (1 Corinthians 3:11 NKJV).

Notice what Jesus said: "I say to you that you are Peter, and on *this rock* I will build My church" (Matthew 16:18, emphasis added). The rock to which Jesus was referring was the revelation that Jesus is the Christ, the Son of the living God. When a sinner has that divine revelation and confesses that Jesus is the Christ, the Son of the living God, he or she becomes part of the true church: "If you confess with your mouth the Lord Jesus and believe in your heart that God has raised Him from the dead, you will be saved" (Romans 10:9 NKJV).

Father, I thank you for building the foundation of your church on Jesus.

The Continual Denial

Jesus said to His disciples, "If anyone wishes to follow Me [as My disciple], he must deny himself [set aside selfish interests], and take up his cross [expressing a willingness to endure whatever may come] and follow Me [believing in Me, conforming to My example in living and, if need be, suffering or perhaps dying because of faith in Me]. For whoever wishes to save his life [in this world] will [eventually] lose it [through death], but whoever loses his life [in this world] for My sake will find it [that is, life with Me for all eternity]."

MATTHEW 16:24–25

The Amplified Bible certainly gives us insight into the original Greek in today's verse. Salvation is a free gift of God; however, being a disciple means that we are disciplined. We no longer live for our own will but take up our cross daily and deny ourselves the pleasures that are offered through the world, the flesh, and the devil. The sinful world with all its enticing pleasures will appeal to our fleshly nature. The love of money, sexual lust, selfishness, and self-indulgence are formidable enemies that, like taunting Goliath, daily weigh upon us. But God is our helper.

Father, I look to you for victory every day.

Worth of the Soul

"What will it profit a man if he gains the whole world [wealth, fame, success], but forfeits his soul? Or what will a man give in exchange for his soul?"

MATTHEW 16:26

Jesus asks a profound question about the value of the human soul compared to worldly gains, such as wealth, fame, and success. His question challenges us to reflect on our priorities and the consequences of our choices.

Earthly possessions and achievements are temporary, whereas the soul represents the eternal essence of a person. By prioritizing transient gains over spiritual health, an individual risks losing something far more valuable and enduring. The rhetorical question, "What will a man give in exchange for his soul?" implies that no worldly possession can redeem or replace the loss of the soul.

This verse emphasizes the importance of seeking a life aligned with God's purpose rather than being consumed by the pursuit of earthly rewards. It encourages a focus on spiritual growth, integrity, and eternal values, because these result in everlasting significance.

Father, today I will consider the worth of my soul.

As Little Children

He called a little child and set him before them, and said, "I assure you and most solemnly say to you, unless you repent [that is, change your inner self—your old way of thinking, live changed lives] and become like children [trusting, humble, and forgiving], you will never enter the kingdom of heaven. Therefore, whoever humbles himself like this child is greatest in the kingdom of heaven."

MATTHEW 18:2–4

We can learn a lot from children. Perhaps the greatest lesson is that children have the utmost faith in their parents. They are not concerned with what they should eat or drink or wear. They are content with life because they trust their parents. Notice that it is after we come to Christ that we are to become as little children.

After we're born again, with a new heart and new desires that long to please the God who gave us life, we are to become as little children. Such a thought is offensive to a proud heart, which prefers adult independence to child dependence on a parent. But for the Christian, the thought that God is my Father and I am his little child is extremely comforting.

Father, it gives me great joy to know that I am your child.

Our Own Sins

"If your brother sins, go and show him his fault in private; if he listens and pays attention to you, you have won back your brother. But if he does not listen, take along with you one or two others, so that every word may be confirmed by the testimony of two or three witnesses. If he pays no attention to them [refusing to listen and obey], tell it to the church; and if he refuses to listen even to the church, let him be to you as a Gentile (unbeliever) and a tax collector."

MATTHEW 18:15–17

It's a sad fact of human nature that we often don't notice our own sins. Like bad breath or body odor, we can notice it in others but not in ourselves. That's why we should diligently make sure we are walking in humility of heart. This is because pride bristles at correction.

But here is the safe attitude of humility of heart: "Let the righteous strike me; it shall be a kindness. And let him rebuke me; it shall be as excellent oil; let my head not refuse it" (Psalm 141:5 NKJV).

Father, help me to see godly correction as a kindness.

Within the Will of God

"I assure you and most solemnly say to you, whatever you bind [forbid, declare to be improper and unlawful] on earth shall have [already] been bound in heaven, and whatever you loose [permit, declare lawful] on earth shall have [already] been loosed in heaven. Again I say to you, that if two believers on earth agree [that is, are of one mind, in harmony] about anything that they ask [within the will of God], it will be done for them by My Father in heaven. For where two or three are gathered in My name [meeting together as My followers], I am there among them."

MATTHEW 18:18–20

It is good to see what Jesus said (translated from the original language) so that we don't think that *everything* we ask in prayer will come to pass. We are given great authority through the name of Jesus. Demons tremble at his name. The Father takes notice of prayers that are in his name.

However, notice that the condition of the prayers that God hears and answers is that "anything that they ask [within the will of God], it will be done for them." Charles Spurgeon said, "When your will is God's will, you will have your will."

Father, may I always pray in your will.

How Many Sins?

Peter came to Him and asked, "Lord, how many times will my brother sin against me and I forgive him and let it go? Up to seven times?" Jesus answered him, "I say to you, not up to seven times, but seventy times seven."

MATTHEW 18:21–22

No doubt Peter thought he was being generous when he spoke of forgiving his brother up to seven times. But Jesus said that we should forgive seventy *times* seven times. That seems like an incredible amount of forgiveness until we consider how many times God forgives us during our lifetimes—both *before* and *after* we are saved.

Upon our conversion, we were forgiven a multitude of sins. Consider what it means if we had sinned as little as ten times a day in our non-Christian life for thirty years. That amounts to over one hundred thousand sins. Then add to that the sins we fall into as Christians—selfishness, a lack of prayer, failing to love our neighbor as much as we love ourselves, and so on. It is the revelation of our own sinfulness that helps us walk with a merciful and forgiving attitude toward those who sin against us.

Father, help me to be a loving and forgiving person.

The Crazy Fairytale

He replied, "Have you never read that He who created them from the beginning made them male and female, and said, 'For this reason a man shall leave his father and mother and shall be joined inseparably to his wife, and the two shall become one flesh'? So they are no longer two, but one flesh. Therefore, what God has joined together, let no one separate.'"

MATTHEW 19:4–6

Jesus addresses a question about divorce by emphasizing the sanctity and permanence of marriage. He begins by pointing to God's original design in creation, quoting Genesis 1:27 and 2:24. God created humans as male and female, establishing a complementary relationship. The union of a man and woman in marriage is depicted as a divine institution, meant to be enduring and inseparable.

The phrase "one flesh" signifies not only physical unity but also emotional, spiritual, and relational oneness, symbolizing a covenant bond. Jesus underscores that this union is God's doing, not merely a human agreement. Therefore, he asserts that marriage should not be dissolved lightly, emphasizing its sacredness and divine intention.

By referring to Scripture, Jesus redirects the conversation from human legalism to God's purpose for marriage. His teaching challenges the audience to view marriage as a reflection of God's faithfulness and commitment, reinforcing that what God joins together, humanity should respect and preserve.

Father, guide me to respect and honor marriage as I should while also acknowledging the relational difficulties that occur in our fallen world.

Keep the Commandments

Jesus answered, "Why are you asking Me about what is [essentially] good? There is only One who is [essentially] good; but if you wish to enter into eternal life, keep the commandments."

MATTHEW 19:17

Jesus' words in today's Scripture quote were in response to an inquiry about how to find everlasting life: "Now behold, one came and said to Him, 'Good Teacher, what good thing shall I do that I may have eternal life?'" (Matthew 19:16 NKJV). Notice the questioner's careless use of the word "good." Most people proclaim their own goodness. And they do this because they're ignorant of the biblical definition of the word. Proverbs 20:6 says, "Most men will proclaim each his own goodness."

So Jesus told the young man that if he wanted to find everlasting life, he had to perfectly keep the moral law. However, no one can do that because the law is spiritual. The law sees lust as adultery and hatred as murder. It leaves us all guilty (Romans 3:19–20; 7:7, 13). The law's function is to act as a schoolmaster, and it drives us to the foot of the cross, where we find the forgiveness of sins.

Father, thank you for saving me from the wrath of the law.

Loving God and Money

Jesus answered him, "If you wish to be perfect [that is, have the spiritual maturity that accompanies godly character with no moral or ethical deficiencies], go and sell what you have and give [the money] to the poor, and you will have treasure in heaven; and come, follow Me [becoming My disciple, believing and trusting in Me and walking the same path of life that I walk]."

MATTHEW 19:21

Many a person has no doubt been left with a misinterpretation of these verses, especially when they have been taken out of context. As some people have claimed, it seems that Jesus was saying that we can purchase everlasting life by selling all our goods, then taking the money and giving it to the poor. If we do that, God will then grant us a place in heaven.

However, in context, that's not what Scripture teaches. The Bible says that everlasting life is a free gift and cannot be purchased by any good works or any amount of money (Ephesians 2:8–9). Jesus was speaking to a young man who *worshiped* his money. And the Bible says you cannot serve God and money. The only way for the rich young man to come to Christ was to forsake that which he loved.

Father, keep me from trusting in and loving money rather than you.

Rich or Poor

Jesus said to His disciples, "I assure you and most solemnly say to you, it is difficult for a rich man [who clings to possessions and status as security] to enter the kingdom of heaven. Again I tell you, it is easier for a camel to go through the eye of a needle, than for a rich man [who places his faith in wealth and status] to enter the kingdom of God."...Jesus looked at them and said, "With people [as far as it depends on them] it is impossible, but with God all things are possible."

MATTHEW 19:23-24, 26

Perhaps the most commonly misunderstood and misquoted verse in the Bible leaves people believing that *money* is the root of all evil. But the Scriptures actually say that it's "the love of money" that is "a root of all kinds of evil" (1 Timothy 6:10 NKJV).

In today's verse, Jesus was saying that it is impossible for a man who loves his money (who puts his trust in his money) to enter the kingdom of God. It's impossible because we cannot serve God and money. In fact, we should not covet anything: "Let your conduct be without covetousness; be content with such things as you have. For He Himself has said, 'I will never leave you nor forsake you'" (Hebrews 13:5 NKJV). Contentment should mark our lives.

Father, never let me trust in money, and help me become content with what I have.

May

The difficulty for a rich man to enter heaven (Matthew 19:24)

The Future Is Known

"Listen carefully: we are going up to Jerusalem; and the Son of Man will be handed over to the chief priests and scribes (Sanhedrin, Jewish High Court), and they will [judicially] condemn him and sentence Him to death, and will hand Him over to the Gentiles (Roman authorities) to be mocked and scourged and crucified, and He will be raised [to life] on the third day."

Matthew 20:18–19

Jesus knew exactly what he was walking into when he went to Jerusalem. He had told his disciples that seven specific things would happen. (1) He would be handed over to the chief priests and scribes. This happened after his arrest. (2) He would be sentenced to death. (3) He would then be handed over to the gentiles. (4) He would be mocked. (5) He would be scourged. (6) The Romans would crucify him. And (7) he would be raised to life on the third day.

He knew all these things because he was divine. While we don't know too many specifics about our future, we do know that we have a hope in Jesus that is sure and steadfast, "an anchor of the soul" (Hebrews 6:19). His kingdom is coming, and his will shall be done on earth as it is in heaven.

Father, I rejoice now in the coming kingdom.

The Way Up

"It is not this way among you, but whoever wishes to become great among you shall be your servant, and whoever wishes to be first among you shall be your [willing and humble] slave; just as the Son of Man did not come to be served, but to serve, and to give His life as a ransom for many [paying the price to set them free from the penalty of sin]."

MATTHEW 20:26–28

Moms can sometimes be embarrassing. Like all good moms, they want the best for their sons, and the mother of Zebedee's sons was no different. Salome came to Jesus along with her two sons James and John, knelt down, and asked Jesus a question: "Grant that these two sons of mine may sit, one on Your right hand and the other on the left, in Your kingdom" (Matthew 20:21 NKJV).

Salome wanted Jesus to promote her sons to the top spots, and it seems that her boys were complicit. Jesus didn't rebuke her; instead, he told her that in the kingdom of God, the way up is the way down. If we want to be great, we should serve. If we want to be first, we should put ourselves last. Jesus' life is our example.

Father, may I humbly serve others this day.

The Son of God

Jesus said to them, "It is written [in Scripture], 'My house shall be called a house of prayer'; but you are making it a robbers' den."

MATTHEW 21:13

God created Adam to commune with God—as a father with his loving son. Scripture even calls Adam "the *son* of God" (Luke 3:38 NKJV). In one sense, he was the first temple of God. But when sin entered the world and Adam (like the sinful prodigal son) ran away from his Father, the temple became defiled.

This is what happened to the temple in Jerusalem. It was created to be a house of prayer, but sinful men had made it a den of thieves. Their love of money had consumed their love of God. What happened to Adam and the temple in Jerusalem is an important lesson for the Christian. "Do you not know that you are the temple of God and that the Spirit of God dwells in you? If anyone defiles the temple of God, God will destroy him. For the temple of God is holy, which temple you are" (1 Corinthians 3:16–17 NKJV). This is why we must forever shut the door to sin.

Father, I ask you this day to help me keep the defilement of sin from my temple.

Speak to the Mountain

Jesus replied to them, "I assure you and most solemnly say to you, if you have faith [personal trust and confidence in Me] and do not doubt or allow yourself to be drawn in two directions, you will not only do what was done to the fig tree, but even if you say to this mountain, 'Be taken up and thrown into the sea,' it will happen [if God wills it]. And whatever you ask for in prayer, believing, you will receive."

MATTHEW 21:21–22

Trust, faith in God, is a steadfast attitude. The Scriptures say of Abraham: "He did not waver at the promise of God through unbelief, but was strengthened in faith, giving glory to God" (Romans 4:20 NKJV).

Caleb was also a man of great faith in God. Look at his faith-filled attitude as he looked at the big problems he would encounter as he entered the promised land: "Now therefore, give me this mountain of which the Lord spoke in that day" (Joshua 14:12 NKJV). Do you have some mountain before you? Then speak to it in prayer. Tell it to move, and it will happen if God wills it.

Father, help me to overcome mountains today by trusting you.

Grace Alone

"Which of the two did the will of the father?" The chief priests and elders replied, "The first one." Jesus said to them, "I assure you and most solemnly say to you that the tax collectors and the prostitutes will get into the kingdom of God before you."

MATTHEW 21:31

Jesus often infuriated his hearers. The first sermon he ever preached caused those who heard him to want to murder him. They took him to a high cliff to toss him off, but it wasn't his time to die.

> All those in the synagogue, when they heard these things, were filled with wrath, and rose up and thrust Him out of the city; and they led Him to the brow of the hill on which their city was built, that they might throw Him down over the cliff. Then passing through the midst of them, He went His way. (Luke 4:28–30 NKJV)

Jesus asked the religious leaders a question, and they answered correctly. The one who did the will of the Father—something they refused to do—would enter the kingdom of heaven. And so, despised tax collectors and openly sinful prostitutes would enter heaven before the chief priests and elders because they humbled themselves and did God's will by trusting in Jesus.

Father, today I trust in your wonderful grace alone.

Humanity's Solution

Jesus replied to him, "'You shall love the Lord your God with all your heart, and with all your soul, and with all your mind.' This is the first and greatest commandment. The second is like it, 'You shall love your neighbor as yourself [that is, unselfishly seek the best or higher good for others].' The whole Law and the [writings of the] Prophets depend on these two commandments."

MATTHEW 22:37–40

Here is the simple answer to the world's complex problems: love God and love people. If the whole world would do that, there would be no more rape, murder, theft, greed, envy, jealousy, lust, or hatred. No one would lie to anyone, nor would they commit adultery. There would be no more war or corruption of any sort. Nor would there be starving people, drunkenness, or drug addiction.

This is because those who love God want his smile, not his frown. Think now who would be out of work if we could live and love the way Jesus taught—the police, judges, lawyers, and prison wardens. But humanity can't make that a reality until the love of God enters the selfish human heart through the new birth.

Father, today I am determined to love you and to love every person I meet.

Clean Cups

"Woe to you, [self-righteous] scribes and Pharisees, hypocrites! For you clean the outside of the cup and of the plate, but inside they are full of extortion and robbery and self-indulgence (unrestrained greed). You [spiritually] blind Pharisee, first clean the inside of the cup and of the plate [examine and change your inner self to conform to God's precepts], so that the outside [your public life and deeds] may be clean also."

MATTHEW 23:25–26

How disgusting it would be to receive a cup that had been cleaned only on the outside, with the inside lined with mold and tiny, filthy, crawling creatures. But the scenario can get far worse than that. The person who gave you the cup could then pour in a beverage and expect you to happily drink it.

That's what the religious hypocrites did with God. They presented themselves as pure vessels, but Jesus said that they were filthy on the inside. And those Pharisees were no different from you and me: "But we are all like an unclean thing, and all our righteousnesses are like filthy rags" (Isaiah 64:6 NKJV). Thank God for the cleansing blood of Jesus.

Father, never let me think of myself as being better than others.

Blind Guides

"You serpents, you spawn of vipers, how can you escape the penalty of hell?"
MATTHEW 23:33

How can any preacher overlook sin and fail to warn his people of its terrible consequences? Yet each of us is no different from those to whom Jesus gave this scathing rebuke in today's Scripture verse. They were the religious leaders who were unfaithful to their office. And that's the sin of many modern preachers. They are being unfaithful by neglecting to warn sinners of the wrath of God. These pastors fail to love their people enough to plead with them to come to the Savior. Listen to the scathing words of Charles Spurgeon:

> Ho, ho, sir surgeon, you are too delicate to tell the man that he is ill! You hope to heal the sick without their knowing it. You therefore flatter them; and what happens? They laugh at you; they dance upon their own graves. At last they die! Your delicacy is cruelty; your flatteries are poisons; you are a murderer. Shall we keep men in a fool's paradise? Shall we lull them into soft slumber from which they will awake in hell? Are we to become helpers of their damnation by our smooth speeches? In the name of God we will not.[3]

Father, make me a true and faithful witness.

---

3 Charles Spurgeon, "Coming Judgment of the Secrets of Man," The Spurgeon Library, Metropolitan Tabernacle Pulpit, vol. 31 (1885), https://www.spurgeon.org/resource-library/sermons/coming-judgement-of-the-secrets-of-man/#flipbook.

The God-Man

"O Jerusalem, Jerusalem, who murders the prophets and stones [to death] those [messengers] who are sent to her [by God]! How often I wanted to gather your children together [around Me], as a hen gathers her chicks under her wings, and you were unwilling."

Matthew 23:37

There are some who, even as professing Christians, don't know that Jesus Christ was God in human form. This is the teaching of the Bible. *All* things were made by Jesus: "All things were made through Him, and without Him nothing was made that was made…And the Word became flesh and dwelt among us" (John 1:3, 14 NKJV).

This isn't an isolated passage from Scripture: "Without controversy great is the mystery of godliness: God was manifest in the flesh" (1 Timothy 3:16 KJV). And look closely at Jesus' words as he spoke of the coming judgment of Jerusalem for murdering those who were sent to them. He spoke as God: "How often I wanted to gather your children together [around Me]." In the incarnation, we see the miracle of God creating for himself a sinless body and filling that body with himself for the purpose of saving humanity from death and hell.

Father, when I think of who Jesus is, it fills me with awe.

The Glory of God

"At that time the sign of the Son of Man [coming in His glory] will appear in the sky, and then all the tribes of the earth [and especially Israel] will mourn [regretting their rebellion and rejection of the Messiah], and they will see the Son of Man coming on the clouds of heaven with power and great glory [in brilliance and splendor]. And He will send His angels with a loud trumpet and they will gather together His elect (God's chosen ones) from the four winds, from one end of the heavens to the other."

MATTHEW 24:30–31

The Bible speaks of the glory of the sun, the moon, and the stars: "There is one glory of the sun, another glory of the moon, and another glory of the stars; for one star differs from another star in glory" (1 Corinthians 15:41 NJKV).

"Glory" is certainly appropriate as we witness a glorious sunrise or sunset, a full moon as it rises over the ocean, or the actual size of tiny stars that twinkle in the heavens. But all this magnificence combined is but a pale and insignificant shadow compared to the glory that will be revealed at the second coming of Jesus Christ. Yet with all his glory and splendor, not one of those who love him will be forgotten.

Father, I live for the coming kingdom.

Jesus Said It

"Heaven and earth [as now known] will pass away, but My words will not pass away. But of that [exact] day and hour no one knows, not even the angels of heaven, nor the Son [in His humanity], but the Father alone."

Matthew 24:35-36

Jesus told us that the heavens and the earth will be made brand-new in the coming kingdom, where there will be no more pain, suffering, or death. The Bible tells us that it will be so magnificent that our mere human imaginations cannot begin to conceive of the wonderful things that God has prepared for those who love him. So much so that any understanding or insight we gain into the goodness and the wonders of God must be directly attributed to the Holy Spirit (1 Corinthians 2:9–10). Jesus said that heaven and earth would pass away before his words passed away. And now two thousand years later, we are still reading them.

When a woman broke an alabaster box of ointment and anointed Jesus, some of Jesus' disciples complained about the waste (Mark 14:4). But Jesus said that wherever the gospel would be preached, what she had done would be remembered (v. 9). More than two thousand years later, what she did is recorded in the best-selling book of all time for hundreds of millions to read. Everything Jesus said has perfectly come to pass.

Father, thank you that no one can resist you and your perfect will.

Godly Priorities

"Be alert [give strict attention, be cautious and active in faith], for you do not know which day [whether near or far] your Lord is coming."
MATTHEW 24:42

There is nothing as important as our faith in Jesus. Every decision that we make, everything we purchase, every conversation, every friendship we have, pales into insignificance when compared to our walk with the Savior. These things are just part of daily life, and they will pass away, but our walk with Jesus determines our eternity. Faith in the Savior should be first and foremost on our minds. Yet to most of the world, it is the last thing.

However, on the day of judgment, nothing else will matter. When anyone passes from this life, whether it be an average person or someone famous, the question that we should ask ourselves is "Were their sins forgiven?"

In a world of busyness, it is very easy for us to put other things before our walk with the Lord, but one of the best ways to ensure this doesn't happen is to spend time every day reading and meditating on God's Word and looking forward to Jesus' second coming.

Father, this day I will seek first your kingdom and your righteousness.

The Mind of God

"The King will say to those on His right, 'Come, you blessed of My Father [you favored of God, appointed to eternal salvation], inherit the kingdom prepared for you from the foundation of the world.'"

Matthew 25:34

Our eternal salvation was prepared before the beginning of time as we know it. The mind of God is absolutely mind-blowing. Think of a massive crowd at the Super Bowl. Among all those faces, each one is different, yet all were made by God. I think about the fact that he knows how many hairs are on every head. He knows every person by name, and he knows the thoughts of their hearts—from the moment they are born until the moment they die. He is intimately familiar with the middle atom in the eyeball of every person…because he made it.

Then multiply that thought by eight billion people and then do the same with every human being who has come and gone in the centuries before us. Add to that the uniqueness of every creature (every bird, fish, elephant, and flea), and we begin to get a tiny glimpse of the mind of God. One other thought: God sees everything, knows everything, and dwells everywhere throughout the infinitude of the universe he created.

Father, with all this, you are the lover of my soul.

Not My Will But Yours Be Done

After going a little farther, He fell face down and prayed, saying, "My Father, if it is possible [that is, consistent with Your will], let this cup pass from Me; yet not as I will, but as You will."

MATTHEW 26:39

Life is full of bitter cups from which we would rather not drink. We cannot help but taste the bitterness of suffering. Jesus knew that cup was waiting for him, and he pleaded with the Father for another way. And yet he yielded to God's will, motivated by love for guilty sinners. We can't begin to imagine the agony of the cross. But what we can do is show our gratitude for what Jesus did by praying the same prayer that Jesus prayed: "Not as I will, but as You will" (v. 39 NKJV).

Many a Christian on his deathbed has no doubt regretted living a life of self-indulgence rather than self-denial. What a sad conclusion to my existence it would be to realize that I have spent my life enjoying legitimate but frivolous pleasures rather than passionately doing the will of God. One of the greatest revelations that we can have as Christians is to have Solomon's understanding of the futility of life. Living for ourselves is indeed "grasping for the wind" (Ecclesiastes 1:14 NKJV).

Father, let me live for you, doing only your will.

Leave the Sword Alone

Jesus said to him, "Put your sword back in its place; for all those who habitually draw the sword will die by the sword. Do you think that I cannot appeal to My Father, and He will immediately provide Me with more than twelve legions of angels?"

MATTHEW 26:52-53

It's easy to panic when things go wrong. And it's then, when we aren't thinking straight, that we take up a sword. We take things into our own hands. We may not pick up a physical sword, but it's in moments of panic when we say things that are cutting and destructive. We should rather take notice of the two-edged sword given to us by God—his Word.

This is what Jesus was saying to Peter. God can handle it when things seem to go wrong. Nothing takes him by surprise. He is always totally in control. In those times of emergency, it is best that we stand still and see what God does to deliver us. That's what Daniel did in the lion's den, and it's what Moses did at the Red Sea, and neither of them was disappointed.

Father, remind me to keep my sword in its sheath.

Have You Come with Swords?

At that moment Jesus said to the crowds, "Have you come out with swords and clubs to arrest Me as you would against a robber? Day after day I used to sit in the porches and courts of the temple teaching, and you did not arrest Me. But all this has taken place so that the Scriptures of the prophets would be fulfilled." Then all the disciples deserted Him and fled.

MATTHEW

It seems that Judas wasn't listening very closely to Jesus for all the years that he followed him. This is evident by the fact that Judas brought a mob armed with swords and clubs to arrest Jesus even though he knew that Jesus had said to love our enemies. Or perhaps Judas thought that the rest of the disciples were like him and would not be peacemakers like Jesus. Perhaps Judas thought they would take things into their own hands.

Peter did take things into his own hands by drawing his sword. After that happened, Jesus told Peter to sheath his sword, and then all the disciples scattered in fear as Scripture had warned they would: "Strike the Shepherd, and the sheep will be scattered" (Zechariah 13:7 NKJV).

Father, may I always listen closely to your Word and be quick to obey it.

The Agony

"My God, My God, why have You forsaken Me?" When some of the bystanders there heard it, they began saying, "This man is calling for Elijah."

MATTHEW

This wasn't a criminal being executed for his crimes. Nor was it an innocent man being executed for crimes he didn't commit. This was the sinless Son of God suffering for the sin of the world. But it was also a display of the wrath of a holy God falling upon Jesus of Nazareth so that we could live forever.

Such thoughts can help us hear the agony in his cry as he fulfilled the prophecy written eight hundred years beforehand in the book of Psalms: "My God, My God, why have You forsaken Me? Why are You so far from helping Me, and from the words of My groaning?" (Psalm 22:1 NKJV). A holy God turned his back on his beloved Son because Jesus actually became sin. "He made Him who knew no sin to be sin for us, that we might become the righteousness of God in Him" (2 Corinthians 5:21 NKJV).

Father, no words can express my gratitude.

The Unspeakable Gift

As they went, suddenly, Jesus met them, saying, "Rejoice!" And they went to Him and took hold of His feet [in homage] and worshiped Him [as the Messiah].

Matthew 28:9

We have good reason to "rejoice evermore" (1 Thessalonians 5:16 KJV). While this initial rejoicing was confined to the disciples at this time, more than two thousand years later we can join them in their joy. Jesus was showing that he did indeed defeat death for *all* who believe so that we can also enjoy pleasure forevermore. His resurrection meant that eventually the day will come when there will be no more tears, pain, suffering, or death.

But notice that the women in Matthew 28:9 didn't throw a party or sing joyful songs. Instead, they fell upon the ground and held onto the feet of Jesus. Their rejoicing was intermingled with humility of heart and a gratitude that they couldn't express in human words. We, too, fall at the feet of Jesus, saying with the apostle Paul, "Thanks be unto God for his unspeakable gift" (2 Corinthians 9:15 KJV). How could we not then run to this dying world, pleading with its people to repent and believe? God, forgive us for complacency.

Father, give me such a love that I cannot but speak that which I've seen and heard.

Do Not Fear

Jesus said to them, "Do not be afraid; go and tell My brothers to leave for Galilee, and there they will see Me [just as I promised]."

Matthew 28:10

The reason Jesus told the women at the tomb not to be afraid was because fear can be paralyzing. The disciples, however, thought they had good reason to be afraid. Their leader had just been executed, and they were his followers. It made sense to believe that the authorities would come after them next so that they could completely eradicate the blasphemous sect. And if the authorities did find the apostles, they wouldn't have a quick death. The followers of Jesus would probably be crucified and left to die in unspeakable agony as a public example not to follow this Jesus of Nazareth. But their fears were, in truth, unfounded.

On the day of Pentecost, we see that God made provision for our fears. He sent the Holy Spirit so that we can be bold in our faith. And that's what we see happen in the life of Peter, who turned from cowardice to courage because of the infilling of the Holy Spirit. That's why the Bible tells us to be filled with the Spirit.

Father, fill me with your Spirit so I may speak boldly about your Son and the salvation he offers.

Thy Kingdom Come

Jesus came up and said to them, "All authority (all power of absolute rule) in heaven and on earth has been given to Me. Go therefore and make disciples of all the nations [help the people to learn of Me, believe in Me, and obey My words], baptizing them in the name of the Father and of the Son and of the Holy Spirit, teaching them to observe everything that I have commanded you; and lo, I am with you always [remaining with you perpetually—regardless of circumstance, and on every occasion], even to the end of the age."

MATTHEW 28:18-20

Look at how the Amplified Bible wonderfully informs us that when Jesus said, "I will be with you always," he was saying that he would be with us perpetually, regardless of the fact that we may be in a lions' den or at the edge of the Red Sea. No matter our circumstances, he promises to be with us until the end of the age.

And when the kingdom of God comes to this earth physically, we will see him face-to-face. The second coming of Jesus is what we live for, but for the wicked, it will be a terrifying day. These sobering thoughts should help us overcome our fears, and as the apostle Paul said, to speak "as [we] ought to speak" (Ephesians 6:20).

Father, we need your help always because without you, we can do nothing.

Godly Sorrow

"The [appointed period of] time is fulfilled, and the kingdom of God is at hand; repent [change your inner self—your old way of thinking, regret past sins, live your life in a way that proves repentance; seek God's purpose for your life] and believe [with a deep, abiding trust] in the good news [regarding salvation]."

Mark 1:15

For the last section of this verse, the New King James Version simply says, "Repent, and believe in the gospel." But look at what repentance and faith actually mean. Repentance is more than just a superficial regret for past "mistakes" we've made. The Bible says for sinners to cleanse their hands and purify their hearts, to let their "laughter be turned to mourning" and their "joy to gloom" (James 4:8–9 NKJV). Judas regretted his wicked betrayal. But it seems he wasn't biblically repentant (Acts 1:25).

The Bible says it's godly sorrow that works repentance unto life (2 Corinthians 7:10). It is therefore important for every Christian to make sure they understand the exceeding depravity of sin. It is that knowledge that helps us to find a place of godly sorrow and true repentance.

Father, this day I will examine myself and see if I'm in the faith.

A Good Doctor

When Jesus heard this, He said to them, "Those who are healthy have no need of a physician, but [only] those who are sick; I did not come to call the righteous, but sinners [who recognize their sin and humbly seek forgiveness]."

MARK 2:17

In today's Scripture passage, Jesus was saying that if we don't recognize our own disease of sin, we won't seek God to be healed. And that's the great delusion that plagues almost all of humanity. So many people think they're morally well when, in reality, they are terminally ill. This is why it's so important for each of us as Christians to confront the world with its sin.

Of course, we do this in a firm and uncompromising gentleness because we are motivated by love and concern. What a coldhearted doctor he would be who refused to confront a dying patient about the severity of his disease! Any doctor who would let someone die would be a traitor to his profession. A good doctor will look the patient in the eye and tell them the bad news. And we must do the same except for the fact that we also have the good news: there is a cure.

Father, may I be a good physician.

Stretch Out Your Hand

After looking around at them with anger, grieved at the hardness and arrogance of their hearts, He told the man, "Hold out your hand." And he held it out, and his hand was [completely] restored.

MARK 3:5

In today's verse, the man at the synagogue had a withered hand. It was useless to him. But he wasn't healed until he obeyed Jesus and held it out—despite the fact that he was surrounded by hard-hearted and arrogant men. Is your hand withered? Do you reach out to the lost, or are you influenced by the hardhearted people around you who have no concern that the world is going to hell?

Think of the sobering last words of the actor and singer David Cassidy, who died in 2017. His daughter reported that as Cassidy was passing into eternity, he said, "So much wasted time." We don't know the reason he said that, but whatever you do, don't let your life be a waste of time. There is no cause more worthy than obedience to the Great Commission: "He said to them, 'Go into all the world and preach the gospel to every creature'" (Mark 16:15 NKJV). Today, obey Jesus and hold out your hand to this dying world.

Father, help me to stretch out my hand to the lost.

He Who Has Ears

He said, "He who has ears to hear, let him hear and heed My words."
MARK 4:9

This is a strange thing for Jesus to say as he began the Parable of the Sower. It seems obvious that if we have ears, we will use them. However, there are multitudes who have an ear for music, an ear for politics, an ear for gossip, and ears for every other sound under the sun, but they don't have an ear for the precious Word of God. As far as they are concerned, the Bible is not worthy of their undivided attention. Many others seem to hear, but because of a proud heart, they remain deaf to the glorious message of everlasting life.

This is why we must cultivate humility and honesty of heart. When Jesus was speaking of his coming suffering, he referred to his disciples' ears: "Let these words sink down into your ears, for the Son of Man is about to be betrayed into the hands of men" (Luke 9:44 NKJV). He said the good soil (the true convert) is the one who "hears the word and understands it" (Matthew 13:23 NKJV). Then, as Jesus concluded the parable, he repeated those words, reminding us to use our ears wisely by always listening closely to the Word of God.

Father, may I always have ears to hear.

The Hidden Things

He said to them, "The mystery of the kingdom of God has been given to you [who have teachable hearts], but those who are outside [the unbelievers, the spiritually blind] get everything in parables, so that they will continually look but not see, and they will continually hear but not understand, otherwise they might turn [from their rejection of the truth] and be forgiven."

Mark 4:11–12

Jesus thanked the Father because God had hidden the mysteries of the kingdom from the wise and prudent (Matthew 11:25). And they are hidden because God "resists the proud, but gives grace to the humble" (James 4:6 NKJV). David said, "My soul shall make its boast in the Lord; the humble shall hear of it and be glad" (Psalm 34:2 NKJV).

The proud aren't glad when God is given glory. They instead get mad. This is because they love their sin and hate the light of righteousness. And the tragic consequence is that they don't understand the unspeakably good news that everlasting life is a free gift (Romans 6:23). No matter how much we lovingly contend with a proud person, they cannot see nor understand the gospel. They look and don't see. They hear and don't understand.

Father, I pray for the multitudes who are blind to the gospel.

Hunger for Knowledge

He said to them, "Pay attention to what you hear. By your own standard of measurement [that is, to the extent that you study spiritual truth and apply godly wisdom] it will be measured to you [and you will be given even greater ability to respond]—and more will be given to you besides. For whoever has [a teachable heart], to him more [understanding] will be given; and whoever does not have [a yearning for truth], even what he has will be taken away from him."

MARK 4:24–25

One virtue of children is that they love to learn, and they do so with wide eyes. They want to learn about the animals they see and the marvels of nature that surround them. And they will become educated according to their own hunger for knowledge.

The same applies within the kingdom of God. Jesus said that we are to become as little children, and so we mingle our faith in the Bible with an insatiable hunger for the things of God. However, we don't want to simply become knowledgeable. Knowledge puffs up. Instead, we should strive to become wise, and the wise will walk in humility of heart. In other words, the wise will use knowledge correctly.

Father, today make me wise. Teach me eternal truths.

The Small Things

He said, "How shall we picture the kingdom of God, or what parable shall we use to illustrate and explain it? It is like a mustard seed, which, when it is sown on the ground, even though it is smaller than all the [other] seeds that are [sown] on the soil, yet when it is sown, it grows up and becomes larger than all the garden herbs; and it puts out large branches, so that the birds of the sky are able to make nests and live under its shade."

MARK 4:30-32

It is a principle of God that he takes small things and grows them for his glory. When King Saul was disobedient, Samuel rebuked him. "Samuel said to Saul, 'Be quiet! And I will tell you what the LORD said to me last night.' And he said to him, 'Speak on.' So Samuel said, 'When you were little in your own eyes, were you not head of the tribes of Israel? And did not the LORD anoint you king over Israel?'" (1 Samuel 15:16–17 NKJV).

The way to stay small is to think of the bigness of God.

Father, remind me daily that I am nothing without you.

Do You Believe?

On that [same] day, when evening had come, He said to them, "Let us go over to the other side [of the Sea of Galilee]."

MARK 4:35

Today's Scripture verse preceded the storm that came on the sea of Galilee and terrified the disciples. Jesus had said that they were going to the other side. If the apostles had truly believed the words of Jesus, they would not have feared.

Those who doubt the words of Jesus open their hearts to fear, anxiety, and eventually despair. In the wonderful allegory *The Pilgrim's Progress*, Christian and his companion Faithful found themselves in Doubting Castle, where they were tormented by Giant Despair. They both doubted God's promises and consequently found themselves in despair.

Never doubt the words of Jesus. Think of what he said to Mary: "I am the resurrection and the life. He who believes in Me, though he may die, he shall live. And whoever lives and believes in Me shall never die. Do you believe this?" (John 11:25–26 NKJV). Do you believe what Jesus said? Do you believe that because of Jesus, you will never die? If you believe, never let fear come near you. You are going to the other side.

Father, though I walked through the valley of the shadow of death, I will fear no evil. You're always with me.

Remember the Battle

Jesus had been saying to him, "Come out of the man, you unclean spirit!"

MARK 5:8

Never forget that the Christian life is a battle against spiritual entities. The Bible says we wrestle "not against flesh and blood," but against "spiritual wickedness in high places" (Ephesians 6:12 KJV). Sometimes discouragement has a spiritual source. So does hatred.

The Bible speaks of the spirit of fear (2 Timothy 1:7). In today's verse, Jesus tells us there is such a thing as an unclean spirit. This is why the Christian is often plagued with unclean thoughts that seem to come out of nowhere. The temptation is to dwell upon these thoughts, and that's when they can lead us down the dark pathway of sin.

Never let that happen. Guard your heart with all diligence. Remember the battle. And then put into practice the commands of Scripture: "Stand therefore, having girded your waist with truth, having put on the breastplate of righteousness, and having shod your feet with the preparation of the gospel of peace; above all, taking the shield of faith with which you will be able to quench all the fiery darts of the wicked one" (Ephesians 6:14–16 NKJV).

Father, remind me to keep my armor on today.

The Word

Taking the child's hand, He said [tenderly] to her, "Talitha kum!"—which translated [from Aramaic] means, "Little girl, I say to you, get up!"

MARK 5:41

Jesus had a habit of speaking to the dead. He did it with Lazarus by saying, "Lazarus, come forth" (John 11:43 KJV). This is because Christ's voice brought life into existence. He said, "The words that I speak are spirit, and they are life" (John 6:63 NKJV). He is even called "the Word" that existed in the beginning who made all things: "In the beginning was the Word, and the Word was with God, and the Word was God. He was in the beginning with God. All things were made through Him, and without Him nothing was made that was made" (John 1:1–3 NKJV).

His voice created everything, and he told us not to marvel because the day would come when his life-creating voice will raise all the dead: "The hour is coming in which all who are in the graves will hear His voice and come forth—those who have done good, to the resurrection of life, and those who have done evil, to the resurrection of condemnation" (John 5:28–29 NKJV). "Today, if you will hear His voice: do not harden your hearts" (Psalm 95:7–8 NKJV).

Father, may I always be open to hearing your voice.

Go Home First

He said to him, "Go home to your family and tell them all the great things that the Lord has done for you, and how He has had mercy on you."

MARK 5:19

Jesus had just delivered a man from a legion of demons, and then we read that the locals came to Jesus and saw the one who had been demon-possessed sitting and clothed and in his right mind. When Jesus was about to leave, the man had one request: "When He got into the boat, he who had been demon-possessed begged Him that he might be with Him" (Mark 5:18 NKJV). It was a legitimate request. The man was thankful and knew that Jesus came from God, so it seems reasonable that he wanted to follow him. However, Jesus said he couldn't. Instead he told the man to go back to his loved ones and share the way of salvation.

This should be our experience as new Christians. While we might want to travel the world and be a missionary to the lost, our first responsibility should be to those we love most. Then we should go far and wide.

Father, may my love for the lost send me deep into the world.

June

Calming the storm (Mark 4:35)

In Times of Trouble

He said to them, "Come away by yourselves to a secluded place and rest a little while"—for there were many [people who were continually] coming and going, and they could not even find time to eat."

MARK 6:31

It had been a really rough week. King Herod had just executed the cousin of Jesus—the greatest man ever born to a woman. It made no sense whatsoever. John the Baptist had said that Jesus must increase and that he must decrease, and that had certainly happened. The twisted king, in an effort to keep an oath, had horrifically murdered John. It was because of who John was that it was a mystery as to why God let it happen.

When Jesus' disciples heard of this tragedy, they gathered around Jesus and told him what had happened. And that's when he told them that they needed to go to a deserted place and rest. When suddenly tragedy strikes in our lives, rather than becoming anxious and fearful, we should simply trust that God allowed it for a reason. And then we should go to a quiet place and rest a little while.

Father, may I learn to come aside in troubled times and rest in Jesus.

Groaning and Sighing

He groaned and sighed deeply in His spirit and said, "Why does this generation demand a sign? I assure you and most solemnly say to you, no sign will be given to this generation!"
MARK 8:12

Scripture captures a moment where Jesus expresses frustration with the Pharisees' demand for a sign to validate his authority. His deep groaning in spirit reflects sorrow and exasperation over their persistent unbelief. Rather than seeking to understand the teachings and the signs he had already provided through his miracles, they demanded further proof, revealing hardened hearts and a lack of genuine faith.

Jesus' response—"No sign will be given to this generation,"—underscores his rejection of their superficial approach. Faith, he emphasizes, should not solely rely on extraordinary signs but even more on trust in God's revelation. This statement also points to their inability to recognize the greatest sign—the presence of Jesus himself as the Messiah.

In context, Jesus critiques a mindset that refuses to see God's work in the everyday and demands spectacular evidence as a condition for belief. This verse invites us to reflect on our own faith and whether it is rooted in trust or in seeking signs.

Father, cause me to take my groaning into prayer for the salvation of the lost.

Bad Doctrine

Jesus repeatedly ordered them, saying, "Watch out! Beware of the leaven of the Pharisees and the leaven of Herod."
MARK 8:15

In Scripture, *leaven* is usually interpreted to mean "unsound doctrine," which puffs up and spreads very quickly. Those who embrace unsound doctrine often do so in a spirit of pride. They are right, and everybody else is wrong. It made sense that Jesus warned his followers to be aware of the bad doctrine of the Pharisees, who made the mistake of cleansing the outside through religious works while inwardly remaining filthy in the sight of a holy God. Jesus had scathing rebukes for them, saying that they strained at the gnat (kept trivial requirements of their tradition) and swallowed the camel (neglected godliness in obvious ways).

Religious rules and regulations tend to choke those who believe in justification through self-righteousness. There is no rest when we're trying to earn our way to heaven. But Jesus also warned of the bad doctrine of Herod. The king gladly listened to John the Baptist (Mark 6:20). But he didn't find a place of genuine repentance and instead gave himself to lust, adultery, and murder. That's the path where bad doctrine can take us. We need to learn a lesson from King David, who traveled a sinful path but later humbled himself in repentance.

Father, remind me to walk in perpetual repentance.

Unbelieving Generation

He replied, "O unbelieving (faithless) generation, how long shall I be with you? How long shall I put up with you? Bring him to Me!"

Mark 9:19

A man in the crowd had brought to Jesus his son, who had a mute spirit. The boy couldn't talk. This demon violently threw him down on the ground and caused him to foam at the mouth, gnash his teeth, and then become rigid. This was no doubt frightening for the parents, so they went to Jesus' disciples in desperation and asked if they could cast the demon out. But they couldn't.

Then Jesus put his finger on the disciples' problem. He said they had no faith in God. He called them an *unbelieving* generation. There was even a hint of anger in the tone of his reply. He said, "How long shall I put up with you?" In other words, they were beginning to irritate him. Unbelief is an irritant. It is a serious insult even to sinful human beings. If someone has no faith in you, that would probably irritate you, especially if you are convinced that you are trustworthy. How much more then should unbelief anger a holy God?

Father, help me to trust you with all my heart.

My Weakness

Jesus said to him, "[You say to Me,] 'If You can?' All things are possible for the one who believes and trusts [in Me]!" Immediately the father of the boy cried out [with a desperate, piercing cry], saying, "I do believe; help [me overcome] my unbelief."

Mark 9:23–24

When a demon in a young boy saw Jesus, it sent the boy into convulsions. He then fell onto the ground and wallowed, foaming at the mouth. When Jesus asked his father how long this had been happening, he replied, "From childhood. And often he has thrown him both into the fire and into the water to destroy him. But if You can do anything, have compassion on us and help us" (Mark 9:21–22 NKJV). When Jesus told the father to trust in him, the desperate father admitted his struggle. He lacked trust, but he didn't want that to hinder his son's deliverance.

Overwhelming trials tend to produce desperate prayers. When we find ourselves in a lion's den, we understand that we are weak and helpless and that our only hope is in heaven's help. Take consolation, dear Christian. God knows our struggles with unbelief. It's part of our sinful nature, but God's love is greater.

Father, forgive me for my failures and help me in my weakness.

Blinded Eyes

"If your eye causes you to stumble and sin, throw it out [that is, remove yourself from the source of temptation]! It would be better for you to enter the kingdom of God with one eye, than to have two eyes and be thrown into hell, where their worm [that feeds on the dead] does not die, and the fire is not put out."

Mark 9:47–48

Sin is frightening because we have a love-hate relationship with it. We long to do that which pleases God, while our sinful nature wants to please itself. But Jesus gives us the key to overcoming sin's power: fear. Though God has not given us the spirit of fear, there is a fear that can help us in our battle with sin.

Look at how Scripture puts the cross right at the heart of this struggle: "In mercy and truth atonement is provided for iniquity; and by the fear of the Lord one departs from evil" (Proverbs 16:6 NKJV). We see God's everlasting mercy at the cross, where Jesus made atonement for sin once and for all. Rather than let our sin-loving eyes have their way, we should quickly run to the cross—to Christ crucified—where we see love and find mercy.

Father, keep the cross before me today.

The More Important Agenda

"Salt is good and useful; but if salt has lost its saltiness (purpose), how will you make it salty? Have salt within yourselves continually, and be at peace with one another."
MARK 9:50

Ephesians 4:3 exhorts us to unify: "Make every effort to keep the unity of the Spirit through the bond of peace" (NIV). The way for any church to have a unity of spirit and a bond of peace is to realize the importance of the Great Commission (Mark 16:15). We are soldiers in the war of all wars, fighting the good fight of faith. No soldier should allow petty differences with his fellow troops to hinder him from fighting the battle. For the sake of the cause, he must unite himself with his fellow soldiers because an army's strength is in its unity of purpose.

We have an Enemy who knows this and who will make every effort to divide and conquer us. And he often does this through misunderstandings and confusion. If we have some sort of misunderstanding or miscommunication with a fellow Christian, we must quickly sort it out. Be quick to let go of your own way and instead think of the good of others—just as a soldier understands that there's an agenda that is more important than his own.

Father, help me to exalt others above myself.

Let the Children Come to Jesus

When Jesus saw this, He was indignant and He said to them, "Allow the children to come to Me; do not forbid them; for the kingdom of God belongs to such as these. I assure you and most solemnly say to you, whoever does not receive and welcome the kingdom of God like a child will not enter it at all."

Mark 10:14–15

By emphasizing that the kingdom of God belongs to those like children, Jesus elevated the status of children, challenging societies who often undervalue them. The qualities of children—such as their wide-eyed innocence, their humility, their gentle trust, and their continual willingness to learn, are presented in today's verses as being essential for entering the kingdom of God. These two verses also suggest that the faith required to enter God's kingdom is very simple and very trusting, akin to a child's faith in a parent, rather than being complex or intellectual.

Jesus' statement served as a rebuke to the disciples, teaching them an important lesson not only about humility but also about the nature of true greatness in God's kingdom.

Father, may I be childlike before you today.

The Love of Money

Looking at him, Jesus felt a love (high regard, compassion) for him, and He said to him, "You lack one thing: go and sell all your property and give [the money] to the poor, and you will have [abundant] treasure in heaven; and come, follow Me [becoming My disciple, believing and trusting in Me and walking the same path of life that I walk]."

Mark 10:21

The rich young man in today's Scripture verse lacked one thing. There was just one thing that stood between him and the gift of eternal life: his sin. He loved his money, and we cannot love both money and God (Matthew 6:24). Jesus therefore loved and pitied the young man because Jesus knew that unless the man rid himself of that inordinate affection, it would take him to hell.

The people of the world have just one thing stopping them from finding the true riches of everlasting life in Christ. It's also their sin. And to find Jesus, they must forsake that sin. Jesus warned his hearers that unless they found a place of repentance, they would perish (Luke 13:2–3). In loving his money, this rich youth had violated the first of the Ten Commandments. He had another god on his throne.

Father, never let any idol come between you and me.

God's Faithfulness

Jesus said, "I assure you and most solemnly say to you, there is no one who has given up a house or brothers or sisters or mother or father or children or farms, for My sake and for the gospel's sake, who will not receive a hundred times as much now in the present age—houses and brothers and sisters and mothers and children and farms—along with persecutions; and in the age to come, eternal life."

MARK 10:29–30

Today's verse is not an invitation to exchange the riches of this life for the riches of the next. We cannot purchase everlasting life because it's without price (Ephesians 2:8–9). It is, rather, a comfort for those who, because they have already received the gift of salvation, give up the things of this world to accommodate it.

A number of disciples gave up fishing for fish so that they could fish for men. One left the security of being a tax collector. They gave up the temporal for the eternal. Hebrews 11 lists those people who gave their all in this life for the riches that endure forever. Rather than a recipe for salvation, these verses are an affirmation that God will supply his children's needs.

Father, I trust you to take care of me in this life and the next.

Servant of Humanity

Calling them to Himself, Jesus said to them, "You know that those who are recognized as rulers of the Gentiles lord it over them; and their powerful men exercise authority over them [tyrannizing them]. But this is not how it is among you; instead, whoever wishes to become great among you must be your servant, and whoever wishes to be first and most important among you must be slave of all. For even the Son of Man did not come to be served, but to serve, and to give His life as a ransom for many."

MARK 10:42–45

Jesus Christ was the ultimate servant, offering hopeless sinners the ultimate service, giving his life on the cross so that we could be free from sin and death. That's why he came to this earth: to give his life as a ransom for many.

Such love should break our hearts and leave us with a burning desire to please God. And we can please him by imitating Jesus. We can serve both the sinner and the saved: the saved by doing them good in any way possible and the sinner by giving them the good news of the gospel.

Father, help me to be your servant today.

Let Me See

Jesus said, "What do you want Me to do for you?" The blind man said to Him, "Rabboni (my Master), let me regain my sight." Jesus said to him, "Go; your faith [and confident trust in My power] has made you well." Immediately he regained his sight and began following Jesus on the road.

Mark 10:51–52

What do you want God to do for you today? Do you have a need that is so pressing that it's blinding you to everything else? Then persist in prayer. Don't give up. Be like the woman of whom Jesus spoke who persisted in her petition to a judge (Luke 18:1–8). He said that because of her persistence, the judge would eventually give her what she so desperately wanted (vv. 4–5). Then he likened this to our consistent petitioning the God who loves us for the things we need (v. 7).

In today's Scripture passage, this blind man's need was obvious. He didn't want anything else but eyesight. But Jesus still required him to articulate this need. He wanted the man to say, "Master, let me regain my sight." So when you continue in importune prayer, make sure Jesus is your master because the need for that is greater than your immediate need—great though it may seem at the time.

Father, you alone are my Lord and Master.

Fearless Faith

"I assure you and most solemnly say to you, whoever says to this mountain, 'Be lifted up and thrown into the sea!' and does not doubt in his heart [in God's unlimited power], but believes that what he says is going to take place, it will be done for him [in accordance with God's will]. For this reason I am telling you, whatever things you ask for in prayer [in accordance with God's will], believe [with confident trust] that you have received them, and they will be given to you."

MARK 11:23–24

Faith in something or in a person will only be as strong as our knowledge of the integrity of the subject. If we have knowledge that a one-hundred-foot-high bridge over jagged rocks is impeccably solid, we base our faith on that particular knowledge.

Life is a high bridge over jagged rocks. Our walk with God through this life will be faith-filled and fearless if we have knowledge of his incredible integrity. And then integrity is based on the pivotal fact that the Bible says it's impossible for God to lie. The bridge is unbreakable.

Father, today I refuse to fear because my faith in you is full.

The Whole World

Jesus answered, "The first and most important one is: 'Hear, O Israel, the Lord our God is one Lord; and you shall love the Lord your God with all your heart, and with all your soul (life), and with all your mind (thought, understanding), and with all your strength.' This is the second: 'You shall [unselfishly] love your neighbor as yourself.' There is no other commandment greater than these."

Mark 12:29–31

Today's verse came as a result of one of the scribes who heard Jesus reasoning with his hearers. When the scribe realized that Jesus had answered the man well, he asked Jesus, "Which is the first commandment of all?" In other words, which one was the most important? "Hear, O Israel," is how Jesus set up his answer to the most important of questions, quoting from Deuteronomy 6:4.

There are those who erroneously think this great commandment is only for Israel. God gave his law to the children of Israel first, but then it was given to the whole world: "Now we know that whatever the law says, it says to those who are under the law, that every mouth may be stopped, and all the world may become guilty before God" (Romans 3:19 NKJV).

Father, help me to use the law to show this world their sin.

The Reason for Persecution

"Be on your guard; they will turn you over to courts, and you will be beaten in synagogues, and you will stand [as accused] before governors and kings for My sake, as a testimony to them. The gospel [that is, the good news regarding the way of salvation] must first be preached to all the [Gentile] nations. When they take you and turn you over [to the court], do not worry beforehand about what to say, but say whatever is given to you [by God] in that hour; for it is not you who speak, but it is the Holy Spirit [who will speak through you]."

MARK 13:9–11

Jesus warned his disciples that persecution would come to them *for his sake*. It is the name of Jesus that is offensive to this wicked world. Hollywood celebrities receive enthusiastic applause when they thank God for their awards. But as soon as the name of Jesus is spoken, many people take instant offense.

After he spoke about his miracles, Jesus said, "Blessed is he who is not offended because of Me" (Matthew 11:5–7 NKJV). The tragic irony is that the only one who can save many from death is the one they hate.

Father, never let me be ashamed of Jesus.

God's Sovereignty

He said to them, "You will no doubt quote this proverb to Me, 'Physician, heal yourself! Whatever [miracles] that we heard were done [by You] in Capernaum, do here in Your hometown as well.'"

LUKE 4:23

The words from today's Scripture verse came just before Jesus grossly insulted his hearers in the synagogue in his hometown. They were so offended that they gnashed on him like rabid dogs. Their hearts were filled with murder. This is because Jesus pointed out that in the Old Testament, God healed a number of gentiles, and in those cases, God ignored his chosen people. To those in the synagogue, the gentiles were unclean and undeserving of God's mercy. However, God has mercy on whomever he wants to have mercy. This is the known as the *sovereignty of God*, and it is offensive to some. Charles Spurgeon said:

> This doctrine of divine sovereignty was not according to the taste of these people, they did not like it, and some of you, I fear, do not like it. They grew very angry, they began to gnash their teeth, and to say, "This young man must be silenced; we will not listen to such doctrine as this from him."[4]

Father, I am both comforted and delighted that you do as you will.

---

4 Charles Spurgeon, Spurgeon's Verse Expositions of the Bible, Luke 4, accessed December 30, 2024, https://www.truthaccordingtoscripture.com/commentaries/spe/luke-4.php.

Earnest Prayer

"In truth I say to you, there were many widows in Israel in the days of Elijah, when the sky was closed up for three years and six months, when a great famine came over all the land."

LUKE 4:25

Elijah had great power with God. The prophet said that there would be no rain, and there came a great drought, which led to famine all over the land. After three and a half years, he then prayed for rain seven times, and it rained, and "the sky became black with clouds and wind, and there was a heavy rain" (1 Kings 18:45 NKJV). The New Testament opens the passage for us: "Elijah was a man with a nature like ours, and he prayed earnestly that it would not rain; and it did not rain on the land for three years and six months" (James 5:17 NKJV).

The inference is that we can have great influence through the power of earnest prayer. And we have a great advantage. We come to God in the name of Jesus, knowing that he hears our prayers. Therefore, pray earnestly for an unprecedented rain of revival to fall upon this sad world and believe God for it to happen.

Father, I long for the day when the knowledge of you covers the Earth as the water covers the sea.

No Fish

When He had finished speaking, He said to Simon [Peter], "Put out into the deep water and lower your nets for a catch [of fish]."

LUKE 5:4

What Jesus said in today's verse didn't make sense at the time. Scripture tells us that Peter had told Jesus that they fished all night and caught nothing. Clearly, there were no fish. Instead of using reason, Peter said to Jesus, "Nevertheless at Your word I will let down the net" (v. 5 NKJV). And that's when they caught a great number of fish—so many that their net began to break. So they signaled to their partners in the other boat to come and help them. And they came and filled both the boats so that they began to sink.

But Peter didn't react by saying, "Lord, this is wonderful. Let's start a fishing company. We'll sign you up as the scout. You tell us where to drop the net, and we'll all make a fortune." Instead, when Peter saw what happened, he fell down at Jesus' knees, saying, "Depart from me, for I am a sinful man, O Lord!" (v. 8 NKJV). Was this because he believed that Jesus was a skilled fisherman? No. Peter recognized that Jesus was the Holy One who created the fish.

Father, keep me from the love of money.

Fishers of Men

He and all his companions were completely astounded at the catch of fish…and so were James and John, sons of Zebedee, who were partners with Simon [Peter]. Jesus said to Simon, "Have no fear; from now on you will be catching men!"

Luke 5:9–10

Jesus said to Peter, "from now on." Things were going to change radically. The big catch of fish wasn't just an exciting supernatural event; it was a foreshadowing of what was going to happen in the future. The fishermen were going to be catching men. And from that moment onward, after the revelation Peter had of his sinfulness, his life would be new.

Has that happened with you and me? Have we fallen at the feet of Jesus? Do we have the knowledge that we have sinned against him? Have we had the revelation that the business of the world is nothing but chasing the wind, and from the moment of our salvation onward, have we wanted to be about our Father's business? If so, then we have no need for fear. Scripture tells us what we should do: "I beseech you therefore, brethren, by the mercies of God, that you present your bodies a living sacrifice, holy, acceptable to God, which is your reasonable service" (Romans 12:1 NKJV).

Father, teach me how to catch individuals for your kingdom.

Childish Sinners

"To what then shall I compare the people of this generation [who set aside God's plan], and what are they like? They are like children sitting in the market place and calling to one another, and saying, 'We played the flute for you [pretending to be at a wedding], and you did not dance; we sang a dirge [pretending to be at a funeral], and you did not weep.'"

LUKE 7:31–32

Most people in this sinful world are like children who have no depth of understanding. They grow physically but never set aside their childish ways. A child is only interested in himself and his appetites, and if he doesn't get his own selfish way, he throws a tantrum. Maturity sometimes comes after the teenage years, but most go through their entire life not thinking about the kindness of God, who gives them life and every other blessing.

But no one can enter the kingdom of God and keep hold of that wicked self-will. We must forsake the old man with its delusion that the world revolves around us. True repentance comes when we leave Sodom without even a tiny wistful glance back at its wickedness.

Father, never let me look back at the pleasures of this world.

The Exaltation of Women

Turning toward the woman, He said to Simon, "Do you see this woman? I came into your house [but you failed to extend to Me the usual courtesies shown to a guest]; you gave Me no water for My feet, but she has wet My feet with her tears and wiped them with her hair [demonstrating her love]. You gave Me no [welcoming] kiss, but from the moment I came in, she has not ceased to kiss My feet. You did not [even] anoint My head with [ordinary] oil, but she has anointed My feet with [costly and rare] perfume."

LUKE 7:44–46

Jesus said to Simon, "Do you see this woman?" Of course he had seen her. But he didn't see her deep humility, depth of character, contrition, and integrity. Most men see women for their outward beauty, but Jesus saw in her an ornament of a "gentle and quiet spirit, which is very precious in the sight of God" (1 Peter 3:4 NKJV).

Consider the experience of the woman who met Jesus at a well (John 4:1–26) or the grace and forgiveness he extended to the woman caught in adultery (John 8:2–11). These verses show that Christianity stands head and shoulders above every other religion in that it honors women.

Father, thank you for the love you have for the daughters of Eve.

The Mystery of the Gospel

He said, "To you [who have been chosen] it has been granted to know and recognize the mysteries of the kingdom of God, but to the rest it is in parables, so that though seeing they may not see, and hearing they may not understand."

LUKE 8:10

When John Newton penned "Amazing Grace," he certainly expressed the most heartwarming experience of every Christian with six words: "Was blind, but now I see." One moment we were in a dark and fearful storm, wide-eyed, seeing the lightning of God's terrible wrath and hearing the thunder of his indignation. But in a moment of time, the gospel said, "Be still," the light of the good news broke through the dark clouds, and the wrath was gone. It was satisfied when Jesus cried from the cross, "It is finished!" The eyes of our understanding were enlightened as we passed from darkness to light. The mystery of life and death was suddenly solved because we knew the truth—and it made us free.

But unbelievers see and don't see. They hear and don't hear. Their understanding is darkened. They are alienated from God because of the ignorance that is in them, because of the blindness of their hearts—until, that is, they experience the opening of their blind eyes, all because of God's amazing grace.

Father, I cry out for the salvation of this lost and blind world.

The Enmity

"Let these words sink into your ears: the Son of Man is going to be betrayed and handed over to men [who are His enemies]."
LUKE 9:44

Jesus delivers a profound and somber statement to his disciples: "Let these words sink into your ears: the Son of Man is going to be betrayed and handed over to men [who are His enemies]." This declaration underscores Jesus' foreknowledge of his coming suffering, betrayal, and death. He refers to himself as the "Son of Man," a Messianic title rooted in Daniel 7:13–14, symbolizing both his divine authority and his role as a servant who suffers for humanity.

Jesus emphasizes the importance of the disciples truly understanding this revelation, urging them to think about the gravity of his fate. His impending betrayal, though orchestrated by human hands, aligns with God's sovereign plan of redemption. The "enemies" represent the forces of sin, corruption, and spiritual blindness that oppose God's purposes.

This verse reminds believers of Jesus' willing sacrifice for humanity and calls for a deep reflection on his mission of love, grace, and redemption through the cross. It also foreshadows the disciples' eventual understanding of Jesus and his mission that largely occurred after his resurrection.

Father, let your words sink into my ears.

The Uniqueness of Jesus

He said to them, "I watched Satan fall from heaven like [a flash of] lightning."
LUKE 10:18

Today's Scripture quote puts to death the erroneous thought that Jesus was just a good man or a great religious teacher who said some good things. Such thoughts don't make sense in the light of a multitude of Scripture passages that tell us that he was preexistent before his birth, that all things were made by him and through him, and that he had power on earth to forgive sin, raise the dead, walk on water, calm storms, multiply food, give sight to the blind, and give hearing to the deaf. He said his words would never pass away, perfectly predicted the future, and quietly added that every human being who has ever lived will be raised from the dead by his voice and stand before him in judgment.

No man had ever spoken like this man. And in today's verse, Jesus told his disciples that he was there when Satan was cast out of heaven like greased lightning. Jesus of Nazareth was either God manifested in human form or the ultimate compulsive liar. There's no fence upon which to sit.

Father, never let me forget the deity of Jesus.

Blessed Eyes

Turning to His disciples, Jesus said privately, "Blessed [joyful, spiritually enlightened, and favored by God] are the eyes which see what you see, for I say to you that many prophets and kings longed to see what you see, and they did not see it; and to hear what you hear, and did not hear it."

LUKE 10:23–24

We have a private audience with the king. Any time we desire, he welcomes us to intimately speak with him as a son or daughter speaks to their beloved father. And listen to what God himself says to us in that private conversation. He tells us that we are blessed because we belong to his Son. In him we are favored and enlightened.

Many of the noble prophets of the Old Testament looked forward with great desire and anticipation to what we now look back on and so clearly see. Through God's precious Word, we see heaven rejoice at the sight of a tiny babe in a manger. We also see Christ grown into a man who was then beaten and crucified for our sins. And we see that three days later, he rose over the power of death—all for us. We are blessed indeed.

Father, thank you for opening my blind eyes to Jesus.

He Sees and Knows

"You foolish ones [acting without reflection or intelligence]! Did not He who made the outside make the inside also?"
LUKE 11:40

How foolish we are to diminish God. And we diminish him in our eyes because we lack reflective, intelligent thought. From a sunrise to a dog's eye to a cat's whisker to a flea's foot—everything screams of the utter genius of Almighty God. How many dog lovers look beyond the revealed emotions they see in their pet canine's eyes and instead see the hand of God? Do they consider their cat's whiskers that grew at predetermined angles to a predetermined length to perform a predetermined function? How could God create such things? Or do they consider the flea's tiny foot and its amazing function, or the human brain—our brains that we are using at this moment to think these thoughts—and how God made it? And if he made it, he can see it functioning.

Listen to the psalmist as he thinks on these things:

> For You formed my inward parts;
> You covered me in my mother's womb.
> I will praise You, for I am fearfully and wonderfully made;
> Marvelous are Your works,
> And that my soul knows very well.
> (Psalm 139:13–14 NJKV)

Father, open my eyes to your greatness.

God's Good Pleasure

"Do not be afraid and anxious, little flock, for it is your Father's good pleasure to give you the kingdom."
LUKE 12:32

It's easy to remember God's love while all is well—when bills are paid and our family is healthy. But when fiery trials come, it's just as easy to forget. It's also easy to forget that the sun is shining when dark angry clouds blot out its warmth and light. But it is still shining.

Thank God for the precious Scriptures that tell us that God himself allows trials so that we may grow in godliness. That wonderful Bible tells us that "all things work together for good to those who love God, to those who are called according to his purpose" (Romans 8:28 NKJV). His love is still shining when we're in a dark storm. And in the midst of these seemingly hopeless situations, we can look to the cross because that is the undeniable evidence of his love. Romans 5:8 assures us, "God demonstrates His own love toward us, in that while we were still sinners, Christ died for us" (NKJV).

Father, never let me doubt for one second your love for me because of the light of the cross.

Glorious Hope

"I have come to cast fire (judgment) on the earth; and how I wish that it were already kindled! I have a baptism [of great suffering] with which to be baptized, and how [greatly] I am distressed until it is accomplished!"

LUKE 12:49–50

Thank God we don't know the future. We don't know what tomorrow will bring. This is why we must approach every day with the solid resolve to trust in God no matter what comes our way. We must build our lives on the firm and solid foundation of the teaching of Jesus because life is filled with unpredictable storms that will shake our house unless it's firmly on the rock.

In today's insightful verse, we see that Jesus did know the future, and because of what the future would bring, we see his intimate thoughts. He was greatly distressed at the thought of what was coming, and he longed for it to be over—for the time when he would utter those glorious words, "It is finished!" They were glorious words not only for Jesus in that his suffering was finished, but they were also glorious for us. We now have a sure and steadfast hope in life after our death.

Father, thank you again (and forever) for the unspeakable gift of salvation.

Satan's Work

The Lord replied to him, "You hypocrites (play-actors, pretenders)! Does not each one of you on the Sabbath untie his ox or his donkey from the stall and lead it away to water it? And this woman, a daughter (descendant) of Abraham whom Satan has bound for eighteen long years, should she not have been released from this bond on the Sabbath day?"

LUKE 13:15–16

One great principle of success in warfare is to know your enemy, to study closely his agenda and how he seeks to accomplish it. In today's passage from Scripture, the Pharisees were complaining that Jesus violated the Sabbath when he healed on that day. The Sabbath was supposed to be a day of rest. But Jesus pointed to the *worth* of the woman he had healed, and then he said that she had been afflicted by Satan for eighteen long years.

It is the Enemy who afflicts us with disease, and the Bible tells us that this is not God's will: "He who sins is of the devil, for the devil has sinned from the beginning. For this purpose the Son of God was manifested, that He might destroy the works of the devil" (1 John 3:8 NKJV). The first step toward victory for any Christian is not to allow sin to have dominion in any part of our lives.

Father, help me to resist sin and the devil today.

Tell That Fox

He said to them, "Go and tell that fox [that sly, cowardly man], 'Listen carefully: I cast out demons and perform healings today and tomorrow, and on the third day I reach My goal.'"

Luke 13:32

The Bible often likens people to animals. Jesus said that we were either sheep (John 10:11; Psalm 23) or goats (Matthew 25:31–46). The Jews called gentiles "dogs." We may interpret that as a good thing, depending on our personal thoughts about our faithful furry friends, but in Jesus' day, the term was derogatory. The Bible further uses dogs to describe unclean or impure people (Philippians 3:2; Revelation 22:15). Jesus is called "the Lion of the tribe of Judah" (Revelation 5:5 NKJV). Conversely, Satan is likened to "a roaring lion, seeking whom he may devour" (1 Peter 5:8 NKJV).

Jesus compared Herod to a fox. Herod was a cunning, sneaky predator. Jesus had something to say to that cunning fox. Because the power of God was with him, Jesus wasn't going to be outwitted by the king, and nothing was going to stop him from accomplishing his goal of the redemption of humanity. And then he was going to rise from the dead on the third day.

Father, thank you that nothing stops you from accomplishing your purposes.

July

The woman at the well (John 4:1–24)

The Wedding Garment

"When you are invited, go and sit down [to eat] at the last place, so that when your host comes, he will say to you, 'Friend, move up higher'; and then you will be honored in the presence of all who are at the table with you."

Luke 14:10

Today's verse might seem to be an instruction about etiquette in life. If we exalt ourselves, we will more than likely be humbled. But if we sincerely humble ourselves, we will almost certainly be exalted. No one would enjoy the humiliation of being told to go to a lower table. However, Jesus spoke of something more important that will take place at the marriage supper of the Lamb.

He said there was a man present who didn't have a wedding garment, and when he was asked why he wasn't dressed appropriately, he was speechless. Then he was cast out of that wedding into outer darkness (Matthew 22:11–13). We should, therefore, make sure that we have on a wedding garment, that we are clothed in a robe of righteousness so that on the great and terrible day of the Lord, we won't be rejected from heaven and cast into hell (7:21–24).

Father, I pray that I will instead hear those words, "Well done, good and faithful servant" (Matthew 25:21 NKJV).

He Isn't Like Us

He said to them, "You are the ones who declare yourselves just and upright in the sight of men, but God knows your hearts [your thoughts, your desires, your secrets]; for that which is highly esteemed among men is detestable in the sight of God."

LUKE 16:15

The psalmist put his finger on humanity's great error. He addressed the wicked, saying that God himself said, "What right have you to declare My statutes, or take My covenant in your mouth, seeing you hate instruction and cast My words behind you?" (Psalm 50:16–17 NKJV). Then God pointed to their violation of a number of the Ten Commandments, including theft, adultery, and lying. He said, "These things you have done, and I kept silent; you thought that I was altogether like you; but I will rebuke you, and set them in order before your eyes" (v. 21 NKJV).

And there's the problem. He said, "You thought that I was altogether like you." Unregenerate humanity thinks that God is just like them, that he has the same moral standards. But he doesn't. He is morally perfect. But the Bible says that in Christ we can have a holy boldness on the day of wrath (1 John 4:17).

Father, thank you that I can face you without shame because of Jesus.

JULY 3

The Mulberry Tree

The Lord said, "If you have [confident, abiding] faith in God [even as small] as a mustard seed, you could say to this mulberry tree [which has very strong roots], 'Be pulled up by the roots and be planted in the sea'; and [if the request was in agreement with the will of God] it would have obeyed you."

LUKE 17:6

Two of the wisest things we can do when reading the Bible are to take our time and to question everything. This does not mean questioning in a skeptical sense but with a desire to dig deeper for the golden nuggets that are hidden in Scripture. In today's verse, Jesus referred to a mulberry tree in a metaphorical context to teach about the importance and power of faith. The question we should ask is "Why did Jesus refer to a tree?" And why did he specifically mention a mulberry tree and talk about it being "uprooted"?

The mulberry tree is known for its deep and extensive root system. It is a nightmare to try to dig a mulberry tree out of a garden. It therefore represents something firmly established and very difficult to move. By using this imagery, Jesus emphasized that faith, even if it appears small, can have extraordinary effects and overcome great obstacles.

Father, I trust you today to move stubborn obstacles.

Worship Jesus

Jesus replied, "I tell you, if these [people] keep silent, the stones will cry out [in praise]!"
LUKE 19:40

If we don't believe that Jesus Christ is God in human form, we are stuck with the ultimate oxymoron. He said that he was meek and lowly of heart. That means that he has a genuinely humble attitude. But look at what he is saying in today's verse. As he rode into Jerusalem on a lowly donkey, people began to lay their cloaks on the ground with palm leaves to honor him. Then they cried out, "Hosanna! Blessed is he who comes in the name of the LORD!" (Mark 11:9 NKJV).

The religious leaders were horrified. The crowd was treating Jesus as though he were the God-promised Messiah. So they told Jesus to tell the crowd to be quiet. And that's when Jesus said that if those human mouths were stopped, the stones would cry out and worship him. What an amazing statement to make! Birds sing his praises, the sun shines in his strength, the heavens declare his glory, the trees raise their arms in worship, the flowers blossom to his glory, and the mountains and hills break for singing. "O come, let us adore Him, Christ, the Lord!"[5]

Father, I long for the day when every knee will bow to Jesus Christ as Lord.

5 John Francis Wade, "O Come, All Ye Faithful," 1743, trans. Frederick Oakeley, 1841, public domain.

JULY 5

Skillful Words

"So make up your minds not to prepare beforehand to defend yourselves; for I will give you [skillful] words and wisdom which none of your opponents will be able to resist or refute."

LUKE 21:14–15

The promise in today's Scripture passage was given to the disciples for when they would suffer persecution by antagonistic, godless authorities. Jesus said that they were not to defend themselves. This is because God was their defense, and if he desired, he would give them the wisdom needed to refute any claims against them.

We should also take this promise to heart. We should make up our minds not to try and justify ourselves if we are persecuted for the name of Christ. Jesus said that if that happens, we should rejoice, be exceedingly glad, and even "leap for joy" (Luke 6:23 NKJV). When Jesus stood before the governor, he didn't justify himself. Instead, he committed himself to the one who judges righteously. And that's what we should do. We are not here to try to justify ourselves. God is the one who will ultimately justify us (Romans 8:33–34). Instead, we are here to preach the everlasting gospel. May God help us to set our face as a flint and do just that.

Father, I look to you as my defense.

The Penitent Thief

Jesus said to him, "I assure you and most solemnly say to you, today you will be with Me in Paradise."

LUKE 23:43

Careless sinners sometimes look to the thief on the cross and conclude that they can live for the pleasures of sin and come to Jesus on their deathbed. However, they don't realize what happened on that cross. This wasn't someone simply changing his mind about Jesus in his final moments of life. There was far more happening. It dawned on this thief that he was sinful and that Jesus was innocent. The thief said that he deserved to be on the cross. In other words, he had a knowledge of sin—that as a thief, he had violated the eighth commandment.

He then turned to Jesus, called him Lord, and asked Jesus to remember him when he came into his kingdom. Clearly the thief believed that Jesus would rise from death. Scripture says that "if you confess with your mouth the Lord Jesus and believe in your heart that God has raised Him from the dead, you will be saved" (Romans 10:9 NKJV). That's what this penitent thief did, and that is why Jesus gave him assurance that he was saved.

Father, thank you that while we are alive, it's never too late to come to Jesus.

Jacob's Ladder

He said to him, "I assure you and most solemnly say to you, you will see heaven opened and the angels of God ascending and descending on the Son of Man [the bridge between heaven and earth]."

JOHN 1:51

Jesus said the words in today's verse to a godly Israelite named Nathaniel. Therefore, there is no doubt that Nathaniel would have been very familiar with Jacob's ladder. Jacob took a stone, used it as a pillow, and then went to sleep. "Then he dreamed, and behold, a ladder was set up on the earth, and its top reached to heaven; and there the angels of God were ascending and descending on it." (Genesis 28:12 NKJV). Jesus was saying that he himself was that ladder by which sinners will ascend to heaven.

He is the only name by which we can be saved. He said, "I am the way, the truth, and the life. No one comes to the Father except through Me" (John 14:6 NKJV). And the Scriptures further say, "For there is one God and one Mediator between God and men, the Man Christ Jesus, who gave Himself a ransom for all, to be testified in due time" (1 Timothy 2:4–6 NKJV).

Father, thank you for providing the ladder to heaven.

The First Miracle

Jesus said to her, "[Dear] woman, what is that to you and to Me? My time [to act and to be revealed] has not yet come."… Jesus said to the servants, "Fill the waterpots with water." So they filled them up to the brim. Then He said to them, "Draw some out now and take it to the headwaiter [of the banquet]." So they took it to him.

John 2:4–8

Jesus and his disciples had been invited to a wedding in Cana of Galilee. And the Bible tells us that his mother was also one of the guests. When the wine ran out, Mary told Jesus about this problem. He then said something that was a little strange: "My hour has not yet come" (v. 4 NKJV). He often said things that didn't make sense until after the fact. He seemed to allude to the suffering of the cross. His mother responded to the servants, "Whatever He says to you, do it" (v. 5 NKJV).

Jesus then told the servants to fill six large pots with water and turned that mundane water into at least 120 gallons of quality wine. Likewise, when we were drinking iniquity like water, Jesus miraculously poured out the new wine of everlasting life. May the joy that we have—of knowing we have eternal life—run over from our cup into this dry and thirsty world.

Father, thank you for the new life we have in Christ.

Zeal for God

His disciples remembered that it is written [in the Scriptures], "Zeal (love, concern) for Your house [and its honor] will consume Me."

John 2:17

Discipline yourself to memorize Scripture. This is because the time will come when recalling the Word of God will be a great source of comfort. This will be the case in the midst of trials and even in the midst of great blessings. We should remember who is in control and therefore know that we need not panic. We should remember who it is that is blessing us and give thanks. Scripture reminds us that God gave us life, and our greatest obligation is to return his love with all our heart, mind, soul, and strength. And remembering this will help us prioritize our time.

Today's wonderful verse came directly after Jesus cleared the temple of the money changers. Maybe this day we will have to use a whip to clear our bodily temple (1 Corinthians 6:19) of what doesn't matter in the light of eternity. If the opportunity doesn't come, we should make it happen. What has eternal value and consequences should consume us, not the merely temporal.

Father, may zeal for your house eat me up today. May your presence and will direct my every step and thought.

The Importance of the New Birth

Jesus answered him, "I assure you and most solemnly say to you, unless a person is born again [reborn from above—spiritually transformed, renewed, sanctified], he cannot [ever] see and experience the kingdom of God."

John 3:3

Today's verse in the King James translation uses the archaic word "verily" twice to emphasize the utter importance of what Jesus was about to say. The original Greek meaning, as quoted above, is "I assure you and most solemnly say to you." But it goes even deeper than that.

> When Jesus leads off with the words *verily, verily* in verses such as Matthew 18:3, Mark 3:28, Luke 23:43, and John 8:51, He is not merely saying, "Believe me, this is true." He is actually saying, "I know this is true firsthand." Since many of these comments are on heavenly, spiritual, or godly issues, Jesus' use of *verily, verily* is part of His consistent claim of divinity. Jesus is not merely aware of these truths: He is the One who originated them![6]

So make sure that you've been born again (that you've truly repented and put your trust alone in Jesus) because it is absolutely essential if you want to enter heaven.

Father, please assure me that I have truly been born again.

---

6 "What Does Jesus Mean When He Says, 'Verily, Verily' or 'Truly, Truly,' in the Gospels?" Got Questions, accessed May 5, 2024, https://www.gotquestions.org.

Born Again

Jesus answered, "I assure you and most solemnly say to you, unless one is born of water and the Spirit he cannot [ever] enter the kingdom of God. That which is born of the flesh is flesh [the physical is merely physical], and that which is born of the Spirit is spirit. Do not be surprised that I have told you, 'You must be born again [reborn from above—spiritually transformed, renewed, sanctified].'"

John 3:5–7

There are those who are absolutely sure that in today's Scripture verse, Jesus was talking about being sprinkled as a baby. They say that's what the reference is to when he said to be born of water and the Spirit. However, this cannot be water baptism because the Bible says, "Repent, and let every one of you be baptized in the name of Jesus Christ for the remission of sins" (Acts 2:38 NKJV). A baby can't repent.

The Bible clearly talks about believers' baptism, not baby baptism. Rather, Jesus was speaking about natural birth, when we are surrounded by water. He emphasized this truth when he said, "That which is born of the flesh is flesh [the physical is merely physical], and that which is born of the Spirit is spirit" (John 3:6).

Father, thank you for giving me a brand-new life in Christ.

Do You Not Know?

Jesus replied, "You are the [great and well-known] teacher of Israel, and yet you do not know nor understand these things [from Scripture]?"

John 3:10

All the study, all the knowledge, and all the theology in the world cannot replace the new birth. Nicodemus had come to Jesus by night. He was perhaps coming at night because as a leader of the Jews, he didn't want to be seen publicly with this controversial new teacher in Israel. But something in him yearned for truth.

Not everyone wants to know the truth as Nicodemus did. Many people spurn it when they hear it, even rail against it. These are the ones "who are perishing…whose minds the god of this age has blinded, who do not believe, lest the light of the gospel of the glory of Christ, who is the image of God, should shine on them" (2 Corinthians 4:3–4 NKJV).

We are living in darkness when we serve sin, no matter how spiritual we may be. That's why we need to be born again and have God open the eyes of our understanding so that we can see this glorious gospel of Jesus Christ. That takes a miracle of God—to transform sin-loving sinners into God-loving saints.

Father, I was blind, but now I see.

The Absolute Truth

"I assure you and most solemnly say to you, we speak only of what we [absolutely] know and testify about what we have [actually] seen [as eyewitnesses]; and [still] you [reject our evidence and] do not accept our testimony."

JOHN 3:11

In a world that is so often filled with nothing but conjecture and lies, there are no words to express how wonderful it is to know the rock-solid truth. If any human being tells us something, it's wise to be skeptical. Multitudes have been left disillusioned and even destitute because they had faith in human nature. The Bible says, "It is better to trust in the LORD than to put confidence in man" (Psalm 118:8 NKJV).

It's better because human beings are not only prone to deceit, but sometimes circumstances mean that we can't keep our word even if we wanted to. But the reason we can put our total confidence in God and his precious Word is because he is absolutely morally pure. He cannot lie (Hebrews 6:18). That means we can trust every word that he has said and rest in the knowledge that it will certainly come to pass.

Father, I trust you with all my heart.

Heavenly Things

"If I told you earthly things [that is, things that happen right here on earth] and you do not believe, how will you believe and trust Me if I tell you heavenly things? No one has gone up into heaven, but there is One who came down from heaven, the Son of Man [Himself—whose home is in heaven]."

JOHN 3:12–13

The gospel we preach is "fantastic" in the truest sense of the word. It sounds like fantasy. We are saying that heaven, hell, angels, and demons exist and that there is an invisible force of evil on this earth that inspires human beings to do things that they know are morally wrong. And this fantasy is epitomized by the fact that we say God in human form died for wicked sinners.

It's hard enough to convince this world of earthly things, let alone heavenly things. But the way to get the gospel to make sense to others is to open up the Ten Commandments, as Jesus did, and show why Jesus had to die on the cross. When people come to Christ and believe the gospel, they will know the truth because the power of God has personally transformed their lives.

Father, give me the wisdom to effectively share the gospel.

Jesus Lifted Up

"Just as Moses lifted up the [bronze] serpent in the desert [on a pole], so must the Son of Man be lifted up [on the cross], so that whoever believes will in Him have eternal life [after physical death, and will actually live forever]."

John 3:14–15

Moses physically preceded Jesus by over one thousand years. And Moses precedes Jesus when we share our faith. If it weren't for the law of Moses, we wouldn't have the cross of Calvary. The eternal law demands retribution for sin, and if sin weren't serious in the sight of God, Jesus wouldn't have had to die on the cross. That's what the struggle in the garden of Gethsemane entailed. Justice demanded equity.

It was not possible that the cup of suffering could pass from Jesus. He *had* to drink of it. Moses lifted up that serpent as a foreshadowing of Jesus being lifted up and becoming a curse for us, to redeem us from the curse of God's law: "Christ has redeemed us from the curse of the law, having become a curse for us (for it is written, 'Cursed is everyone who hangs on a tree')" (Galatians 3:13 NKJV).

Father, let me remember the cross during the busyness of today.

His Sovereign Hand

A woman from Samaria came to draw water. Jesus said to her, "Give Me a drink."

John 4:7

The sovereign hand of God is such a wonderful mystery. Jesus' conversation with the woman in today's Scripture verse occurred as he sat on the well in Samaria two thousand years ago, but it was foreseen and instigated by God. His hand guided her there to speak with Jesus about water and, consequently, about her eternal salvation. "No one can come to Me unless the Father who sent Me draws him; and I will raise him up at the last day. It is written in the prophets, 'And they shall all be taught by God.' Therefore everyone who has heard and learned from the Father comes to Me" (John 6:44–45 NKJV).

God sometimes overrides human free will. "For the Scripture says to the Pharaoh, 'For this very purpose I have raised you up, that I may show My power in you, and that My name may be declared in all the earth.' Therefore He has mercy on whom He wills, and whom He wills He hardens" (Romans 9:17–18 NKJV). He not only knows the path we will take, but in his great love, he draws us to Jesus.

Father, thank you for your sovereign hand in my salvation.

They Shrink from the Light

"For every wrongdoer hates the Light, and does not come to the Light [but shrinks from it] for fear that his [sinful, worthless] activities will be exposed and condemned."

John 3:20

This powerful verse highlights a fundamental spiritual truth: human nature tends to resist the Light—a metaphorical title of Jesus that symbolizes truth, purity, and the presence of God. The "wrongdoer" refers to anyone who indulges in sin. Such individuals often avoid the Light because it exposes their sinful actions, bringing them into view for judgment and correction.

The "Light" in this context represents Jesus Christ and his teachings, who and which illuminate what is good and reveal what is sinful. Rather than confronting and repenting for their sins, sinners shrink away in fear of condemnation, preferring to remain in darkness where their actions can go unnoticed and unchecked. This tendency underscores the human inclination to prioritize self-preservation and comfort over accountability and transformation.

Ultimately, the verse calls the world to examine their hearts and embrace the Light, trusting that God's grace enables repentance and renewal rather than fear and hiding. It emphasizes the importance of truth and transparency for spiritual growth and redemption.

Father, thank you for pursuing me and giving me the Light.

This Was Well-Spoken

For His disciples had gone off into the city to buy food—The Samaritan woman asked Him, "How is it that You, being a Jew, ask me, a Samaritan woman, for a drink?" (For Jews have nothing to do with Samaritans.)

John 4:8–9

Here is a significant interaction between Jesus and a Samaritan woman, highlighting cultural and social boundaries in first-century Israel.

While Jesus' disciples were away buying food, he engaged a Samaritan woman in conversation at a well. His request for a drink broke multiple societal norms. Jews traditionally avoided Samaritans due to long-standing religious and ethnic tensions, considering them impure because of their intermarriage with gentiles and differing worship practices. Furthermore, Jewish men typically avoided direct interaction with women, especially in public settings.

The Samaritan woman's surprise reflects these cultural divides. Her question, "How is it that You, being a Jew, ask me, a Samaritan woman, for a drink?" underscores the depth of the separation between Jews and Samaritans. Yet Jesus' approach demonstrated his disregard for such barriers, showing his mission to reach all people regardless of background. This encounter emphasizes the inclusive nature of his message, foreshadowing the breaking of barriers between people through the gospel.

Father, give me a "woman at the well" experience today.

If You Knew

Jesus answered her, "If you knew [about] God's gift [of eternal life], and who it is who says, 'Give Me a drink,' you would have asked Him [instead], and He would have given you living water (eternal life)."

John 4:10

The Bible says that God's people are destroyed through lack of knowledge (Hosea 4:6). We can lose our lives by not knowing something. If you don't know where the exit is in a hotel that's on fire, you may perish. And at the moment, most people in this sad world haven't any idea what's going to happen to them after they die. They don't know that "the gift of God is eternal life" through trusting in Jesus alone (Romans 6:23 NKJV). They think they can instead earn eternal life by their good works.

If only they knew what we have in Christ, they would ask us about the way of salvation. And that's what Jesus was saying to this woman. If she knew who Jesus was—the very source of life itself in human form—she would ask him, and he would give her living water, everlasting life. How will this world hear without a preacher? May God help us to forget about ourselves and share the truth in love.

Father, I need your love and wisdom today.

He Will Never Thirst Again

Jesus answered her, "Everyone who drinks this water will be thirsty again. But whoever drinks the water that I give him will never be thirsty again. But the water that I give him will become in him a spring of water [satisfying his thirst for God] welling up [continually flowing, bubbling within him] to eternal life."

John 4:13–14

When we're thirsty and begin to drink water, there comes a time during the drinking process when the thirst is completely satisfied. But with natural water, we will thirst again and need another drink. Not so with the water that Jesus gives. Living water gives satisfaction.

Before we came to Christ, we thirsted for pleasures that never lasted. They were transient, and like an alcoholic or a drug addict goes back for more, we had to continually go back to the world, the flesh, and the devil. But because God has given us a new heart that loves him, the thirst for sin has become distasteful. As the Amplified Bible says, the living water satisfies our thirst for God "welling up [continually flowing, bubbling within]" us to eternal life.

Father, use me this day to further your kingdom.

The Power of Belief

Jesus replied, "Woman, believe Me, a time is coming [when God's kingdom comes] when you will worship the Father neither on this mountain nor in Jerusalem."

John 4:21

"Woman, *believe Me*." Here are just two simple words that carry the deepest of implications. Jesus was telling the woman at the well to "believe" what he was about to say. This is because our beliefs will govern the direction we take in life. If you were told that there was a land mine directly in front of you and you believed, you would go around it. But if you didn't believe, you would step right onto it and suffer the consequences of unbelief.

In essence, we are simply saying to this evil world, "Believe Jesus." We are telling them to trust in him as a person, to believe his words and his sober warnings. And if they genuinely believe that he is the Christ, the Son of the living God, they will bow to his sovereignty and wisely do the things that he tells them to do. This was the experience of the woman at the well.

Father, I believe the words of Jesus and will trust in him today and forever.

She Spoke Truthfully

At this, Jesus said, "Go, call your husband and come back." The woman answered, "I do not have a husband." Jesus said to her, "You have correctly said, 'I do not have a husband'; for you have had five husbands, and the man you are now living with is not your husband. You have said this truthfully."

JOHN 4:16–18

It's a huge revelation to understand that God is intimately familiar with us as human beings. He knows how many hairs are on our heads, and he knows the thoughts that are in deep within our hearts. Nothing is hidden from the eyes of him to whom we have to give an account (Hebrews 4:13). The woman in today's Scripture passage had violated the seventh commandment, and Jesus mentioning her husband was a test of her honesty. And she was honest.

That's all we ask of someone when we take them through the Ten Commandments. We want them to be honest. If they're not honest and try to cover their sins, they will not come to repentance. The Scriptures say, "He who covers his sins will not prosper, but whoever confesses and forsakes them will have mercy" (Proverbs 28:12 NKJV). Nobody ever truly repented who considered themselves to be a good person.

Father, help me to always be honest.

Worship God

"But a time is coming and is already here when the true worshipers will worship the Father in spirit [from the heart, the inner self] and in truth; for the Father seeks such people to be His worshipers. God is spirit [the Source of life, yet invisible to mankind], and those who worship Him must worship in spirit and truth."

JOHN 4:23-24

Skeptics sometimes ask why God commands us to worship him, and they often imply in a derogatory way that God has the ultimate inflated ego. While the following analogy is sorely lacking, it may help us to understand a principle of worship.

Imagine a man painted a painting that was so magnificent it outshined Rembrandt, Monet, and Picasso. When it was displayed in public, crowds looking at it gasped at its beauty and immediately lavished praise on the painter. The praise wasn't coerced. They couldn't help but praise him. And so it is with the creator of sunrises, sunsets, beautiful trees, flowers, and birds. The more we see of creation, the more we cannot help but praise the Creator. This isn't coerced. It spills from a humble heart as we begin to understand the power and genius of God.

Father, it gives me great joy to spontaneously worship you.

It Went Well

Jesus said to her, "I who speak to you, am He (the Messiah)."
John 4:26

Jesus was speaking to a Samaritan woman, something that wasn't a social norm. And he did this because he cared about this woman's individual worth. Today's verse marks a significant moment when Jesus explicitly revealed his identity as the Messiah. It's one of the few times in the Gospels when he directly stated who he was. But he revealed himself to someone whom most Jews despised—an adulterous female Samaritan outcast. His open declaration of his identity was not only a fulfillment of Old Testament prophecy about the coming Messiah; it also left no ambiguity about his identity.

In many instances, Jesus asked people to keep his identity a secret. Here, he openly declared it, suggesting the importance of this particular encounter. Although he spoke of the kingdom of God to massive crowds, here he engaged with one individual in an intimate and meaningful conversation that led to her conversion and the conversion of many others. She became a witness to her community—sharing about Jesus. This highlights how one personal encounter with him can lead to broader evangelistic impact.

Father, may my testimony about Jesus touch others this day.

Bread of Heaven

He told them, "I have food to eat that you do not know about."
John 4:32

The disciples had gone to buy food, and no doubt, eating that food was on their minds when they returned to Jesus. But they found him speaking with a Samaritan woman. They presumed that he would end the conversation and join them in a meal. But he wasn't interested and told them that he had his own private food. This wasn't a natural nourishment but one that fed him spiritually. It was the same food that gave him strength when he resisted the temptation to turn stones into bread. In that case, he said to the devil, "Man shall not live by bread alone, but by every word that proceeds from the mouth of God" (Matthew 4:4 NKJV). The satisfying food of which Jesus spoke was the food of doing his Father's will. Zeal for God's house had eaten him up, and that included his natural appetite. God's work was both his joy and his strength.

Today's verse underscores Jesus' dedication to his divine mission and obedience to God's perfect will. For believers, this encourages us to seek spiritual sustenance and fulfillment by doing God's work.

Father, my desire for today is to do your will.

Raise Your Eyes

Jesus said to them, "My food is to do the will of Him who sent Me and to completely finish His work. Do you not say, 'It is still four months until the harvest comes?' Look, I say to you, raise your eyes and look at the fields and see, they are white for harvest."

John 4:34-35

Jesus said to his disciples that it was still four months away from the harvest. Then he added that his disciples should raise their eyes. In other words, they should look up from what was occupying their attention and look closer at the fields to see that, in reality, the crops were ready for harvesting.

If we don't also raise our eyes from the many distractions around us and look at the field of this godless world, we will think that they aren't interested in the gospel. But they would be if they knew that "Jesus Christ…has abolished death" (2 Timothy 1:10). And that's why we should appeal to their God-given will to live—just as Jesus did with the woman at the well (John 4:10). That will change the dynamic.

Father, today I will lift up my eyes and look on the fields.

Someone Planted

"Already the reaper is receiving his wages and he is gathering fruit for eternal life; so that he who plants and he who reaps may rejoice together...I sent you to reap [a crop] for which you have not worked. Others have worked and you have been privileged to reap the results of their work."

John 4:36-38

When one sinner comes to Christ, all heaven rejoices (Luke 15:7). Although the Scriptures tell us "[neither] he who plants is anything, nor he who waters, but God who gives the increase" (1 Corinthians 3:7), we can rejoice in the fact that God uses us to reach this world. We are colaborers with him (1 Corinthians 3:9). And if we have the joy of leading someone to the Savior, we can be sure that, though someone else planted the seed of the Word of God in their heart, God caused it to grow.

No one can come to the Son unless the Father draws him or her, and it is God who grants repentance (2 Timothy 2:25). If we look back on our own path to the cross, no doubt we remember that someone (or something) planted a seed in our heart that in time grew until we came to the Savior.

Father, thank you for drawing me to yourself and granting me repentance.

John's Simple Message

Jesus said to him, "Unless you [people] see [miraculous] signs and wonders, you [simply] will not believe."

JOHN 4:48

It's common for skeptics to say that if God would just do a miracle in front of them, they would believe. Jesus did many miracles—including raising the dead several times, healing the sick, giving sight to the blind, and giving hearing to the deaf. But the crowd still cried out for him to be crucified. This is why it's important not to convince anyone of the gospel by appealing to their intellect alone. There must be a knowledge of sin preceding the new birth. No one is going to seek for God's forgiveness unless they believe they *need* his forgiveness. The convincing agent is the law of God.

The Bible says that sin is transgression of the law (1 John 3:4). John the Baptist simply preached that sinners should repent and put their trust in the coming one. He was a forerunner to Jesus. We preach after the fact, but we have the same message—repent, believe in the one who came two thousand years ago, and escape the wrath to come.

Father, remind me to always preach the simplicity of the gospel: that Christ died for sinners.

He Believed Jesus

Jesus said to him, "Go; your son lives!" The man believed what Jesus said to him and started home.

JOHN 4:50

This man was a royal official. He had an important position in society, but his son was dying. Despite the authority he possessed, he was helpless. The Bible tells us, "When he heard that Jesus had come out of Judea into Galilee, he went to Him and implored Him to come down and heal his son, for he was at the point of death…The nobleman said to Him, 'Sir, come down before my child dies!'" (John 4:47, 49 NKJV).

This incident happened in Cana of Galilee, where Jesus had turned the water into wine. No doubt the nobleman had heard of this miracle, and that may have motivated him to beg Jesus to heal his beloved son. And when Jesus said, "Go; your son lives," notice that the official believed what Jesus said, and the evidence of that faith was that he went home. And there he found that his son had been healed. He didn't keep imploring Jesus; he simply went home trusting Jesus' word. That's the sort of faith that moves mountains.

Father, may my faith in you move mountains today.

Laying Hopeless and Helpless

When Jesus noticed him lying there [helpless], knowing that he had been in that condition a long time, He said to him, "Do you want to get well?"

John 5:6

The entire world is like that impotent man—hopeless and helpless in the face of his impending death. And after death took him, he would have to face God and give an account for every thought, word, and deed: "As it is appointed for men to die once, but after this the judgment" (Hebrews 9:27 NKJV). When speaking of the first coming of Jesus, the Scriptures address this helplessness of all humanity: "The people who sat in darkness have seen a great light, and upon those who sat in the region and shadow of death Light has dawned" (Matthew 4:16 NKJV).

Sinners sit helplessly in the shadow of death. They're not going anywhere. They're on a freeway, an eighteen-wheeler is heading for them, and they don't know how to get off. But the next verse tells us what they must do: "From that time Jesus began to preach and to say, 'Repent, for the kingdom of heaven is at hand'" (v. 17 NKJV). May God help them.

Father, help me today to follow in the footsteps of Jesus.

Sin No More

Jesus said to him, "Get up; pick up your pallet and walk."
John 5:8

This man had been sick for thirty-eight years. The fact that Jesus healed him and told him to pick up his bedding was an evident miracle. But instead of rejoicing, the religious leaders said that the healed man was violating the Sabbath day by carrying his bed. After they confronted the healed man about his Sabbath violation (vv. 10–13), Jesus then found the man and said these fearful words: "Don't sin as you did before, or something even worse may happen to you" (v. 14 TLB).

These words should put a healthy fear of God in every Christian because there are many who toy with sin, not knowing that it has the bite of a deadly serpent. This man was without strength, and Jesus had given it to him. He now had a choice. Should he now use his newfound strength to sin, or should he walk in perpetual repentance? We have the same choice: "What shall we say then? Shall we continue in sin, that grace may abound? God forbid. How shall we, that are dead to sin, live any longer therein?" (Romans 6:1–2 KJV).

Father, never let me play the hypocrite. Instead, may I walk in continual repentance.

August

Raising Lazarus from the dead (John 11:38–44)

Imitation of Jesus

Jesus answered them by saying, "I assure you and most solemnly say to you, the Son can do nothing of Himself [of His own accord], unless it is something He sees the Father doing; for whatever things the Father does, the Son [in His turn] also does in the same way. For the Father dearly loves the Son and shows Him everything that He Himself is doing; and the Father will show Him greater works than these, so that you will be filled with wonder."

JOHN 5:19–20

These verses from John's gospel show us that Jesus and the Father are indeed one. They show a unity of purpose. And they act as a model for the Christian life. Our will should be one with God's will. Our desires should be the same as his. We should be unwilling that any should perish but that all should come to repentance.

These verses also reveal a reliance that Jesus had on the Father. Again, this is an example to help us have a complete reliance upon God—to trust in the Lord with all our heart and not lean to our own understanding (Proverbs 3:5). If you lack that reliance, meditate for a few moments on the integrity of God's holy character—on the fact that it's impossible for him to lie (Hebrews 6:18) and that in Christ he promises to never leave nor forsake you (Hebrews 13:5).

Father, I affirm this day that I will trust you with all my heart.

The Power of God

"Just as the Father raises the dead and gives them life [and allows them to live on], even so the Son also gives life to whom He wishes."

JOHN 5:21

The religious leaders called the Sadducees mocked the thought of the resurrection by giving Jesus a scenario. They recounted a situation where seven brothers successively married the same woman due to the Levirate marriage law, which required a man to marry his brother's widow to produce offspring. Each brother died without having children, and eventually, the woman also died. The Sadducees then asked Jesus whose wife she would be in the resurrection since all seven were married to her. This scenario was meant to challenge the concept of resurrection and highlight what they saw as a logical inconsistency (Matthew 22:23–28).

Jesus' answer to the Sadducees pointed to their lack of understanding "the Scriptures [which teach the resurrection]" and "the power of God [for He is able to raise the dead]" (Matthew 22:29).

God always tells the truth, even about the future. And he has the power to bring about anything he declares will come to be, which includes the resurrection of the dead. Disbelief in these truths is evidence that humanity is truly blind. All one has to do is look around at this incredible universe and be in wonder and awe at the power of its Creator. A being who can create such complexity and beauty can certainly raise the dead. In him we can trust.

Father, I am in awe of your great power.

AUGUST 3

Great Is the Mystery of Godliness

"The Father judges no one, but has given all judgment [that is, the prerogative of judging] to the Son [placing it entirely into His hands]."

John 5:22

Once again in today's verse, we see evidence in the words of Scripture that Jesus of Nazareth was the Creator in human form. He said that the Father judges no one because he gave all judgment to the Son. This claim must have astounded his hearers. This is because Jesus was the mere son of a local carpenter—one man who was limited to time and space, needing to eat, to drink, and to sleep. His words were senseless to the highest degree—nonsensical, that is, unless we accept what Scripture says about who Jesus actually was.

He was the very source of life who took to himself a full sinless human nature for the purpose of suffering for the sin of the world so that the door of immortality could be opened to the sons and daughters of Adam. "Without controversy great is the mystery of godliness: God was manifested in the flesh, justified in the Spirit, seen by angels, preached among the Gentiles, believed on in the world, received up in glory" (1 Timothy 3:16 NKJV).

Father, today may I consider this great mystery.

Honor the Son

"All will give honor (reverence, homage) to the Son just as they give honor to the Father. [In fact] the one who does not honor the Son does not honor the Father who has sent Him."

JOHN 5:23

If God has given all judgment to the Son, we should give honor, reverence, and homage to the Son as we would the Father.

The Jehovah's Witnesses created their own version of the Scriptures to fit their own erroneous doctrine. They say that Jesus was a created being. However, Jesus himself said that he was preexistent: "For I have come down from heaven, not to do My own will, but the will of Him who sent Me" (John 6:38). And in John 8:58, Jesus claimed the very name of God: "Most assuredly, I say to you, before Abraham was, I AM." Jesus made it clear that he was the same eternal God who revealed himself to Moses many centuries before.

The Bible says that the Son of God was manifested to destroy the works of the devil, the one who had the power of death. When Jesus rose from the dead, he snatched the keys from the hands of the devil and said, "I am he that liveth, and was dead; and, behold, I am alive for evermore, Amen; and have the keys of hell and of death" (Revelation 1:18 KJV).

Father, I honor Jesus as I honor you.

Skim-Reading Scripture

"I assure you and most solemnly say to you, the person who hears My word [the one who heeds My message], and believes and trusts in Him who sent Me, has (possesses now) eternal life."

JOHN 5:24

Once again in today's Scripture verse, the Amplified Bible gives us wonderful insight into the meaning of the original language. Our daily reading of the Scriptures can be enriched if we slow down and take a magnifying glass and look closer. If we put a leaf or a tiny bug under a microscope, it will take us into a whole new world. And the same applies with Scripture.

We cheat ourselves when we superficially read the Bible. Meditation involves slowing down and taking a closer and more thoughtful look at passages of Scripture. The practice is often highlighted in the book of Psalms. We miss so much if we quickly devour a chapter as a dog gulps its food. Take the time to chew over each verse, break it down, absorb it into the soul, and then let it energize you through your day. And of all the verses that should put joy into our hearts, this one is among the best. Those who trust in Jesus alone possess eternal life here and now.

Father, feed me now and evermore.

Absolute Assurance

"The person who hears My word...and believes in Him who sent me, has (possesses now) eternal life [that is, eternal life actually begins—the believer is transformed], and does not come into judgment and condemnation, but has passed [over] from death into life."

JOHN 5:24

It is common for unbelievers to say, "You can't *know* when it comes to the afterlife." They believe this because they are unbelievers. They choose not to believe Jesus and entrust themselves to him. If they did, they, too, could have absolute assurance that they have everlasting life.

That assurance is based on two powerful truths. The first is internal. God in Christ makes us brand-new on the inside. The promise of the Old Testament was that he would write his law upon our hearts and cause us to walk in his statutes (Jeremiah 31:33). In other words, God would cause us to love him and long to do what is right. That's a very powerful personal miracle for a sin-loving sinner.

The second truth is the external foundation that "it is impossible for God to lie" (Hebrews 6:18 NKJV). Therefore, if God makes a promise, we can believe it without a hint of doubt, and that gives us blessed assurance.

Father, thank you for absolute assurance of everlasting life in Christ.

Those Who Hear

"I assure you and most solemnly say to you, a time is coming and is [here] now, when the dead will hear the voice of the Son of God, and those who hear it will live."

JOHN 5:25

Jesus said the time is coming *and* is here now. He was saying that this will happen in the future, and it is happening right now. When any sinner is born again, trusting alone in Jesus, they hear the voice of the Son of God. And through their repentance and faith in Jesus, God seals them with his Holy Spirit. He grants them the gift of everlasting life (Romans 6:23). Right now. Then the time will come in the future when Jesus comes, and his voice will raise every human being who has lived and died.

Those who have responded will, on that day, hear his voice and be raised from the dead to everlasting life. But those who refused to hear his voice and remain in their sins will be raised to be judged and will justly be damned. On that day, wealth, fame, and status will mean nothing because no man or woman is above the law. These sober thoughts should guide us every day to warn the ungodly.

Father, today give me courage to speak to the unsaved.

God's Self-Existence

"For just as the Father has life in Himself [and is self-existent], even so He has given to the Son to have life in Himself [and be self-existent]. And He has given Him authority to execute judgment, because He is a Son of Man [sinless humanity, qualifying Him to sit in judgment over mankind]."

John 5:26–27

The thought that God had no beginning and has no end is extremely hard to comprehend. Yet we can accept it with simple childlike faith. This basic acceptance may seem like a cop-out to some until they realize that accepting by faith is what we do when it comes to the endlessness of space. No matter what direction we point, space goes on forever. It has no end—in every direction.

Logic tempts us to conclude that there *must* be an end. Yet if there is an end—a big wall with "The End" written on it—what is behind the wall? And so we are forced to say (with childlike faith) that we simply believe that space has no end because we have no alternative. This is how the psalmist dealt with God's greatness. "Such knowledge is too wonderful for me; it is high, I cannot attain it" (Psalm 139:6 NKJV).

Father, my mind is continually in awe of your greatness.

Don't Be Surprised

"Do not be surprised at this; for a time is coming when all those who are in the tombs will hear His voice, and they will come out—those who did good things [will come out] to a resurrection of [new] life, but those who did evil things [will come out] to a resurrection of judgment [that is, to be sentenced]."

JOHN 5:28–29

In today's verse, Jesus qualifies the statement he's about to say. In the King James Version, Jesus says not to "marvel" at this. In other words, do not let the fantastic nature of what he's about to say leave you in disbelief because it's too much to believe. When King Solomon philosophized about life, pointing to all his riches and fame, he said that it was all futile and chasing after wind. All because the reality of death was coming to him.

This is the revelation every human being needs. This life is chasing the wind if we've not found peace with God. Solomon finished his philosophy with these wise words:

> Let us hear the conclusion of the whole matter:
> Fear God and keep His commandments,
> For this is man's all.
> For God will bring every work into judgment,
> Including every secret thing,
> Whether good or evil. (Ecclesiastes 12:13–14 NKJV)

Father, never let me forget what I've been saved from.

The Praise of Men

"I can do nothing on My own initiative or authority. Just as I hear, I judge; and My judgment is just (fair, righteous, unbiased), because I do not seek My own will, but only the will of Him who sent Me. If I alone testify about Myself, My testimony is not valid. There is another [My Father] who testifies about Me, and I know [without any doubt] that His testimony on My behalf is true and valid."

JOHN 5:30-32

We live in a world that seeks the praise of men. The opinions of our peers can easily shape our tastes for music, sports, or clothing. We often put on clothes and think to ourselves, *I wonder how I will look to other people*? This is because we think that their opinions matter. If someone says they don't like what we're wearing, it can ruin our day. Or if someone says that a particular article of clothing looks great on us, it can lift our spirits and make our day.

However, human opinions should come secondary to the opinion of God. We should, above all else, make our every decision with reference to his pleasure. This is what Jesus did, and that's what we should imitate if we've fully yielded our will to him.

Father, I only want your smile today.

Far Greater Testimony

"The testimony I receive is not from man [a merely human witness]; but I say these things so that you may be saved [that is, have eternal life]...But the testimony which I have is far greater than the testimony of John; for the works that the Father has given Me to finish—the very same works [that is, the miracles and proofs of My deity] that I am [now] doing—testify about Me, [by providing evidence] that the Father has sent Me."

JOHN 5:34, 36

Jesus here clarifies that he didn't rely on human testimony for validation, such as that of John the Baptist. Although John's testimony was important and trustworthy, Jesus emphasizes that his purpose in speaking is to lead people to salvation and eternal life.

He then explains that his works—his miracles, teachings, and actions—serve as a far greater testimony than John's words. These works were given to him by the Father as part of his mission, demonstrating his divine authority and identity. The miracles are evidence that Jesus was sent by the Father and that he operated with divine power and purpose.

Essentially, Jesus contrasts human testimony with the divine evidence found in his life and works. By performing the will of the Father, he reveals his true nature and invites belief in him as the Son of God. His ultimate goal is to bring people into a saving relationship with God.

Father, thank you for the utterly unique life of Jesus.

The Ultimate Treasure

"The Father who sent Me has Himself testified about Me. You have never heard His voice nor seen His form [His majesty and greatness—what He is like]. You do not have His word (Scripture) abiding in you [actually living in your hearts and minds], because you do not believe in Him whom He has sent. You search and keep on searching and examining the Scriptures because you think that in them you have eternal life; and yet it is those [very Scriptures] that testify about Me."

John 5:37–39

The religious leaders of Jesus' day searched the Scriptures because they believed that in God's Word they had everlasting life. But the Bible is simply the map that leads to hidden treasure. It is of great importance, but it is not the treasure. The treasure is Jesus of Nazareth. There is no treasure on this earth that compares to him because he is life itself.

The Bible refers to the believer who has the indwelling Christ as possessing incalculable treasure: "We have this treasure in earthen vessels, that the excellence of the power may be of God and not of us" (2 Corinthians 4:7 NKJV). May we guard that treasure: "Behold, I am coming quickly! Hold fast what you have, that no one may take your crown" (Revelation 3:11).

Father, nothing and no one on this earth compares to you.

They Would Not Come

"Still you are unwilling to come to Me so that you may have life. I do not receive glory and approval from men; but I know you and recognize that you do not have the love of God in yourselves."

JOHN 5:40–42

How crazy it is for anyone to be *unwilling* to come to the Savior for everlasting life! If a sinful world refuses God's mercy in Christ, God lets them have their own way and even lets them perish. When Israel of old lusted for meat in the desert, he gave them their hearts' desires even though it wasn't his will (Exodus 16:1–21; Numbers 11:4–34). Similarly, he gave Israel a king in King Saul when it wasn't his perfect will (1 Samuel 8).

Jesus said to the religious leaders that they were unwilling to come to him that they might have life. They wanted their own will rather than the divine will. David affirmed this great truth. "The wicked, through the pride of his countenance, *will* not seek after God: God is not in all his thoughts" (Psalm 10:4 KJV, emphasis added). The proud sons and daughters of Adam will not seek after God. It's not that they *can't* find him but that they *refuse* to seek him.

Father, thank you for softening my hard heart.

Others Will Be Received

"I have come in My Father's name and with His power, and you do not receive Me [because your minds are closed]; but if another comes in his own name and with no authority or power except his own, you will receive him and give your approval to an imposter."

JOHN 5:43

The contentious Jewish leaders continued to question the authority and divinity of Jesus. This is because he claimed to come in his Father's name, which implied that his divine mission and authority came from God. Then Jesus pointed out that the Jewish leaders did not accept him, highlighting their spiritual blindness and resistance to his message.

The contrast between coming "in my Father's name" and "in his own name" emphasizes the authenticity and divine backing of Jesus versus the self-promotion of false leaders. This rejection and acceptance of false messiahs fulfilled Old Testament prophecies about Israel's response to true and false prophets (Deuteronomy 18:15–19; Jeremiah 23:21–22). The above verse serves as a warning to future generations to discern true messengers of God from false ones, stressing the importance of spiritual vigilance.

Father, may my mind always be open to you.

AUGUST 15

Believe Moses

"How can you believe [in Me], when you [seek and] receive glory and approval from one another, and yet you do not seek the glory and approval which comes from the one and only God?"

John 5:44

After Jesus asked the question in today's verse, he then told the Jewish leaders that there was one who accused them. It was Moses, the one in whom they trusted. If they had believed Moses, they would have believed in Jesus, the one Moses had predicted. Very little has changed over two thousand years. The religious leaders relied on Moses for their salvation, just as do many today.

"Moses" is a reference to the law of Moses—the Ten Commandments, which God gave to Moses. Despite many thinking that keeping the Ten Commandments is the way to heaven, Moses can't save us. But he can show us the Savior. The Commandments show us the nature of sin. They mirror our sinful hearts. This is what the world needs to hear, and if they believe Moses, they will believe in Jesus. This is what the apostle Paul was saying when he said that the law is our schoolmaster to bring us to Christ (Galatians 3:24).

Father, help me today to point sinners to Jesus.

What It Means to Believe

"If you do not believe his writings, how will you believe My words?"
JOHN 5:47

The proud are often offended at the very thought of having "faith." They erroneously think that faith is believing something despite the lack of evidence, but biblical faith is no such thing. We intellectually have faith that God exists because of creation. It is impossible for creation to exist without a creator. That sort of faith rests on the evidence. But when the Bible speaks of faith *in* God, it is speaking of trusting in his promises and having faith in his impeccable integrity.

The Bible is filled with exceedingly great and precious promises that become applicable to us the moment we repent and put our trust in Jesus. It is very simple (even childlike) to "believe" in him, but it has massive eternal implications.

Nevertheless, there are many who say they believe in Jesus, but their lifestyles of willful sin show that their belief is merely intellectual rather than an implicit trust in him for their salvation. They don't have the evidence of regeneration—the "things that accompany salvation" (see Hebrews 6:9).

Father, may the evidence of regeneration come through my life clearly so I can even more effectively point others to the salvation they so desperately need.

We Need Never Be Afraid

Jesus said to them, "It is I (I AM); do not be afraid."
JOHN 6:20

The disciples were in a boat rowing across the Sea of Galilee when a great wind put them in danger. Suddenly, they saw Jesus walking on the sea and drawing near the boat, and they were afraid. But he said to them, "It is I; do not be afraid" (John 6:20 NKJV).

Look at how the Amplified Bible reveals what Jesus was saying. It was far more than, "It's I, Jesus." When Moses asked God for his name so that he could tell the children of Israel who sent him, God replied "I AM" (Exodus 3:13–14 NKJV). That answer was truly profound. As human beings, we are bound by time. We have to wait for it to pass. But not so with God. He is not bound by what he created. He walked on water, stilled the storm with his voice, raised the dead to life, and he moves through time as easily as you and I flick through the pages of a history book. Jesus was telling us disciples that he is God in human form. That's why we need never be afraid.

Father, today I will look to Jesus, the author and finisher of my faith.

The 24/7 Battle

Jesus answered, "I assure you and most solemnly say to you, you have been searching for Me, not because you saw the signs (attesting miracles), but because you ate the loaves and were filled. Do not work for food that perishes, but for food that endures [and leads] to eternal life, which the Son of Man will give you; for God the Father has authorized Him and put His seal on Him."

John 6:26–27

Probably the most difficult battle for most of us as Christians is our battle against the carnal mind. This is what we often refer to as the Adamic nature, the nature we inherited from Adam. The battle against it will remain until we are completely transformed. That's when we will be free from the continual pull of the flesh toward the pleasures of this sinful world.

But that battle goes even deeper in that we are tied to our natural senses. We look to the things that we see rather than that which is unseen. As Jesus' followers, we need to fill ourselves with him and his teaching, with all that will outlast this temporal world. Only that will truly satisfy our deepest longings.

Father, help me to set my eyes upon that which is eternal.

Trust in Jesus

Jesus answered, "This is the work of God: that you believe [adhere to, trust in, rely on, and have faith] in the One whom He has sent."

JOHN 6:29

Today's verse describes God's perfect will for the whole of humanity. If asked what God requires of them, most people will give a list of things that they suspect he requires based upon portions of Scripture they know, while others will say that God hasn't any requirements—that we should just live each day doing the best we can.

We are, of course, to love the Lord our God with all of our heart, mind, soul, and strength, and we are to love our neighbor as ourselves. When we look at what that entails, we all fall woefully short (Romans 3:11–12, 23). Think of how the Samaritan loved a complete stranger—that's how much we should love others (Luke 10:25–37). And it's the knowledge of how far short we fall of the glory of God that sends us to Jesus. He is the one who can wash away our sins and give us peace with God. It's as simple as trusting in the Savior.

Father, today I trust in Jesus as my Lord and Savior.

The True Bread

Jesus said to them, "I assure you and most solemnly say to you, it is not Moses who has given you the bread out of heaven, but it is My Father who gives you the true bread out of heaven. For the Bread of God is He who comes down out of heaven, and gives life to the world."

John 6:32–33

After speaking the words in today's verse, Jesus then told the listening crowd that he was the Bread of Life and that anyone who came to him would never hunger or thirst. During the time of Moses, when the children of Israel were wandering in the wilderness, God miraculously provided manna from heaven for them. But this was merely a foreshadowing of the true bread that would come down from heaven.

Bread is sometimes called the "staff of life." It is a staple that most of us include in a healthy diet. Jesus is the real Staff of Life. He is the Living Bread that came down for the specific purpose of giving his life for the world. When we are born again, we partake of that bread. It's then that we "taste and see that the Lord is good" (Psalm 34:8 NKJV).

Father, may the bread of heaven feed me now and evermore.

Blessed Assurance

"As I told you, you have seen Me and still you do not believe. All that My Father gives Me will come to Me; and the one who comes to Me I will most certainly not cast out [I will never, never reject anyone who follows Me]."

JOHN 6:36–37

What a wonderful comforting thought that in this world where so many of us are afraid of rejection, God will never reject us. Notice that in today's verse Jesus said, "The one who comes to me…." The prodigal son went into a far country to get away from his father so that he could spend his money on prostitutes. When a famine came and his money ran out, he found himself feeding pigs—even desiring to eat the pigs' food. When he came to himself, he determined to return to his father and say, "I've sinned against heaven and before you" (Luke 15:18 NKJV). When his father saw him returning, he ran to him, fell upon him, and kissed him, saying that once his son was dead, but now he is alive.

Come to Jesus in that repentant way, and you can be assured he will never ever leave you nor forsake you.

Father, thank you for the wonderful assurance that you'll never leave me.

The Last Day

"For I have come down from heaven, not to do My own will, but to do the will of Him who sent Me. This is the will of Him who sent Me, that of all that He has given Me I lose nothing, but that I [give new life and] raise it up at the last day."

JOHN 6:38-39

The last day is the day of resurrection, when Jesus will call from death all those who died in him and live on this earth with pleasure forevermore. God's kingdom is coming to earth, and the Genesis curse will be removed. That means no more pain, suffering, disease, loneliness, or fear, and the last enemy to be swallowed up is death (1 Corinthians 15:26). To that we whisper, "Hallelujah."

How we long for that day. How we groan for the kingdom of God to come to this earth. And how our hearts must break for the ungodly who don't have this blessed hope. Death to them is a terror beyond words, not a joy to be looked forward to as it is for the Christian. May compassion cause us to run to them with the good news of the gospel.

Father, please use me as a vessel to take the gospel to the lost.

A Lamp to Our Feet

"This is My Father's will and purpose, that everyone who sees the Son and believes in Him [as Savior] will have eternal life, and I will raise him up [from the dead] on the last day." Now the Jews murmured and found fault with Him because He said, "I am the Bread that came down out of heaven."

John 6:40–41

After Jesus spoke the startling words in today's Scripture verse, his hearers then began to ask how someone they knew—Jesus, the son of Joseph—could say such strange things like "I have come down from heaven"? We can almost sympathize with the Jews because they *knew* Jesus and his earthly father, and here he was saying that he came down from heaven!

His statement was understandably fantastic, outrageous, and nonsensical—unless they knew the Scriptures that prophesied where Jesus would be born and even gave his lineage. Had they read and believed the Scriptures that God gave them describing the Messiah in great detail, they wouldn't have rejected him. This is why we must know the Scriptures. They are a lamp to our feet and a light to our path (Psalm 119:105), and without them, we will be in darkness and eventually stumble.

Father, thank you for your Word that gives us light.

Those Who Have Seen God

"Not that anyone has seen the Father, except He [who was with the Father and] who is from God; He [alone] has seen the Father."

JOHN 6:46

Be wary of those who find fame by saying that they have seen God. They apparently died on the operating table, were taken up to heaven, chatted with God, and had conversations with Jesus. The Bible tells us that "no one has seen God at any time" (John 1:18 NKJV). God told Moses that he couldn't see God and live. This is because, like us, Moses was sinful, and if he stood in God's presence, God's goodness would have fallen on him in wrath.

When Moses asked to see God's glory, God hid him in the cleft of a rock, and Moses was allowed to look only upon where God had been (Exodus 33:20–23). And the Scriptures tell us that the glory of God so shone from the face of Moses that the children of Israel were afraid to go close to him (34:29–30). In the Old Testament, some saw a manifestation of God, but no one has seen his essence. We should therefore be very skeptical when we hear people say they've seen God.

Father, only the pure in heart will see you (Matthew 5:8).

Hard Sayings

Jesus said to the twelve [disciples], "You do not want to leave too, do you?"
JOHN 6:67

In today's reading, Jesus had just said some "hard" sayings. If taken literally, they are more than hard, and it caused many to leave Jesus. "Jesus said to them, 'Most assuredly, I say to you, unless you eat the flesh of the Son of Man and drink His blood, you have no life in you. Whoever eats My flesh and drinks My blood has eternal life, and I will raise him up at the last day'" (John 6:53–54 NKJV).

This, of course, is not a reference to the disciples eating the flesh of Jesus and drinking his blood. This is not only repulsive, but it is also forbidden in Scripture (Leviticus 19:26). They are clearly spiritual statements. When we are born of God's Spirit (born again), we "taste and see that the LORD is good" (Psalm 34:8 NKJV). Jesus made it clear that he was speaking spiritually: "It is the Spirit who gives life; the flesh profits nothing. The words that I speak to you are spirit, and they are life" (John 6:63 NKJV).

Father, I never ever want to leave Jesus. He is my life.

One of You Is a Devil

Jesus answered them, "Did I not choose you, the twelve [disciples]? And yet one of you is a devil (ally of Satan)."
John 6:70

In today's Scripture verse, Jesus was responding to the wonderful words of Peter. Jesus had asked his disciples if they were also going to leave him after he had shared some very hard sayings. Peter said, "Lord, to whom shall we go? You have the words of eternal life. Also we have come to believe and know that You are the Christ, the Son of the living God" (John 6:68–70 NKJV).

There are many things in Scripture and in life that cause some to fall away from following Jesus. But where are they going to go? Only Jesus of Nazareth has the words of eternal life. How foolish we would be to turn our backs on him, as did Judas. And the problem that Judas had was that he played the hypocrite. He was a thief who so lacked a fear of God that he stole from the disciples (John 12:4–6). He never knew who Jesus was. He didn't see him as the precious source of life. To Judas, Jesus was worth only about thirty pieces of silver.

Father, never let me be deceived by sin as was Judas.

Any Time Is Right

Jesus said to them, "My time has not yet come; but any time is right for you...Go up to the feast yourselves. I am not going up to this feast because My time has not yet fully come."

John 7:6, 8

Jesus had used a phrase similar to today's passage at the beginning of his public ministry. Mary had brought to his attention the fact that the wedding that they were attending had run out of wine. That's when Jesus responded by saying, "My hour has not yet come" (John 2:4 NKJV). This was a gentle rebuke to remind Mary that the time that he would begin his public ministry was in the hands of his heavenly Father, not his earthly mother.

Jesus had come for the specific purpose of suffering and dying for the sin of the world. But Jesus said that his disciples weren't bound by this terrifying schedule. And so you and I are free to serve God in any way we choose. That's why we should use every day we have to let our light shine by sharing the gospel with dying sinners. Any time is right for us to do this.

Father, direct me today to some lost sinner and give me the wisdom I need to share the gospel.

Taste and See

Jesus answered them by saying, "My teaching is not My own, but His who sent Me. If anyone is willing to do His will, he will know whether the teaching is of God or whether I speak on My own accord and by My own authority. He who speaks on his own accord seeks glory and honor for himself. But He who seeks the glory and the honor of the One who sent Him, He is true, and there is no unrighteousness or deception in Him."

JOHN 7:16–18

The moment we are born of the Spirit, we enter a supernatural realm. The Bible says, "He has delivered us from the power of darkness and conveyed us into the kingdom of the Son of His love" (Colossians 1:13). The Scriptures tell us that we have passed from death to life. We now *know* the truth, and the truth makes us free (John 8:32).

If you are a skeptic and you're standing on the outside looking in, how can you know this is true? Jesus here gives the answer: "If anyone wills to do His will, he shall *know* concerning the doctrine, whether it is from God or whether I speak on My own authority" (John 7:17 NKJV, emphasis added). The old maxim is true: The proof of the pudding is in the tasting. Simply obey the gospel—confess and forsake your sins, put your trust in Jesus, and you will come to know the Lord—you have his promise on that. (See John 14:21 for further details.)

Father, thank you for not leaving me in darkness about the most important of issues.

A Form of Godliness

Jesus called out as He taught in the temple, "You know Me and know where I am from; and I have not come on My own initiative [as self-appointed], but He who sent Me is true, and Him you do not know. I know Him Myself because I am from Him [I came from His very presence] and it was He [personally] who sent Me."

JOHN 7:28–29

The sin of the religious leaders of Jesus' time was great. Jesus reveals in today's verse that the offense the Pharisees committed was not out of ignorance. They knew who Jesus was and where he was from. The inference is that this was not just the knowledge that he was the son of a local carpenter. They knew that he had come down from heaven, and they hated him because he exposed their hypocrisy.

They hated God without cause. They drew near to him with their lips, but their hearts were far from him. And Jesus told them so. He said that they didn't know him. We are surrounded by a world that has a form of godliness, but they keep God at arm's length. The truth is that they love the darkness and hate the light.

Father, please extend your mercy toward those who don't know you.

You Cannot Come

Jesus said, "For a little while longer I am [still] with you, and then I go to Him who sent Me. You will look for Me, and will not [be able to] find Me; and where I am, you cannot come."

JOHN 7:33-34

This statement reflects Jesus' foreknowledge about his impending death, resurrection, and ascension. Here he speaks to a group that includes religious leaders opposing him, explaining that his time on earth is temporary. He indicates that he will soon return to "Him who sent Me," referring to God the Father. This highlights his divine mission and heavenly origin.

Jesus' words, "You will look for Me, and will not…find Me," underscore the idea that after his departure, those who reject him will be unable to find him or access the presence of God through him. Their inability to follow him to "where I am" reflects the separation caused by their unbelief.

The passage serves as a profound call to seek Jesus while he is near. It emphasizes that faith in him as the Son of God is essential for access to eternal life and reconciliation with God. Jesus' statement challenges his audience—and readers today—to consider their spiritual response to his invitation for salvation.

Father, thank you that Jesus ever lives to make intercession for me in your presence.

If Anyone Thirsts

Now on the last and most important day of the feast, Jesus stood and called out [in a loud voice], "If anyone is thirsty, let him come to Me and drink! He who believes in Me [who adheres to, trusts in, and relies on Me], as the Scripture has said, 'From his innermost being will flow continually rivers of living water.'"

John 7:37–38

Jesus here speaks on the final and most significant day of the Feast of Tabernacles, a Jewish festival celebrating God's provision. He boldly invites the spiritually thirsty to come to him for spiritual satisfaction. By declaring, "If anyone is thirsty, let him come to Me and drink," Jesus presents himself as the ultimate source of spiritual life, echoing God's promise to quench deep, soul-level needs.

Jesus explains that belief in him leads to a transformation, referencing the Scriptures to promise that "rivers of living water" will flow from within believers. This imagery signifies the Holy Spirit, who would later be given to all who trust in Christ. The Spirit provides ongoing spiritual vitality, empowerment, and renewal, likened to abundant, life-giving streams.

Jesus' words underscore that he alone fulfills humanity's longing for purpose and connection with God. By faith, believers receive an eternal source of divine life, enabling them to share God's grace with others, creating a ripple effect of spiritual refreshment.

Father, I'm so grateful for your thirst-quenching Holy Spirit.

September

Jesus's arrest in the garden of Gethsemane (Matthew 26:36–46)

Blind World

Once more Jesus addressed the crowd. He said, "I am the Light of the world. He who follows Me will not walk in the darkness, but will have the Light of life."

John 8:12

Look at the absolute surety of this promise in today's verse. Jesus said, "I am the Light of the world." Jesus *is* the Light of the World. Only our Creator could make such a phenomenal claim. In the beginning, he created physical light: "Then God said, 'Let there be light'; and there was light. And God saw the light, that it was good; and God divided the light from the darkness" (Genesis 1:3–4 NKJV). And in Christ we receive spiritual light that divides us from the darkness of sin.

This whole sinful world lives and walks in darkness. Many people are blind to the things of God. But when any sinner trusts in Jesus, God opens the eyes of their understanding. When Jesus spoke these words, he was speaking to a limited crowd two thousand years ago. But this promise is as relevant and real for the billions who are alive on this earth today as it was when Jesus said it so long ago. If they follow Jesus, they will have the light of life.

Father, keep me in the light today.

Fruit of Repentance

Jesus was saying to the Jews who had believed Him, "If you abide in My word [continually obeying My teachings and living in accordance with them, then] you are truly My disciples. And you will know the truth [regarding salvation], and the truth will set you free [from the penalty of sin]."

JOHN 8:31-32

There are many today who say that all any sinner needs to do to be saved is to merely 'believe' in Jesus. But we are not saved by just 'believing.' In fact, we are not saved by *anything* we do—that is, we cannot earn our way to God. Instead, we are saved by God's grace alone. And he has established how we receive his grace, and that's through repentance and faith (Ephesians 2:8–9). As Jesus said, "Repent [change your inner self—your old way of thinking, regret past sins, live your life in a way that proves repentance; seek God's purpose for your life], for the kingdom of heaven is at hand" (Matthew 3:2).

As evidence of repentance, we walk in obedience to God's Word. Those who believe but continue to serve sin are playing the hypocrite and shouldn't have assurance of salvation. They don't have the "things that accompany salvation" (Hebrews 6:9–12). Let's make sure that we have those things and do as Scripture says by making our calling and election sure (2 Peter 1:10).

Father, today I will examine my heart for any hypocrisy.

The Trap of Sin

Jesus answered, "I assure you and most solemnly say to you, everyone who practices sin habitually is a slave of sin."
JOHN 8:34

Sin is a Venus flytrap. It sends out an aroma that attracts our evil hearts. It turns our head as the flytrap turns the head of an unthinking and vulnerable insect. When David turned his sinful eyes toward another man's wife, he began to go toward the Venus flytrap until it snapped and caught him in a death-trap (2 Samuel 11). Bathsheba-like temptation is around every corner waiting for your vulnerable eyes. Lust wants to turn your head and feed your heart with thoughts that make you smile but make God frown. And if you love God, the thought of his displeasure should turn your heart from sin. Jesus said, "Whoever looks at a woman to lust for her has already committed adultery with her in his heart" (Matthew 5:27 NKJV).

We may fall into sin, and if we do, we will quickly get back up and seek God's forgiveness (1 John 1:9). But Jesus said that if we *habitually* practice sin, we become its slave. We are "taken captive" by Satan "to do his will" (2 Timothy 2:26 NKJV). That's when we become trapped in its deathly grip. This is why we continually look to Jesus. Keep your eyes on him and your nose out of sin.

Father, don't let sin deceive me today.

Free Indeed

"If the Son makes you free, then you are unquestionably free."
John 8:36

Freedom was the fruit of the sexual revolution of the 1960s. That's when a generation threw off the shackles of slavery to what they considered an outdated morality. The sexual revolution gave people freedom to enjoy the pleasure of sex with no marital commitment. It gave them liberty to follow a sinful heart without fear or guilt. But there was one problem. Sin is the bedfellow of death. It has wages (Romans 6:23). It delivers pleasure, but only for a season.

But the freedom of which Jesus spoke is something far different. It's a promised liberty from the cold clutch of death, freedom from the deadliest of enemies. Look at this wonderful promise God gave to humanity eight hundred years before Jesus came to this earth in the form of a little babe: "He will swallow up death forever, and the Lord God will wipe away tears from all faces" (Isaiah 25:8 NKJV). One faint heartbeat in the lifeless body of the Son of God as he lay in that tomb flung open the doorway to everlasting life. That's the freedom we have in Jesus. O happy day when Jesus washed my sins away![7]

Father, thank you for not leaving us in death.

---

7 A paraphrase of lyrics from the song "Oh, Happy Day," written by Edwin Hawkins, performed by the Edwin Hawkins Singers, track 5 from their album *Let Us Go into the House of the Lord*, released April 1968.

The Experience

"I assure you and most solemnly say to you, if anyone keeps My word [by living in accordance with My message] he will indeed never, ever see and experience death."

John 8:51

It wasn't too long ago that we didn't exist. But God opened our mother's womb, and there we were—alive and kicking. Over the next few years, we instinctively ate food, drank, and slept. Then we learned to walk and talk. And we can't recall any of that learning. We don't remember the first few years of life.

And now we all face impending death. For most of the world, it's a terrifying and dark mystery. But look at what Jesus said in today's verse. If *anyone* obeys him, they will indeed never see or experience death. Death is the biggest event any human being will experience. It dwarfs our birth, choosing a vocation, or getting married. But what does Scripture mean when it speaks of *experiencing* death? We really don't know, but one thing we do know is that every instinct we have pulls back from it. But we won't know that experience if we belong to Jesus.

Father, words cannot express my gratitude for deliverance from having to experience death.

The I AM

Jesus replied, "I assure you and most solemnly say to you, before Abraham was born, I Am."

JOHN 8:58

Every philosophical word written or spoken by great human beings combined is nothing but light dust on the scales of truth. However, the words of Jesus of Nazareth crushed the scales to dust itself. His words were both weighty and without precedent. Truly, never a man spoke like this man. Not Aristotle, not Plato, not Socrates.

This most profound "I Am" truth came in response to the continual questioning of Jesus by the religious leaders. At one point, they even said that he was demon-possessed:

> Then the Jews said to Him, "Now we know that You have a demon! Abraham is dead, and the prophets; and You say, 'If anyone keeps My word he shall never taste death.' Are You greater than our father Abraham, who is dead? And the prophets are dead. Who do You make Yourself out to be?" (John 8:52–53 NKJV)

They asked, so he told them. He was the God of Israel in human form: "Then they took up stones to throw at Him; but Jesus hid Himself and went out of the temple, going through the midst of them, and so passed by" (John 8:59 NKJV).

Exalt Jesus today, both in your mind and in your words, to everyone around you, including the unsaved.

Father, how wonderful that you became one human being in Jesus.

They Will Never Perish

"I am the Door; anyone who enters through Me will be saved [and will live forever], and will go in and out [freely], and find pasture (spiritual security)...I am the Good Shepherd, and I know [without any doubt those who are] My own and My own know Me [and have a deep, personal relationship with Me]...The sheep that are My own hear My voice and listen to Me; I know them, and they follow Me. And I give them eternal life, and they will never, ever [by any means] perish; and no one will ever snatch them out of My hand."

John 10:9, 14, 27–28

Seeing the depth of meaning of the words of Jesus translated from the original language should bring us to tears of joy. The apostle Paul called it "joy unspeakable" (1 Peter 1:8 KJV). We have everlasting life! We have pleasure forevermore!

The living hope we have in him is both sure and steadfast, "an anchor of the soul" (Hebrews 6:19 NKJV). And look at who holds the anchor. After he gives us everlasting life, he assures us that "they will never, ever [by any means] perish; and no one will ever snatch them out of My hand." Many don't go through the door. They never get a handle on who Jesus is. He is the way, the truth, and the life (John 14:6). He alone is the entrance into the kingdom of heaven.

Father, I rest in your wonderful promise of everlasting life.

The Power of Words

Jesus said, "Take away the stone." Martha, the sister of the dead man, said to Him, "Lord, by this time there will be an offensive odor, for he has been dead four days! [It is hopeless!]" Jesus said to her, "Did I not say to you that if you believe [in Me], you will see the glory of God [the expression of His excellence]?"

John 11:39–40

The Bible tells us that this world is "dead in trespasses and sins" (Ephesians 2:1 NKJV). Their righteous deeds "are like filthy rags" in the sight of God (Isaiah 64:6 NKJV). Notice in today's reading that Jesus didn't miraculously cause the stone to roll away from the entrance of Lazarus' grave. He told human beings to remove it. And God has chosen human beings and the foolishness of preaching to save sinners from death.

The task before us is formidable because we are weak. But God in his great wisdom can use our words to remove the hindrance between Jesus and those who are dead in their trespasses. Never underestimate your words on behalf of the kingdom. They may be part of God's plan to bring someone into the kingdom of light.

Father, may you be pleased to use me today.

Faithful Prayer

They took away the stone. And Jesus raised His eyes [toward heaven] and said, "Father, I thank You that You have heard Me. I knew that You always hear Me and listen to Me; but I have said this because of the people standing around, so that they may believe that You have sent Me [and that You have made Me Your representative]."

JOHN 11:41–42

Almost every Christian prays with the tradition of having their eyes closed. This is possibly because we are easily distracted by things we see if we have our eyes open when we pray. We often bow our heads at the same time as a token of reverence and humility toward the Lord. But Jesus here lifted his eyes up toward heaven. And in the opening sentence of his prayer, he not only calls God his Father, but he also shows the faith that he has in that he knew that God heard his prayers.

Scripture teaches that sin can hinder God from hearing us (Psalm 66:18). However, Jesus was sinless and therefore had direct access to the ear of his Father. He not only affirmed that God was hearing him, but he also affirmed that God *always* heard him.

Father, may I always approach you full of faith in your integrity.

Graveclothes

When He had said this, He shouted with a loud voice, "Lazarus, come out!" Out came the man who had been dead, his hands and feet tightly wrapped in burial cloths (linen strips), and with a [burial] cloth wrapped around his face. Jesus said to them, "Unwrap him and release him."

JOHN 11:43–44

Jesus not only told those who were at Lazarus' graveside to roll the stone away, but he also told them to unwrap the burial cloths that were around the face of Lazarus. Until this was done, Lazarus wasn't completely free.

Often when a sinner comes to Christ, those of us who are more mature can come alongside them and unwrap the burial cloth that still hinders their walk. We need to disciple them into fellowship, into reading the Word daily, and into sharing their faith with the lost. By doing this, we can make the Christian life easier for them, particularly when it comes to sharing their faith. We need to tell them how to present the gospel biblically, how to approach sinners without being offensive, and the importance of having a loving and gentle tone as they share the gospel.

Father, please give me a sensitivity with new believers.

Mind Your Own

Jesus said, "Let her alone, so that she may keep [the rest of] it for the day of My burial. You always have the poor with you, but you do not always have Me."

John 12:7–8

In today's verse, Jesus responded to Judas after Judas complained that a woman had been extravagant when she broke an alabaster box of expensive ointment and poured it on Jesus as an act of worship. When Jesus said to leave her alone, he was telling Judas to mind his own business. The Bible tells us not to be busybodies. In other words, we shouldn't meddle in other people's business.

One time, Jesus even gave a strong "Mind your own business" to Peter. "Peter, turning around, saw the disciple whom Jesus loved following, who also had leaned on His breast at the supper, and said, 'Lord, who is the one who betrays You?' Peter, seeing him, said to Jesus, 'But Lord, what about this man?' Jesus said to him, 'If I will that he remain till I come, what *is* that to you? You follow Me'" (John 21:20–22 NKJV). The lesson is that if I am about my Father's business, it will keep me from putting my nose into other people's affairs.

Father, keep me busy doing your business.

Dying Daily to Be Fruitful

Jesus answered them, "The hour has come for the Son of Man to be glorified and exalted. I assure you and most solemnly say to you, unless a grain of wheat falls into the earth and dies, it remains alone [just one grain, never more]. But if it dies, it produces much grain and yields a harvest."

John 12:23–24

Was Jesus speaking about his ascension to heaven in today's verse, or was he making reference to the suffering of the cross? Whatever the case, he used the analogy of a tiny seed falling to the earth and dying. Just as one seed falling to the earth and coming alive has the potential to produce literally millions of trees, so the death of Jesus on the cross was the seed that gave life to millions of believers down through the ages.

If you and I wish to become fruitful, we must die to ourselves and to this world so that we can produce fruit to the glory of God. We gladly die now that we may live later: "But someone will say, 'How are the dead raised up? And with what body do they come?' Foolish one, what you sow is not made alive unless it dies" (1 Corinthians 15:35–36 NKJV).

Father, this day, I reckon myself dead to sin.

Unless You Hate

"The one who loves his life [eventually] loses it [through death], but the one who hates his life in this world [and is concerned with pleasing God] will keep it for life eternal."

JOHN 12:25

The teachings of Jesus are often hyperbolic (Luke 14:26). We know that as Christians, we shouldn't hate the life that God has given us. However, Jesus was again speaking of having "inordinate affection," which involves a lavishing of affection upon the gift and ignoring the Giver. Jesus spoke of the man who built bigger barns for himself but was not rich toward God (Luke 12:21).

How tragic it is for those who don't see the depth of their sin and find a place of true repentance. The revelation of what we had in the world and what we have in Christ makes it easy to put our hand to the plow and not even look back. For the true convert, to longingly look back at Sodom is repulsive. It's to tread the blood of Christ underfoot. This is why we must never forget how much we depend on the cross, and we won't forget that if we always remember the depth of our sinful heart.

Father, may I depend always on your mercy.

Serving Jesus

"If anyone serves Me, he must [continue to faithfully] follow Me [without hesitation, holding steadfastly to Me, conforming to My example in living and, if need be, suffering or perhaps dying because of faith in Me]; and wherever I am [in heaven's glory], there will My servant be also. If anyone serves Me, the Father will honor him."

John 12:26

Scripture emphasizes the commitment and devotion required to serve and follow Jesus. To serve him, we must live a life of faithful discipleship, reflecting his teachings and example without hesitation. This involves steadfast obedience, a willingness to endure challenges, and even the potential cost of suffering or death for one's faith. It calls for complete alignment with Jesus in actions and heart, demonstrating trust in his leadership.

The verse also provides a promise of eternal fellowship: wherever Jesus is, his faithful servants will be with him. This assurance gives us hope and purpose. Additionally, Jesus declares that those who serve him will receive honor from God the Father. This underscores the profound value and eternal significance of faithful service to Christ.

In essence, the verse calls for unwavering commitment to Jesus, assuring believers of heavenly fellowship and God's honor for their faithful dedication. It reflects the deep relationship between service, sacrifice, and divine reward.

Father, use me this day to serve you.

The Unthinkable Thought

"Now My soul is troubled and deeply distressed; what shall I say? 'Father, save Me from this hour [of trial and agony]'? But it is for this [very] purpose that I have come to this hour [this time and place]. [Rather, I will say,] 'Father, glorify (honor, extol) Your name!'" Then a voice came from heaven saying, "I have both glorified it, and will glorify it again."

John 12:27–28

It's unthinkable—and a scenario that should make us shudder—that Jesus could have changed his mind about the suffering of the cross. If that had been the case, we would be of all people most miserable because we would have no hope after death. Instead, in today's verses, we are privy to the inner battle that went on in the heart of Jesus.

We see that he was troubled and deeply distressed, but he never lost sight of the fact that he was born for the most terrible suffering and death. He overcame the temptation to choose his own will above the will of the Father. And it was his perfect love for you and me that caused him to cast out all fear. How can we not be broken by such love?

Father, glorify your name through my life.

Face-to-Face

Jesus answered, "This voice has come for your sake, not for mine. Now judgment is upon this world [the sentence is being passed]. Now the ruler of this world (Satan) will be cast out. And I, if and when I am lifted up from the earth [on the cross], will draw all people to Myself [Gentiles, as well as Jews]."

John 12:30–32

Jesus had said, "Now My soul is troubled, and what shall I say? 'Father, save Me from this hour'? But for this purpose I came to this hour. Father, glorify Your name" (John 12:27–28 NKJV). That's when God spoke audibly from heaven, saying, "I have both glorified it and will glorify it again" (v. 28 NKJV). The people who heard the voice either thought that it thundered or that an angel had spoken to Jesus.

As Christians we are restricted to walking by faith and not by sight. But oh, the excitement of hearing God's voice! How we yearn for the supernatural. And because of what Jesus did on the cross, one day we will see him face-to-face (1 John 3:2). We will see God as he is. What a day that will be!

Father, I long to see you face-to-face.

Light and Darkness

Jesus said to them, "The Light is among you [only] a little while longer. Walk while you have the Light [keep on living by it], so that darkness will not overtake you. He who walks in the darkness does not know where he is going [he is drifting aimlessly]. While you have the Light, believe and trust in the Light [have faith in it, hold on to it, rely on it], so that you may become sons of Light [being filled with Light as followers of God]." Jesus said these things, and then He left and hid Himself from them.

JOHN 12:35–36

Jesus would only be with his people for a short time. He therefore gave them and us the Holy Spirit to help us overcome the darkness of sin. The Bible continually speaks of this battle between the light and darkness: "You are a chosen generation, a royal priesthood, a holy nation, His own special people, that you may proclaim the praises of Him who called you out of darkness into His marvelous light" (1 Peter 2:9 NKJV).

Look at his words: "So that darkness will not overtake you." Darkness naturally comes when light is removed. That's why we need to stay close to the one who said that he is the Light of the World (John 8:12). And the way to stay in the light is to cultivate a tender conscience toward God.

Father, help me always to be guided by my conscience in the light of your Word.

Trust in the Lord

Jesus replied to him, "You do not realize now what I am doing, but you will [fully] understand it later."

John 13:7

We know that the Christian life is founded upon trust. We trust that God knows what he's doing in our lives—even when we have no idea what he's doing at the time. "Trust in the Lord with all your heart, and lean not on your own understanding; in all your ways acknowledge Him, and He shall direct your paths" (Proverbs 3:5–6 NKJV).

It's *natural* for our human understanding to want to know the details, but we instead choose the *supernatural* and trust in the Lord. And his will is often to take us into the lions' den and then to work it out for our good (Romans 8:28). More often than not, it's only when we come out of the fiery trial that we understand. In the meantime, faith produces a joy that God is in control, and the joy of the Lord is our strength: "Though the fig tree may not blossom, nor fruit be on the vines;…I will joy in the God of my salvation" (Habakkuk 3:17–18 NKJV). Listen to Jesus speak about joy: "These things I have spoken to you, that My joy may remain in you, and that your joy may be full" (John 15:11).

Father, today and tomorrow I will trust you with my mind and heart.

SEPTEMBER 19

God Resists the Proud

Peter said to Him, "You will never wash my feet!" Jesus answered, "Unless I wash you, you have no part with Me [we can have nothing to do with each other]."

John 13:8

The fact that God resists the proud and gives grace to the humble is an unbending biblical truth. The Scriptures tell us that *everyone* who is "proud in heart is an abomination to the Lord" (Proverbs 16:5 NKJV). The Bible also says that the wicked through the pride of his face will not seek after God (Psalm 10:4). We must remember that pride can come in subtle disguises. Someone may say they're humble, but that confession is rooted in pride. Others may say that they're proud, and they may be right or they may actually be humble.

However, God is the discerner of the thoughts and intents of our heart. Only he can see if we are truly humble or if we are steeped and pride. What Peter was saying in today's verse sounded humble, but the sharp rebuke from Jesus shows us that Peter's heart wasn't right. If we want God to use us to further his kingdom, we must continually have a humble heart.

Father, this day I humble myself before you.

Most Blessed

"If you know these things, you are blessed [happy and favored by God] if you put them into practice [and faithfully do them]."
JOHN 13:17

In today's verse, look at how the translation from the original language tells us that it's not enough just to know the great truths that Jesus taught. We must know them and put them into practice to experience the blessedness of which Jesus spoke. Washing the feet of others is the key. This isn't necessarily a physical washing. It is rather being a humble servant to everyone we meet. This includes family, friends, strangers, and enemies. We must do this if we want to experience the fulfilled Christian life.

Libraries and bookstores are full of books on how to obtain success. However, Jesus here gives us the recipe for finding a different type of gratification. This comes from seeing others as better than ourselves. Again, this means that we become a servant to everyone we meet—whether they are Christian or non-Christian. This is because it's more blessed to give than to receive. Give of yourself to others and you will find an inner satisfaction that can't be duplicated by the world and its selfish and superficial pleasure.

Father, remind me to be a lowly servant to those I meet today.

Gospel Authentication

"I am not speaking of all of you. I know whom I have chosen; but [this has happened] in order that the Scripture may be fulfilled: 'He who eats My bread has raised up his heel against Me [as My enemy].' From now on I am telling you [what will happen] before it occurs, so that when it does take place you may believe that I am He [who I say I am—the Christ, the Anointed, the Messiah]."

John 13:18–19

One of the greatest proofs that the Bible is the Word of God is that it contains prophecy. In today's Scripture verse, Jesus was telling his disciples of something that will come to pass in the future. Only God knows the future. Weather forecasters only make an estimated guess on the data they have. And so we should use prophecy to convince the ungodly of the authenticity of the gospel that we preach.

This was the practice of the apostle Paul. "When they had appointed him a day, many came to him at his lodging, to whom he explained and solemnly testified of the kingdom of God, persuading them concerning Jesus from both the law of Moses and the Prophets, from morning till evening" (Acts 28:23 NKJV).

Don't hesitate to speak about the evident signs of the times (lawlessness, turmoil in the Middle East, the possession of Jerusalem, etc.) because they can be effective bait to get the fish nibbling.

Father, it gives me great comfort to know that you know the future.

Satan Entered Him

Jesus answered, "It is the one to whom I am going to give this piece [of bread] after I have dipped it." So when He had dipped the piece of bread [into the dish], He gave it to Judas, son of Simon Iscariot.

John 13:26

The Bible tells us that at the Last Supper, after Judas had taken the piece of bread from Jesus, Satan entered him. Then Jesus said to him that what he was about to do, he should do quickly. Judas was a marked man the moment he stole money from Jesus and the disciples. Sin opened the door to Satan, and now Satan wanted possession of the house.

Notice that the devil entered just after Judas had taken the piece of bread from Jesus. It was common to offer a guest a morsel of bread as a gesture of love and friendship. Jesus was honoring Judas and extending his loving hand to him. How evil of Judas to take the bread with the intent to offer himself as a guide to those who planned to kill Jesus. That gave the devil possession of the house. Never give place to the devil. Keep your heart free from sin, and that will keep the door closed and locked (James 4:7).

Father, I submit to you with my whole heart.

Love One Another

"I am giving you a new commandment, that you love one another. Just as I have loved you, so you too are to love one another."

JOHN 13:34

Jesus told his friends that everyone would know that they were his disciples if they had love and unselfish concern for one another. No doubt these words resonated within the hearts of the disciples *after* they understood the love expressed on the cross. Jesus said, "A new commandment I give to you, that you love one another." But this wasn't new. Jesus had spoken of love many times. But the love that they would have for one another would be in the light of his suffering.

The world has a measure of love. Secular people can be kind and loving. But the love of Christ in us remains steadfast in the face of hatred. It is the love that Stephen expressed toward those who were stoning him to death (Acts 7:59–60). It is love that is patient and kind, never jealous, proud, selfish, or rude (1 Corinthians 13). If we can show this sort of love to those who live in darkness, it can be worth a thousand sermons.

Father, let your love shine through me this day.

I Am Not Ashamed

Simon Peter said to Him, "Lord, where are You going?" Jesus answered, "Where I am going, you cannot follow Me now; but you will be able to follow later."

JOHN 13:36

Peter asked why he couldn't follow Jesus, saying that he would lay down his life for Jesus. That's when Jesus asked if Peter would really lay down his life for him and warned him that he would deny Jesus three times before a rooster crowed. Peter made a promise he couldn't keep. He was quick with his mouth but slow with his heart. His spirit was willing, but his flesh took over when push came to shove.

But he did have some sort of excuse. He wasn't born again as we are. He didn't yet have the indwelling Holy Spirit to give him the power to stand against his fears. We do. "For God has not given us a spirit of fear, but of power and of love and of a sound mind" (2 Timothy 1:7 NKJV). May we never deny Jesus, especially in the light of the cross. We love him because of the evidence that he first loved us and gave himself as an atonement for our sins.

Father, help me to be unashamed and bold about my faith in Jesus.

Believe Also in Me

"Do not let your heart be troubled (afraid, cowardly). Believe [confidently] in God and trust in Him, [have faith, hold on to it, rely on it, keep going and] believe also in Me."

John 14:1

These words of Jesus in today's Scripture verse show us that we are the ones who are in control of both our faith and our fear. He said, "Do not let your heart be troubled." Guard your heart with all diligence. The translation from the original language shows us that the fear referred to here is a "cowardly" fear. The way to keep cowardly fear out of our heart is to have a predetermined and steadfast resolution to trust in God—to hold on to him, rely on him, and to continue to do so.

Then Jesus redirects our faith. He says, "Believe also in Me." Many have a belief in God, and others trust in him, but Scripture teaches us that eternal salvation comes through Jesus and Jesus alone (John 14:6). God provided a Savior. "This is eternal life, that they may know You, the only true God, and Jesus Christ whom You have sent" (John 17:3 NKJV).

Father, I trust in you and in Jesus for my salvation.

New World Coming

"In My Father's house are many dwelling places. If it were not so, I would have told you, because I am going there to prepare a place for you."

JOHN 14:2

Jesus spoke of his second coming, saying that he would return and was leaving "to prepare a place" for us. This world is not our home. We have a home in the heavens that Jesus has made ready for those who love him. "For we know that if our earthly house, this tent, is destroyed, we have a building from God, a house not made with hands, eternal in the heavens" (2 Corinthians 5:1 NKJV).

But there's a problem. Our fallen minds fall way short of grasping the unspeakable magnificence of heaven. It's beyond our intellectual grasp. The Scriptures put it this way: "Eye has not seen, nor ear heard, nor have entered into the heart of man the things which God has prepared for those who love Him" (1 Corinthians 2:9 NKJV).

Think of the most beautiful things on this amazing earth—hummingbirds, blue skies, waterfalls, rainbows. They are nothing but an emptied trash can compared to what God has in store for those who love him.

Father, thank you for our glorious hope in Jesus.

The Only Way

Jesus said to him, "I am the [only] Way [to God] and the [real] Truth and the [real] Life; no one comes to the Father but through Me."

JOHN 14:6

This one statement in today's Bible passage infuriates the pride of man. But there is no ambiguity here. There's no wiggle room. When Jesus said that he is the only way to God, he meant that he is the only way to God. This is because God is holy and cannot have fellowship with sin. Jesus forgives us our sins, washes us clean, and makes us holy in the sight of our Creator. As the only Savior, Jesus restores our fellowship with God that was lost in the beginning, and no one can come to the Father except through him.

This is a hard truth for us to swallow until we understand the exceedingly sinful nature of sin. Knowing we have to jump out of a plane makes us value a parachute, and knowing that we have to pass through death and face a holy God shows us that we need to "put on the Lord Jesus Christ" (Romans 13:14 NKJV). And he's the only parachute being offered.

Father, I am eternally grateful for your mercy.

The Invisible God

Jesus said to him, "Have I been with you for so long a time, and you do not know Me yet, Philip, nor recognize clearly who I am? Anyone who has seen Me has seen the Father."

JOHN 14:9

Philip had asked Jesus if they could see God. He wanted Jesus to show the disciples the Father, and he added that seeing God would satisfy them. In reality, he didn't know what he was asking. As we have seen, the Bible says no man can see God and live (Exodus 33:20). We know that Moses was allowed to look at where God had been, but he had to be sheltered in the cleft of a rock as he did so.

However, it is because of this outlandish question from Philip that we have this wonderful answer from Jesus. He is God in human form (1 Timothy 3:16), made "a little lower than the angels, for the suffering of death crowned with glory" (Hebrews 2:9 NKJV). The invisible God created a visible body in Jesus of Nazareth: "He is the image of the invisible God, the firstborn over all creation" (Colossians 1:15 NKJV). This biblical truth magnifies our understanding of Scripture as we read of the life of Jesus, particularly in the Gospels.

Father, thank you that we can see the invisible in Jesus.

Greater Works

"I assure you and most solemnly say to you, anyone who believes in Me [as Savior] will also do the things that I do; and he will do even greater things than these [in extent and outreach], because I am going to the Father."

John 14:12

Jesus told his disciples that whatever they asked in his name would be done so that the Father may be glorified in the Son. The Amplified Bible brings some common sense to those who think they're going to do greater things than Jesus did. The word "greater" means that we have larger outreach with the gospel because we have been given the Holy Spirit as our helper.

As one man, Jesus was limited to time and space. He had to travel to reach his audience. Not so with the body of Christ worldwide. Christians can reach billions around the world through preaching to large crowds or witnessing one-on-one via the printed page, television, film, radio, and social media. Owing to these mediums, we have amazing advantages that no other generation has had before us.

Father, open doors for us to use these amazing mediums to reach the lost.

The Gauntlet

"The person who has My commandments and keeps them is the one who [really] loves Me; and whoever [really] loves Me will be loved by My Father, and I will love him and reveal Myself to him [I will make Myself real to him]."

JOHN 14:21

Here is our most powerful gauntlet:

First, here is a universal call to all of humanity: "The person who has My commandments and keeps them." The gospel is not confined particularly to Jew or to gentile. It reaches out to all human beings.

Second, this amazing verse is the gauntlet we throw at the feet of any skeptic. How can a person know if Jesus truly is the risen Son of God? Simply obey his words, and both the Father and the Son will miraculously make themselves known to the skeptic. Many a Doubting Thomas has become a believer the moment he put this into practice.

Third, if we love God, we will keep his commandments. We are not obedient *to be* saved; we are obedient *because* we're saved.

Therefore, whatever category in which you find yourself today, don't let unbelief hold you back from making peace with God by trusting in Jesus.

Father, thank you for revealing yourself to me.

October

The conversion of Saul of Tarsus (Acts 9:1–19)

The Helper

"The Helper (Comforter, Advocate, Intercessor—Counselor, Strengthener, Standby), the Holy Spirit, whom the Father will send in My name [in My place, to represent Me and act on My behalf], He will teach you all things. And He will help you remember everything that I have told you."

John 14:26

Jesus was speaking of the coming of the Holy Spirit, which happened on the day of Pentecost. Then, after the resurrection, he added specifics: "You shall receive power when the Holy Spirit has come upon you; and you shall be witnesses to Me in Jerusalem, and in all Judea and Samaria, and to the end of the earth" (Acts 1:8 NKJV).

The Holy Spirit was specifically given to us to give us power to be witnesses of Christ when we proclaim the gospel. If you ever feel fearful when it comes to sharing the gospel with the unsaved, make it a habit of not listening to your fears. This is because the Holy Spirit will assist you. He will teach you the biblical truths, and he will bring back to your remembrance things that Jesus said. That's the promise of Scripture. Make sure you believe it.

Father, thank you for giving me your Holy Spirit.

Putting Perfect Peace into Practice

"Peace I leave with you; My [perfect] peace I give to you; not as the world gives do I give to you. Do not let your heart be troubled, nor let it be afraid. [Let My perfect peace calm you in every circumstance and give you courage and strength for every challenge.]"

JOHN 14:27

Look at the conditions of this wonderful promise: "You will keep him in perfect peace, whose mind is stayed on You, because he trusts in You" (Isaiah 26:3 NKJV). God will keep us in perfect peace if we keep our mind stayed on him—that is, if we trust in him.

The perfect peace of which the Bible speaks isn't the absence of war or the absence of noise. It is an inner knowledge that Jesus is always with us, and whatever comes our way, God will work it out for our good (Romans 8:28). Storms tend to stir up waves. They trouble the ocean. But if we will let it, the peace of God, which passes all understanding, will keep us calm as we sit beside still waters. And the way to let it is to keep our mind "stayed" on God, because the mind is the battlefield.

Father, today I determine to keep my mind stayed on you.

Made a Little Lower

"You heard Me tell you, 'I am going away, and I am coming back to you.' If you [really] loved Me, you would have rejoiced, because I am going [back] to the Father, for the Father is greater than I. I have told you now before it happens, so that when it does take place, you may believe and have faith [in Me]."

JOHN 14:28

The fact that Jesus said, "I am going to the Father, for the Father is greater than I," is one of the arguments of the Jehovah's Witnesses against the deity of Jesus. They believe that in today's verse, Jesus is saying that he's not God. This is the danger of not interpreting Scripture with Scripture. Many people have made errors by taking one verse and building a doctrine on it.

The Scriptures tell us, "We see Jesus, who was made a little lower than the angels, for the suffering of death crowned with glory and honor, that He, by the grace of God, might taste death for everyone" (Hebrews 2:9 NKJV). In his humanity, he became thirsty, hungry, depressed, sorrowful, and he wept. The Father was not only greater than Jesus in his human form, but so were the angels.

As God, however, Jesus and the Father are coequals with the Holy Spirit. This is the Christian doctrine of the Trinity: three persons existing and relating together in the same divine nature. A tripersonal God.

A mystery? Yes. True? Absolutely. This is why we can trust and follow and worship Jesus: he is truly God, just as he is truly human. The God-man. The very Son of God in human form.

Father, may I always see Jesus in the light of your Word.

No Power over Me

"I will not speak with you much longer, for the ruler of the world (Satan) is coming. And he has no claim on Me [no power over Me nor anything that he can use against Me]."
JOHN 14:30

Satan is the god of this world. When we do anything evil, we imitate him. The Bible tells us that he once had the power of death over humanity, but look at what happened:

> Inasmuch then as the children have partaken of flesh and blood, He Himself likewise shared in the same, that through death He might destroy him who had the power of death, that is, the devil, and release those who through fear of death were all their lifetime subject to bondage. (Hebrews 2:14–15 NKJV)

Because of the suffering, death, and resurrection of Jesus, Satan lost the power of death. We rose in victory with Jesus. His victory became ours. "Now if we died with Christ, we believe that we shall also live with Him, knowing that Christ, having been raised from the dead, dies no more. Death no longer has dominion over Him" (Romans 6:8–9 NKJV). And now Satan has no power over us. When we submit to God and resist the devil, he must flee (James 4:7).

Father, thank you for the victory we have in Jesus.

Much Fruit

"Remain in Me, and I [will remain] in you. Just as no branch can bear fruit by itself without remaining in the vine, neither can you [bear fruit, producing evidence of your faith] unless you remain in Me."

John 15:4

Jesus told his disciples that his Father was glorified when they bore much fruit. That was evidence that they were truly his disciples. The same is true for us. Unfortunately, contemporary churches are filled with false converts. These are tares among the wheat, foolish virgins among the wise, bad fish among the good, and goats among the sheep. These will be sorted out on judgment day. Tragically, there are many who don't understand the reality of true and false conversion. Some think that Christians can lose their salvation while others think that we can live like the devil and still go to heaven.

In reality, a false convert plays the hypocrite and serves sin while a genuine convert's heart is free from sin. Those who trust in Jesus and walk in perpetual repentance can have absolute assurance that they are saved because no one can pluck them from God's hand (John 10:28). They bear much fruit, and the thought of falling away is repulsive to them.

Father, thank you for keeping me in your hand.

Trust and Obey

"No one has greater love [nor stronger commitment] than to lay down his own life for his friends."

JOHN 15:13

How amazing is today's verse, where Jesus alluded to the love he would express at the cross. However, in the following verses, he put a condition on his friendship. He said that we are his friends *if* we keep on doing what he commanded us to do. If we call him Lord but refuse to obey him and instead love this world, we are not his friend; in fact, we are his enemy. Look at these strong words directed at those who still have an affection for sin and this evil world: "Adulterers and adulteresses! Do you not know that friendship with the world is enmity with God? Whoever therefore wants to be a friend of the world makes himself an enemy of God" (James 4:4 NKJV).

Scripture is very clear that a saved person is obedient to Jesus: "Though He was a Son, yet He learned obedience by the things which He suffered. And having been perfected, He became the author of eternal salvation to all who obey Him" (Hebrews 5:8–9 NKJV).

Father, may I always value my friendship with you.

We Are Not of This World

"If the world hates you [and it does], know that it has hated Me before it hated you."

John 15:18

Jesus said that if his followers were still part of the world, the world would treat us with affection. But he brought us out of the kingdom of darkness and into the kingdom of light, so it shouldn't come as a surprise that those of the world despise us. Jesus told us to rejoice when we are despised for his name's sake (Matthew 5:11). This is because their hatred is evidence that we belong to God.

If I'm a police officer, I shouldn't expect the wicked criminal world to speak well of me. If they do, something is radically wrong. The reason criminals hate police officers is because the law stands for what is right and just. And as Christians, we stand against lawlessness, everything evil this world loves—sexual promiscuity, adultery, abortion, homosexuality, lust, the love of money, blasphemy, and so on. The Scriptures warn that everyone who lives a godly life as a Christian "will suffer persecution" (2 Timothy 3:12 NKJV).

Father, help me to keep my head up when I am persecuted as a Christian.

Preaching Jesus Crucified

"If I had not come and spoken to them, they would not have [the guilt of their] sin; but now they have no excuse for their sin."

John 14:22

Jesus boldly spoke to the religious leaders about their sin, exposing their continual violations of God's law. The Old Testament said that he would do just that—that he would "exalt the law and make it honorable" (Isaiah 42:21 NKJV). This is why we must do the same by proclaiming "Jesus Christ and Him crucified" (1 Corinthians 2:1–2 NKJV). When we tell others about Jesus Christ, we expound his words and emphasize the cost he paid. We do this because he opened up the *spiritual* nature of God's law: "You have heard that it was said to those of old, 'You shall not commit adultery.' But I say to you that whoever looks at a woman to lust for her has already committed adultery with her in his heart" (Matthew 5:27–28 NKJV).

And it's the law that brings "the knowledge of sin" (Romans 3:20 NKJV) and produces a personal sense of guilt (Romans 7:7), which then shows sinners that they need God's forgiveness that comes through the cross.

Father, may my faithful witness always center on Jesus.

Persecuted for Christ

"They will put you out of the synagogues and make you outcasts. And a time is coming when whoever kills you will think that he is offering service to God."
JOHN 16:2

After warning his disciples that they would face persecution, Jesus then explained that people would do these things because they knew neither him nor his Father. He added that he had told the disciples these things so that when they came to pass, it would strengthen their faith.

This warning of coming persecution is one of the most frightening portions of Scripture. What Jesus said would happen did happen throughout church history, even starting as early as the initial preaching of the gospel by the apostles in Jerusalem soon after the coming of the Holy Spirit (Acts 4). Those who stoned Stephen to death thought they were offering service to God (Acts 7:54–60). As Saul of Tarsus held the clothes of those who murdered Stephen, Saul no doubt thought that God was pleased.

Much of the persecution that comes to genuine Christians comes from religious people who have their own image of God. Consequently, they are offended by the talk of sin and what they see as fearmongering when hell is preached. To them, God is only love, and ironically, they are the ones who often become violent in their erroneous convictions.

Father, help me to be patient and loving when I'm scorned for the gospel.

The Power of "But"

"But now I am going to Him who sent Me; and none of you asks Me, 'Where are You going?' But because I have said these things to you, sorrow has filled your hearts [and taken complete possession of them]."

John 16:6–7

The word "but" is a very small word, but it has huge implications. The world often uses it to destroy a positive and usher in a negative. They will agree with the gospel by saying something like, "I agree with everything that you said about Christ dying for our sins and destroying death, *but* I have a problem with…." In today's Scripture verse, Jesus said that even though he was leaving the disciples, something hugely positive was happening because of it. He was going to the right hand of God to ever intercede for the church.

We don't understand the implications of his intercession, but it is a great consolation to know that, according to Scripture, Jesus is praying for you and me right now. "Therefore He is also able to save to the uttermost those who come to God through Him, since He always lives to make intercession for them" (Hebrews 7:25 NKJV).

Father, thank you for the intermediary and intercessory ministry of the Savior.

To Our Advantage

"I tell you the truth, it is to your advantage that I go away; for if I do not go away, the Helper (Comforter, Advocate, Intercessor—Counselor, Strengthener, Standby) will not come to you; but if I go, I will send Him (the Holy Spirit) to you [to be in close fellowship with you]."

John 16:7

God always works for the advantage of those who love him. Jesus said it's the Father's good pleasure to give us the kingdom. He is the one who tells us that it's more blessed to give than to receive. In other words, God is blessed when he blesses us. We can see this in the natural realm with the warmth of the sun, the sound of birds, the magnificence of trees, the deliciousness of food that is lavished upon us, the pleasure of love and laughter, friends, and family. All these things are the gifts from the God who is benevolence itself.

In today's verse, Jesus was telling his sorrowful disciples that even though he was leaving them, he wasn't leaving them alone because they were going to have a great advantage of having the Holy Spirit as their Comforter, Advocate, Intercessor, Counselor, Strengthener, and Standby. And we are also blessed to have this great advantage.

Jesus, thank you that you didn't leave us alone.

The Holy Spirit

"He, when He comes, will convict the world about [the guilt of] sin [and the need for a Savior], and about righteousness, and about judgment."

John 16:8

Jesus gave us an insight into what we should preach. We should speak of the nature of sin, the perfection of righteousness, and the surety of judgment. Listen to Paul's message to Felix: "Now as he reasoned about righteousness, self-control, and the judgment to come, Felix was afraid and answered, 'Go away for now; when I have a convenient time I will call for you'" (Acts 24:25 NKJV).

While God has chosen the foolishness of preaching to save those who believe, we know that without the help of Jesus, we can do nothing. Whatever we preach without the influence of the Holy Spirit will be a dead letter. When we take someone through the Ten Commandments to bring the knowledge of sin, we know that it's the Holy Spirit who causes them to tremble. He convicts them of their sins, shows them God's perfect righteousness, and makes them fearful of the judgment to come so that they desire to flee to the Savior. This is why we must always pray for his help, especially when speaking to the lost.

Father, remind me that without you, I can do nothing.

Guided by God

"I have many more things to say to you, but you cannot bear [to hear] them now."

John 16:12

Jesus spent years teaching his disciples, and we know from Scripture that we only have the tip of the iceberg of the things that he said and did. "There are also many other things that Jesus did, which if they were written one by one, I suppose that even the world itself could not contain the books that would be written. Amen" (John 21:25 NKJV).

However, we have the four wonderful Gospels that tell us all that we need to know: there is going to be a terrifying day of judgment, but God in his great mercy provided a Savior. And now everlasting life is a free gift for guilty sinners who repent. Jesus said he had many more things to tell his disciples, but they couldn't bear them. However, Jesus said that when the Holy Spirit came, he would "guide" them into all truth. That speaks of drip-feeding rather than a tidal wave of truth. As we read the Scriptures daily, the Holy Spirit nourishes our souls, giving us food to eat of which the world knows nothing.

Father, thank you for the nourishment of your Word.

He Cares

"A little while, and you will no longer see Me; and again a little while, and you will see Me."
JOHN 16:16

The Scriptures tell us that some of the disciples talked among themselves, questioning what Jesus could have meant with his "a little while" statement in today's verse. They were confused by its seeming ambiguity. However, for some unknown reason, they didn't go directly to him for the answer. They chose to ask one another. Why didn't they just go to Jesus? And why do we carry worrisome burdens on our own shoulders or seek the help of others rather than taking them to the Lord in prayer? Is it because we don't think to do so? Is it because we don't think God is interested? We need to think again.

If we have cares and troubles, we should always give them to God because he cares for us. "Casting all your care upon Him, for He cares for you" (1 Peter 5:7 NKJV). King David said the same thing: "Cast your burden on the LORD, and He shall sustain you; He shall never permit the righteous to be moved" (Psalm 55:22 NKJV).

Father, I love you because you first loved me and you care for me.

He Turned My Mourning into Joy

They were saying, "What does He mean when He says, 'A little while?' We do not know what He is talking about.'"

John 16:18

Jesus knew that his disciples were questioning what he had said, and he repeated his rather strange statement about disappearing and then reappearing. Then he said, "Most assuredly, I say to you that you will weep and lament, but the world will rejoice; and you will be sorrowful, but your sorrow will be turned into joy" (John 16:20 NKJV).

When all of the disciples scattered like frightened sheep when Jesus was arrested in the garden of Gethsemane, we don't know what they said to each other as they hid themselves. No doubt they felt both fear and shame. Then as the hours passed, the unthinkable happened. Jesus, the miracle worker, was crucified and died like a common thief. We do know from these words Jesus spoke that these grown men wept and grieved "in great mourning" (v. 20). However, their great lamentation lasted only for three days, and in a moment of time, joy came in the morning, and their sorrow was indeed turned into an even greater joy.

Father, Jesus turned my mourning into everlasting joy.

Labor Pains

"A woman, when she is in labor, has pain because her time [to give birth] has come; but when she has given birth to the child, she no longer remembers the anguish because of her joy that a child has come into the world."

John 16:21

No one can take from us the joy that we have (even in the midst of life's pains) in knowing that Jesus conquered death. A woman who gives birth forgets the pains of labor the moment that precious new life is placed into her arms. And the moment we are born again and realize the value of the precious new life we have in Christ, we can forget the labor that brought us to the Savior. But we should remember it for the sake of sinners who are laboring and heavy-laden under the weight of sin.

We remember so that we can say with James, "Wash your hands, you sinners; and purify your [unfaithful] hearts, you double-minded [people]. Be miserable and grieve and weep [over your sin]. Let your [foolish] laughter be turned to mourning and your [reckless] joy to gloom" (James 4:8–9). And we say that because sorrow for sin produces genuine repentance, leading to everlasting life (2 Corinthians 7:10).

Father, thank you for delivering me from death.

Prayers of the Humble

"In that day you will not [need to] ask Me about anything. I assure you and most solemnly say to you, whatever you ask the Father in My name [as My representative], He will give you."

John 16:23

Listen to the prayers of this unregenerate world. Such prayers are usually selfish because people's conception of God is that he is a divine genie, and very rarely do they ask in the name of Jesus for what they need. But we come directly to God the Father knowing that he hears us because we come in the name of his Son. We are no longer motivated by selfishness. We know what we are without the grace of God. We know where we came from—so our prayers are soaked in a genuine humility and a steadfast faith in the integrity of God, knowing that he keeps his promises.

We are saved by grace, and it's only by grace that we have his listening ear. "God resists the proud, but gives grace to the humble" (James 4:6 NKJV). And it is in that grateful humility that we keep on asking, knowing that we will receive, so that our joy may be full and complete.

Father, I know you hear my prayers.

The Hidden Truths

"I have told you these things in figurative language (veiled language, proverbs); the hour is now coming when I will no longer speak to you in figures of speech, but I will tell you plainly about the Father."

JOHN 16:25

The Bible says that when Jesus walked on the water to the disciples who were in the boat, he was going to pass them by (Mark 6:48). However, Peter called out to him (Matthew 14:28). And the parables and much of what Jesus said will pass us by if we don't have an inquiring mind. The parables are veiled truth, but a persistent faith will pull the veil back. Many of the parables that Jesus told are famous, and the world sometimes refers to them, but they do not always understand the spiritual truths behind them.

John Wesley said of today's verse, "'So that seeing they see and do not perceive'—They would not see before now they could not, God having given them up to the blindness which they had chosen." Once we are born again, Jesus tells us plainly about the Father. The eyes of our understanding are enlightened, and the parables of the Bible come alive. They are no longer hidden from us who were blinded by the god of this world.

Father, thank you for opening the eyes of my understanding.

The Safest Place

Jesus answered them, "Do you now [at last] believe?"
JOHN 16:31

In the next verse after today's Scripture verse, Jesus was specific: "Indeed the hour is coming, yes, has now come, that you will be scattered, each to his own, and will leave Me alone. And yet I am not alone, because the Father is with Me" (v. 32 NKJV). The disciples made the mistake of having a measure of confidence that would crumble under pressure. They believed in Jesus, and they called him "Lord," but their hearts were still unregenerate. When Judas showed up with soldiers and weapons, they ran like frightening rabbits.

But thanks to these prophetic words of Jesus, we see where they ran. They scurried home. They'd had no permanent abode for three years, and now they went home with nothing but memories of miracles and an overwhelming sadness and confusion about what had happened to Jesus. Where do we go when everything goes wrong? Do we want to go back to our past life, or do we go to our knees? We should go to God in prayer. That's the safest place to be because it's there where we find the perfect peace that passes our understanding.

Father, in you and in you alone I have perfect peace.

A New City

"In the world you have tribulation and distress and suffering, but be courageous [be confident, be undaunted, be filled with joy]; I have overcome the world." [My conquest is accomplished, My victory abiding.]

JOHN 16:33

We now find tribulation, distress, and suffering in a world whose pleasures we once enjoyed. The moment we were born of the Spirit, we were made new creatures in Christ with a love of righteousness. Like dead fish floating downstream, we were made alive, we turned, and we began to swim against the flow. Thank God that he has given us a new heart that wants to serve him, and with these new desires, he has given us courage and a supernatural, bold confidence, making us more than conquerors in Christ (Romans 8:37).

Even though we have trials and tribulations, we already have the victory. Paul wrote, "Yet in all these things we are more than conquerors through Him who loved us" (Romans 8:37 NKJV). And in another letter, he said, "Thanks be to God, who gives us the victory through our Lord Jesus Christ" (1 Corinthians 15:57 NKJV). Dear Christian, be confident, be undaunted, be filled with joy. Stay close to Jesus and wait for the city that cannot be moved, whose foundations have been built by God (Hebrews 11:10).

Father, help me today to resist sin.

Raise Our Eyes to Heaven

When Jesus had spoken these things, He raised His eyes to heaven [in prayer] and said, "Father, the hour has come. Glorify Your Son, so that Your Son may glorify You."

John 17:1

One of the greatest gifts that God has given to each of us is a free will. We are free to do what we desire each day. We can become involved in legitimate pursuits of pleasure, such as playing sports, spending time with our family, or enjoying the wonderful array of food that God has placed upon our tables.

But whatever we do, at the end of each day, we should raise our eyes up to heaven in prayer. This is because we only enjoy sports because God has given us the physical ability to do so. He is the one who gave us life, a family, such an amazing variety of food, and tastebuds to enjoy them. This is why we should always be cognizant of who gave us life during these joyful times of pleasure. It's simply a matter of keeping God and his requirements first in our minds. "Seek first the kingdom of God and His righteousness, and all these things shall be added to you" (Matthew 6:33 NKJV).

Father, I'm ever thankful for your blessings that the world often takes for granted.

Come, Lord Jesus

"Just as You have given Him power and authority over all mankind, [now glorify Him] so that He may give eternal life to all whom You have given Him [to be His—permanently and forever]."

John 17:2

We can easily take for granted that in reading Scripture, we are given the incredible privilege of being a fly on the wall—listening to an intimate conversation between Jesus and Almighty God. Think of the great nations of the earth with their wealth and their massive militaries. To God, all that power of the nations combined is nothing but a tiny drop of water left in an empty bucket. "Behold, the nations are as a drop in a bucket, and are counted as the small dust on the scales; look, He lifts up the isles as a very little thing" (Isaiah 40:15 NKJV).

And that divine power and authority over all mankind the Father gave to Jesus. And the Bible says that he will exert that authority upon his return, with an unbending "rod of iron" (Revelation 2:27 NKJV). What a glorious day that will be when our Savior puts a stop to all evil and judges the world in righteousness!

Father, save the lost and hasten that day.

This Is Eternal Life

"Now this is eternal life: that they may know You, the only true [supreme and sovereign] God, and [in the same manner know] Jesus [as the] Christ whom You have sent."

JOHN 17:3

We are like a blind worm that has been lifted from the dirt and held in the hand of God, and even as Christians, we are still limited in our knowledge of the eternal. If asked for a definition of "eternal life," we would probably say that it is perpetual life. But in today's verse, we have the biblical definition of what it is.

Jesus said that eternal life isn't a thing. It's knowledge of a person. It doesn't exist outside of God. And when he fellowships with us, we have everlasting life in that relationship. It is a marriage. "This is the testimony: that God has given us eternal life, and this life is in His Son. He who has the Son has life; he who does not have the Son of God does not have life. These things I have written to you who believe in the name of the Son of God, that you may know that you have eternal life" (1 John 5:11–13 NKJV).

Father, words cannot express my thanks to you for having saved me from death.

Amazing Grace

"I have manifested Your name [and revealed Your very Self, Your real Self] to the people whom You have given Me out of the world; they were Yours and You gave them to Me, and they have kept and obeyed Your word."

John 17:6

If we've been born again (John 3:1–5), we belonged to God long before that happened and even before we were created, "just as He chose us in Him before the foundation of the world, that we should be holy and without blame before Him in love" (Ephesians 1:4 NKJV).

According to Scripture, we have been chosen by God and therefore belong to him. We have been bought with a price (the precious blood of Christ) and have no obligation to this evil world—"therefore glorify God in your body, and in your spirit, which are God's" (1 Corinthians 6:20). That's when he wrote his law upon our hearts and miraculously gave us a willingness to follow Jesus. He caused us to want to walk in his statues (Ezekiel 36:27). We couldn't even come to Jesus without God drawing us to himself (John 6:44), and neither could we repent without his assistance. "If God perhaps will grant them repentance, so that they may know the truth" (2 Timothy 2:25 NKJV).

Father, without your grace, I would still be sitting in the shadow of death.

We Know That We Know

"Now [at last] they know [with confident assurance] that all You have given Me is from You [it is really and truly Yours]."
John 17:7

In his prayer to the Father, Jesus said that he had given his followers the words which God gave him, and they received them "and have known surely that I came forth from You; and they have believed that You sent Me" (v. 8 NKJV). The old hymn by Fanny Crosby says, "Blessed assurance, Jesus is mine." How thankful we are that God didn't leave us doubting as to who Jesus is. He didn't leave us doubting when it comes to whether or not he conquered death. He didn't leave us doubting that all our sins were washed away the moment we put our trust in Jesus.

This is because being Christian doesn't mean having an intellectual assurance. It is rather an *experiential knowledge*—in the same way we know fire is hot by touching it. This is why we can have the sure knowledge—right now, here on this earth—that we have everlasting life so that we can face death without fear.

> Blessed assurance, Jesus is mine;
> Oh, what a foretaste of glory divine!
> Heir of salvation, purchase of God,
> Born of His Spirit, washed in His blood.

Father, thank you for the assurance of eternal salvation.

His Glorious Bride

"I pray for them; I do not pray for the world, but for those You have given Me, because they belong to You; and all things that are Mine are Yours, and [all things that are] Yours are Mine; and I am glorified in them."

JOHN 17:9–10

Jesus is glorified in us because we have been cleansed from our filthiness, and he is coming back for a spotless bride, "that He might present her to Himself a glorious church, not having spot or wrinkle or any such thing, but that she should be holy and without blemish" (Ephesians 5:27 NKJV).

What groom doesn't burst with joy when he sees his bride walking toward him as he waits at the altar? The analogy is a picture of Jesus coming for his beloved. "'Let us be glad and rejoice and give Him glory, for the marriage of the Lamb has come, and His wife has made herself ready.' And to her it was granted to be arrayed in fine linen, clean and bright, for the fine linen is the righteous acts of the saints" (Revelation 19:7–8 NKJV). Jesus is coming again. Paul wrote, "In a moment, in the twinkling of an eye, at the last trumpet. For the trumpet will sound, and the dead will be raised incorruptible, and we shall be changed" (1 Corinthians 15:52 NKJV). Are you ready?

Father, I am ready.

In the World

"I am no longer in the world; yet they are still in the world, and I am coming to You. Holy Father, keep them in Your name, the name which You have given Me, so that they may be one just as We are."

John 17:11

When Jesus ascended into heaven, he was accompanied by clouds, power, and great glory (Acts 1:9–11). We know this because the Bible says that he will come again in the same way as he had gone to heaven. The two men who appeared at his ascension asked, "Men of Galilee, why do you stand gazing up into heaven? This same Jesus, who was taken up from you into heaven, will so come in like manner as you saw Him go into heaven" (v. 11 NKJV).

What a sight it must have been for the disciples, and yet it must have broken their hearts to know that Jesus would no longer be physically with them. He was passing the torch to his church. But we're not alone in this grand endeavor. He has given us his Holy Spirit as our helper to empower us to fulfill his will on earth. May we never forget the trust placed in us.

Father, help me to fulfill your will today.

Not One Lost

"While I was with them, I was keeping them in Your name which You have given Me; and I guarded them and protected them, and not one of them was lost except the son of destruction, so that the Scripture would be fulfilled."

JOHN 17:12

While today's verse is clearly about the disciples and how Jesus kept them during the time he was with them on this earth, it has a much broader application. Jesus said that no one shall pluck us from his hand (John 10:28). God saves "to the uttermost those who come to God" through Jesus (Hebrews 7:25 NKJV). He is able to keep us from falling and present us "faultless before the presence of His glory with exceeding joy" (Jude 24 NKJV).

Think about that. Jesus is going to present us faultless to God—with exceeding joy. The best of us was guilty, with a multitude of sins, and yet we will be guiltless on that day. Jesus is indeed treasure in earthen vessels, and in him, we will have pleasure forevermore (Psalm 16:11). May God help us to never be discouraged in our trials or in our labors for him because of that joy which is set before us (Hebrews 12:2).

Father, never let me be discouraged by this world.

The Two Worlds

"Now I am coming to You; and I say these things [while I am still] in the world so that they may experience My joy made full and complete and perfect within them [filling their hearts with My delight]."

John 17:13

After saying the words in today's verse, Jesus spoke of his mission. He had given the disciples God's Word, and he warned them that because of that, they would be hated by an evil world that loved darkness.

A faithful police officer lives in a different world from that of criminals. Everything the officer lives for is a direct antithesis to everything that is important to the criminal. The goal of the police is to see that justice is done. The goal of the criminal is to try and get away with violating the law for his own gain—whether it is to gain power and prestige or to get wealth.

The kingdom of light and the kingdom of darkness are two completely different worlds, and if we have been born again, we are in the kingdom of light, and we will never compromise with darkness. "Whoever therefore wants to be a friend of the world makes himself an enemy of God" (James 4:4 NKJV).

Father, never let me compromise with this evil world.

True and Faithful

"I do not ask You to take them out of the world, but that You keep them and protect them from the evil one."
JOHN 17:15

Jesus didn't ask the Father to take the disciples out of the world, because that would've defeated his purposes. He asked God to protect and preserve them from the devil. And you and I haven't been taken out of the world either. Rather, we have been left here for a definite purpose. We are to be preserved from evil and to shine as "the light of the world." "You are the light of the world. A city that is set on a hill cannot be hidden…Let your light so shine before men, that they may see your good works and glorify your Father in heaven" (Matthew 5:14–16 NKJV).

Jesus left us in the world to be a witness to those who are sitting helplessly in the shadow of death. This is why we must plead with God to rid us of our fears, and then (like the early disciples) be true and faithful witnesses to the light of the gospel. This is not only an incredible honor. It's a sobering task.

Father, help me to faithfully let my light shine today.

Daily Sanctification

"Sanctify them in the truth [set them apart for Your purposes, make them holy]; Your word is truth."

John 17:17

When we have our daily battle with the Enemy with temptations to sin and we overcome those temptations, we can give ourselves a little pat on the back for that victory. We take the credit. This is because it's easy to forget that, in reality, the victory happened as an answer to this specific prayer of Jesus. He asked the Father to sanctify us. He asked him to set us apart for his purposes and make us holy.

The apostle Paul gives us insight into what invisibly takes place in the spiritual realm. "No temptation has overtaken you except such as is common to man; but God is faithful, who will not allow you to be tempted beyond what you are able, but with the temptation will also make the way of escape, that you may be able to bear it" (1 Corinthians 10:13 NJKV). Therefore, when we are tempted to sin, we should thank God there and then for already making a way of escape—for helping us overcome that temptation.

Father, lead me not into temptation, but deliver me from evil.

November

The woman caught in the act of adultery (John 8:1–11)

The Prayer of Jesus

"For their sake I sanctify Myself [to do Your will], so that they also may be sanctified [set apart, dedicated, made holy] in [Your] truth."

JOHN 17:19–21

Once again in today's verse, we are privileged to eavesdrop on the most intimate of conversations between Jesus and the Father. After asking for the sanctification of his disciples, Jesus makes it clear that he isn't confining his prayers to them. He prays for all those who will be born into the kingdom—that we will be unified so that the world may know we represent the true God. Our salvation is the fruit of this prayer.

Two thousand years ago, Jesus asked the Father that we would be set apart, dedicated to him, and made holy. The eternal God in Christ had you and me in mind on that day. It was his love for us that drove him to the cross, but he was looking further than just you and me. Jesus desired "that the world may believe [without any doubt] that You sent Me" (v. 21). This is speaking of those who don't yet believe. So be an answer to his prayer by taking the gospel to an unbelieving world today.

Father, use me today as an answer to Jesus' prayer.

The Lost

"I have given to them the glory and honor which You have given Me, that they may be one, just as We are one."
JOHN 17:22

After reading today's Scripture verse, let's look at why Jesus then said, "that they may be made perfect in one, *and that the world may know that You have sent Me,* and have loved them as You have loved Me" (John 17:23 NKJV, emphasis added).

Jesus had great concern for those who were still in their sins. Zeal for God's house had eaten him up. This zeal wasn't confined to keeping the temple clean of thieves and robbers. It was a love for the world that took Jesus to the cross, and it was love for the world that caused him to command us to "go into all the world and preach the gospel to every creature" (Mark 16:15 NKJV). Just as the god of this world has hidden the gospel from the unsaved, the Great Commission to preach the gospel to every creature is hidden from many in the modern church. This is clear from the lack of concern that most contemporary Christians have for the unsaved. The lost are last and least on their long list of priorities. This ambivalence should not characterize us. And it doesn't have to if we will just trust in our Lord and speak the truth always, especially to those who need to hear it and accept it the most.

Father, cause me to run to the world with the gospel.

Pure of Heart

"Father, I desire that they also, whom You have given to Me [as Your gift to Me], may be with Me where I am, so that they may see My glory which You have given Me, because You loved Me before the foundation of the world."

John 17:24

At the end of our lives, we will get to see what Moses couldn't see when he asked to see God's glory (Exodus 33:18–20). God told Moses that he couldn't look upon God and live. As we have seen, this is because the goodness of God would have consumed Moses in wrath if he stood in God's presence. Perfect justice demands absolute retribution, and the only way Moses could ever see the glory of God was to be morally perfect.

Jesus referred to this when he said, "Blessed are the pure in heart, for they shall see God" (Matthew 5:8 NKJV). The same sin that ran through the veins of Moses runs through our veins. We, too, would be consumed by wrath if we stood in the presence of God. However, because of the wondrous work of the cross, you and I have been made perfectly righteous in the sight of a holy God.

Father, one day I will look upon your glory.

Darkened Understanding of the Lost

"O just and righteous Father, although the world has not known You and has never acknowledged You [and the revelation of Your mercy], yet I have always known You; and these [believers] know [without any doubt] that You sent Me."

JOHN 17:25

The world gravitates toward idolatry like a compass points to the north. People will always want to go there because their thoughts about God are erroneous. In speaking of the darkened mind of the ungodly, Scripture says that "their understanding [is] darkened, being alienated from the life of God, because of the ignorance that is in them, because of the blindness of their heart" (Ephesians 4:18 NKJV).

Unbelievers will gladly say that God is loving, gentle, merciful, and kind, but rarely will they say that he's just and righteous. This is because that brings in the question of moral accountability. And because many people recoil from admitting that they are morally responsible, they will never have a revelation of God's mercy. The truth of what happened at the cross will be hidden from them. However, if we faithfully stir their conscience with the law, we will give them light and help them to see why God sent Jesus to the cross.

Father, never let me lose sight of your justness and righteousness.

If It Is Your Will

Then Jesus, knowing all that was about to happen to Him, went to them and asked, "Whom do you want?"
John 18:4

Today's verse takes place in the garden of Gethsemane. The religious leaders said that they were seeking Jesus of Nazareth, to which he replied, "I am He" (v. 5). Jesus knew what was about to happen. Evil men were about to arrest and murder him in the cruelest manner. And yet, he had a serene demeanor, and his words were calm. He willingly identified himself, showing his submission to the Father's plan. This willingness to lay down his life is evidence of his sincerity, whereas earlier, he had wrestled in prayer and gave up his own will, saying, "Father, if it is Your will, take this cup away from Me; nevertheless not My will, but Yours, be done" (Luke 22:42 NKJV).

This is where the real battle took place, and it's the key to you and me overcoming our fears and then fulfilling God's will in our lives. The knowledge of this key in the life of every Christian is why Paul was so passionate in his plea: "I beseech you therefore, brethren, by the mercies of God, that you present your bodies a living sacrifice, holy, acceptable to God, which is your reasonable service" (Romans 12:1 NKJV).

Father, may my will never conflict with yours.

The Kingdom

Jesus replied, "My kingdom is not of this world [nor does it have its origin in this world]."

John 18:36

The King of kings, whose kingdom was foreign to this world, was unlawfully arrested and tried for crimes he didn't commit. And yet he didn't resist his death but rather surrendered to it. He had earlier said, "You are from beneath; I am from above. You are of this world; I am not of this world" (John 8:23 NKJV). And it's because of the wonderful submission of the Lamb of God that you and I have been taken out of the kingdom of darkness and brought into the kingdom of light (Colossians 1:13).

We are now citizens of a kingdom that is eternal—one that *cannot* be moved. "Therefore, since we are receiving a kingdom which cannot be shaken, let us have grace, by which we may serve God acceptably with reverence and godly fear. For our God is a consuming fire" (Hebrews 12:28–29 NKJV). Kingdoms come and go and disappear in time. But not this one. We will inherit this earth and see the fulfillment of God's master plan for the once fallen sons and daughters of Adam.

Father, I am honored beyond words to be part of your kingdom.

Salt and Light

Jesus replied, "My kingdom is not of this world nor does it have its origin in this world]. If My kingdom were of this world, My servants would be fighting [hard] to keep Me from being handed over to the Jews; but as it is, My kingdom is not of this world."

John 18:36

Sometimes Christians use today's verse to say that we should have nothing to do with politics. Our kingdom isn't of this world, they say; therefore, we should completely wash our hands of it. But that's not biblical. Jesus said that we should be salt and light. Salt preserves, and we must do everything we can to preserve righteousness because "righteousness exalts a nation" (Proverbs 14:34 NKJV).

Who of us doesn't rejoice when godly men and women get into places of political authority and pass legislation that outlaws the killing of the unborn and laws that stop children from being sexually brainwashed? However, we mustn't rest on passing godly legislation as a means of establishing the kingdom of God on earth. It's the gospel that does that, and that gospel is our spearhead. It is the only effective way to hold back the darkness of sin.

Father, may I never lose sight of the power of the gospel.

The King of All Kings

Pilate said to Him, "Then You are a King?" Jesus answered, "You say [correctly] that I am a King. This is why I was born, and for this I have come into the world, to testify to the truth."

JOHN 18:37

As Pontius Pilate sat in judgment over Jesus of Nazareth, he must have been thinking about the words of warning that came from his wife as she cautioned him about dealing with this Jewish preacher. "While he was sitting on the judgment seat, his wife sent to him, saying, 'Have nothing to do with that just Man, for I have suffered many things today in a dream because of Him'" (Matthew 27:19 NKJV).

It is strange that his wife didn't give details of the dream. But it does seem that it was a nightmare that caused her much suffering. Could this have been a warning from God? If it was, it was unexpected because the coming suffering of Jesus was his will. Was it a merciful warning for her husband? We really don't know, but we can be sure Pilate never forgot it when the King of kings stood before him on that darkest of all nights. And may we never forget for a moment the one who gave his life that we might live.

Father, may we be like Pilate's wife and warn sinners about their rejection of Jesus.

The Truth in Jesus

Pilate said to Him [scornfully], "What is truth?"
JOHN 18:38

After Pilate asked the famous question, "What is truth?," he went back to the Jews and said to them, "I find no fault in Him at all" (v. 38 NKJV). What is truth? That is arguably the deepest and most philosophical question that can come from human lips. It encompasses *Why are we here? Is there an afterlife? What is life's purpose?* and so much more. Without Jesus Christ, who *is* the truth (John 14:6), the world is founded on ever-shifting sand. Sinners don't even know why they are alive. They're just here. Neither do they know the purpose for their existence. Foolish worldly philosophy has left them with no rhyme or reason to even exist. No wonder so many take their own lives to get out of what they consider to be a meaningless existence.

Pilate asked the question with the answer standing right in front of his very eyes, and, like the governor, so many have Jesus before them, but they don't see him as he is. "You have not so learned Christ, if indeed you have heard Him and have been taught by Him, as the truth is in Jesus" (Ephesians 4:20–21 NKJV). May we daily speak the truth and do so in love.

Father, I'm so grateful that the truth made me free.

Sadness and Joy

Pilate said to Him, "You do not speak to me? Do You not know that I have authority to release You, and I have authority to crucify You?"
JOHN 19:10

Jesus told Pilate that he could have no power unless God had given it to him, adding, "Therefore the one who delivered Me to you has the greater sin" (v. 11 NKJV). More than eight hundred years earlier, the Scriptures had perfectly prophesied this very moment when Jesus of Nazareth would stand before Pontius Pilate. Little did the Roman governor know that this was the precious sacrificial Lamb of God standing in silent submission to his terrible fate.

> He was oppressed and He was afflicted,
> Yet He opened not His mouth;
> He was led as a lamb to the slaughter,
> And as a sheep before its shearers is silent,
> So He opened not His mouth. (Isaiah 53:7 NKJV)

What mixed emotions we have at this amazing sight. As we see this scene through the eyes of faith, an overwhelming sadness is mingled with an unspeakable joy as we think that Jesus went through the agony of the cross—all for us. Will you take a moment to thank him for his selfless sacrifice?

Father, we will never forget the love expressed on the cross.

Motherly Love

The soldiers did these things. But standing by the cross of Jesus were His mother, His mother's sister [Salome], Mary the wife of Clopas, and Mary Magdalene.

JOHN 19:25

We can't help but wonder if, at that moment, Mary thought back to more than thirty years prior, when she and Joseph presented the child Jesus in the temple, and Simeon had said to her, "Behold, this Child is destined for the fall and rising of many in Israel, and for a sign which will be spoken against (yes, a sword will pierce through your own soul also), that the thoughts of many hearts may be revealed" (Luke 2:34–35 NKJV).

Mothers have an intuitive tender spot for their little children. They feel their pains as they fall in life. But this was no ordinary child. Mary had seen the child Jesus grow into a man, perform miracles, and show nothing but love and kindness—even to his enemies. And here he was, impaled like a stricken animal, being cruelly mocked by the religious leaders and hardened soldiers while he was on the cross. The agony must've indeed been like a sword cutting into Mary's very soul. So she stood by the cross helpless, refusing to abandon her son.

It's such empathy and commitment that should inspire us to reach out to those who don't understand what happened on that cross so long ago.

Father, help me to always enter into the pains of others.

Mothers and Brothers

Jesus, seeing His mother, and the disciple whom He loved (esteemed) standing near, said to His mother, "[Dear] woman, look, [here is] your son!"
JOHN 19:26

While hanging on the cross in agony, Jesus spoke to his apostle John about Mary, directing John to protect and provide for her as his own mother. Mary had at least five other children (Matthew 13:55–57), but Jesus didn't mention them from the cross. This may have been because he wanted his mother to be under a godly covering. But this was more than John taking Mary into his home and looking after her. Jesus was saying that John should adopt her as his mother.

Believers in the faith are part of a larger family. As John was to regard Mary, so should we regard one another. We are more than fellow believers. We are members of the same family of faith. "[Jesus] answered…, 'Who is My mother and who are My brothers?' And He stretched out His hand toward His disciples and said, 'Here are My mother and My brothers! For whoever does the will of My Father in heaven is My brother and sister and mother'" (Matthew 12:48–50 NKJV). Each of us has a multitude of brothers and sisters and mothers and fathers in the faith.

Father, thank you for the wonderfully close-knit family we have in Christ.

I Thirst

After this, Jesus, knowing that all was now finished, said in fulfillment of the Scripture, "I am thirsty."

John 19:28

King David, when writing of the coming Messiah, gives us an insight into the agonies Jesus was going to go through on the cross. The three words in today's verse Jesus spoke at the culmination of his suffering, but we see from Psalm 22 that it was more than thirst for a drink of water.

> I am poured out like water,
> And all My bones are out of joint;
> My heart is like wax;
> It has melted within Me.
> My strength is dried up like a potsherd,
> And My tongue clings to My jaws;
> You have brought Me to the dust of death.
> (Psalm 22:14–15 NKJV)

Jesus came into our world, made a little lower than the angels (Hebrews 2:9), so he could pay the price for our redemption. His execution was brutal and carried out before the people and their governing authorities. His crucifixion was made a public spectacle outside of the main gates of Jerusalem as an example to others not to follow in his steps. But the cross, which was designed to be a local and very dark warning, has become a universal display of the love of God, a love that carries on two thousand years later. He suffered the cross as an expression of God's love for us. How great a love we have in Jesus!

Father, thank you that Jesus suffered out of his love for us.

Finally Finished

A jar full of sour wine was placed there; so they put a sponge soaked in the sour wine on [a branch of] hyssop and held it to His mouth. When Jesus had received the sour wine, He said, "It is finished!"

John 20:29–30

Today's verse from John's gospel is a fulfillment of a Messianic prophecy.

> Reproach has broken my heart,
> And I am full of heaviness;
> I looked for someone to take pity, but there was none;
> And for comforters, but I found none.
> They also gave me gall for my food,
> And for my thirst they gave me vinegar to drink.
> (Psalm 69:20–21 NKJV)

When David's sin with Bathsheba was uncovered, the king cried out in penitent prayer, "Purge me with hyssop, and I shall be clean; wash me, and I shall be whiter than snow" (Psalm 51:7 NKJV). When God delivered the children of Israel from the angel of death, he had Moses tell them to take the blood of the lamb and apply it to the doorposts with a hyssop branch (Exodus 12:22). Because of the cross, we can now take the blood of the lamb and apply it to the doorposts of our lives, and God will cause the angel of death to pass over us. Our redemption is finished.

Father, thank you for the finished work of the cross.

Why Are We Weeping?

After saying this, she turned around and saw Jesus standing there, but she did not know that it was Jesus. Jesus said to her, "Woman, why are you crying? For whom are you looking?"
John 20:14–15

Mary Magdalene had been standing outside of the tomb weeping. And as tears continued to well in her eyes, she stooped down and looked into the tomb, no doubt expecting to see the corpse wrapped in graveclothes (John 20:11 NKJV). That's when she instead saw two angels clothed in white, one sitting at the head and the other at the feet where the body of Jesus should have been (v. 12). When they asked Mary a strange question—"Woman, why are you weeping?"—she replied, "Because they have taken away my Lord, and I do not know where they have laid Him" (v. 13).

Then Jesus asked her that same strange question. Why was she in tears? Had she and the disciples truly believed what he had told them, there would have been no need for tears. When a Christian dies—in all seriousness—it's nothing serious. We weep because we will miss them, but why are we weeping when death has lost its sting?

Father, help me to overcome grief. Give me joy instead of mourning.

He Knows Our Name

Jesus said to her, "Mary!"
JOHN 20:16

Have you ever taken the time to look at a crowd at a large sporting event? As camera operators do close-ups of portions of the crowd, have you considered how many different faces there are on earth? Other than identical twins, everyone is different. And we don't just have different faces; we also have different ears, hair, skin, heights, shapes, fingerprints, and personalities. And God knows every one of us deeply. Have you ever considered how God knows the secret thoughts of every human heart? And he is even intimately familiar with the middle atom that makes up each eyeball—because he made it.

Such thoughts can help us to see the unspeakable greatness of God, but they can also make us feel insignificant among the multitudes. We can remember that in that one moment on the morning of the resurrection, Mary Magdalene heard the familiar voice of Jesus saying her name, and suddenly all was well. Death didn't and couldn't hold him (Acts 2:24). And as with Mary, Jesus knows our names. He's the lover of our souls, and he promises never to leave or forsake us. "I will praise You, for I am fearfully and wonderfully made; marvelous are Your works, and that my soul knows very well" (Psalm 139:14 NKJV).

Father, today I will think about how you intimately know me.

My Brethren

She turned and said to Him in Hebrew, "Rabboni!" (which means, Teacher). Jesus said to her, "Do not hold Me, for I have not yet ascended to the Father; but go to My brothers and tell them."

John 20:16–17

Scripture captures a profound moment between Mary Magdalene and the risen Jesus. After discovering the empty tomb, Mary encounters someone she initially assumes to be the gardener. When Jesus calls her by name, "Mary," she recognizes him and responds with "Rabboni," an affectionate term for "Teacher" in Hebrew, reflecting her respect and deep personal connection to him.

His response, "Do not hold Me, for I have not yet ascended to the Father," reveals his transitionary state between resurrection and ascension. He gently redirects Mary's focus from clinging to his physical presence to embracing the mission ahead.

Jesus then told her to inform his disciples—whom he referred to as "My brothers"—about his resurrection and his upcoming ascension to God the Father. This highlighted the transformation in their relationship through Jesus' victory over death, elevating the disciples from servants to siblings in God's family.

These verses emphasize the importance of recognizing Jesus and shifting from a physical attachment to a spiritual relationship and mission.

Father, I'm honored to be born into your family and given a mission to tell others about you.

The First Evangelist

"I am ascending to My Father and your Father, and to My God and your God."

John 20:17

Jesus speaks these words to Mary Magdalene after his resurrection. This verse highlights the profound relational change between God and humanity through Jesus' victory over sin and death.

By saying "I am ascending to My Father and your Father," Jesus emphasizes the shared relationship believers now have with God. Through his sacrifice and resurrection, he has opened the way for humanity to call God "Father" in a personal and intimate sense. This signifies the restoration of fellowship with God, made possible through faith in Jesus.

When Jesus adds "and to My God and your God," he affirms both his unique divine nature and his solidarity with humanity. As the Son of God, Jesus has a unique relationship with the Father. Yet, as the incarnate Savior, he also identifies with believers, acknowledging God as their God. This underscores the unity and shared access believers have to God through Christ.

The verse is a profound declaration of reconciliation and shared identity. Jesus' ascension points to his glorification and the continuation of his mission as intercessor, paving the way for the coming of the Holy Spirit and the fulfillment of God's redemptive plan.

Father, may I never lose sight of this victory.

Peace to You

When it was evening on that same day, the first day of the week, though the disciples were [meeting] behind barred doors for fear of the Jews, Jesus came and stood among them, and said, "Peace to you."

John 20:19

There was another time when Jesus suddenly appeared to his disciples and told them not to be afraid: "But immediately Jesus spoke to them, saying, 'Be of good cheer! It is I; do not be afraid'" (Matthew 14:27 NKJV). He said this as he was walking on water during a terrifying storm. And on the occasion in today's Scripture verse, his appearance was also supernatural and came during another terrifying storm that left the disciples in fear of perishing.

The Jews had murdered Jesus, and no doubt, the disciples believed it was just a matter of time until the Jewish leaders came for them. "The fear of man brings a snare" (Proverbs 29:25). It holds us behind locked doors and torments us with thoughts of what may happen. But Jesus is in our midst and gives us the peace of God which passes all understanding. Never let the fear of man keep you from sharing the gospel with this dying world.

Father, may your peace and your love for sinners free me from the fear of man.

The Evidence

After He said this, He showed them His hands and His side. When the disciples saw the Lord, they were filled with great joy. Then Jesus said to them again, "Peace to you; as the Father has sent Me, I also send you [as My representatives]."

JOHN 20:20–21

The disciples were filled with unbelief (Mark 16:11). They heard that Jesus had risen from the dead, and despite the fact that he had told them that he would rise on the third day, they didn't believe. They needed physical evidence. And so Jesus gave it to them.

Christianity does not lack evidence. There are some who believe that faith fills in where evidence lacks. This is not true. The greatest evidence any sinner can have is a transformed life. In a moment of time, God changes our heart and gives us a love for righteousness. This is a personal miracle that only God can do. He takes his law and writes it upon our hearts so that we love to walk in his statutes: "Therefore, if anyone is in Christ, he is a new creation; old things have passed away; behold, all things have become new" (2 Corinthians 5:17 NKJV).

Father, thank you for the undeniable evidence of the new birth.

Only God

"If you forgive the sins of anyone they are forgiven [because of their faith]; if you retain the sins of anyone, they are retained [and remain unforgiven because of their unbelief]."

JOHN 20:23

Jesus told his disciples that if they forgave the sins of any, those sins would be forgiven; and if they didn't forgive, those sins wouldn't be forgiven. This is contrary to Scripture if it means that mortal men have the power on earth to forgive sins. Only God can do that: "Why does this Man speak blasphemies like this? Who can forgive sins but God alone?" (Mark 2:7 NKJV).

The Scriptures tell us that there is only "one Mediator between God and men," and that Mediator is Jesus Christ (1 Timothy 2:5 NKJV). What we *can* do as Christians is give assurance that those who put their faith in Jesus for the forgiveness of their sins will have their sins forgiven. And we can warn them that if they remain in unbelief and refuse to trust in him (and die in their sins), they will perish. This authority is given to every Christian. We can tell them, "If we confess our sins, He is faithful and just to forgive us our sins and to cleanse us from all unrighteousness" (1 John 1:9 NKJV).

Father, thank you for the forgiveness we have in Jesus.

Walking through Locked Doors

Eight days later His disciples were again inside the house, and Thomas was with them. Jesus came, though the doors had been barred, and stood among them and said, "Peace to you."

John 20:26

It would seem that Jesus, even though he had a physical body that could be touched and handled, could walk through closed and barred doors. And why would anyone have a problem believing that God could perform the miraculous? If he can create the sun, the moon, the stars, flowers, birds, trees, the seasons, the marvel of the human eye, and the miracle of childbirth—all from nothing—then he can do anything.

Upon coming to earth, Jesus could walk on water, multiply loaves and fishes, raise the dead, give the blind their sight, and restore hearing to the deaf. And miracle of miracles, he can even take blind, unregenerate, sin-loving, God-hating sinners and transform them in a moment of time so that they love him with all their heart, mind, soul, and strength. "With God nothing shall be impossible" (Luke 1:37 KJV). That's why we need not stress at the edge of the Red Sea or when we are in a lion's den. God still performs the miraculous.

Father, I completely trust you in everything I do.

Doubting Thomas

He said to Thomas, "Reach here with your finger, and see My hands; and put out your hand and place it in My side. Do not be unbelieving, but [stop doubting and] believe."
John 20:27

More than two thousand years after the fact, we still call a skeptic "a Doubting Thomas." Here's why he gained that reputation:

> Now Thomas, called the Twin, one of the twelve, was not with them when Jesus came. The other disciples therefore said to him, "We have seen the Lord."
>
> So he said to them, "Unless I see in His hands the print of the nails, and put my finger into the print of the nails, and put my hand into His side, I will not believe." (John 20:24–25 NKJV)

It's not that Thomas could not believe but that he *would* not believe. Thomas *refused* to believe. It's an insult to you and me as human beings if someone refuses to trust us, so it is a terrible sin to doubt the promises of our sinless Creator: "He who believes in the Son of God has the witness in himself; he who does not believe God has made Him a liar, because he has not believed the testimony that God has given of His Son" (1 John 5:10 NKJV). Let us therefore believe in God and, of course, in Jesus, who said, "Believe [confidently] in God and trust in Him, [have faith, hold on to it, rely on it, keep going and] believe also in Me" (John 14:1).

Father, my wholehearted trust will be in you today.

Do You Now Believe?

Thomas answered Him, "My Lord and my God!"
JOHN 20:28

All it took for Thomas to acknowledge that Jesus was both Lord and God and then bow his knee in worship was three years of seeing breathtaking miracles. All it took was three years of him hearing the gracious and unprecedented words that came from the mouth of Jesus, seeing him walk on water, calm the storm, raise people from the dead, perfectly prophesy the future, raise himself from death, and walk through walls. And finally, when this hardheaded, hardhearted Thomas put his unbelieving finger into the holes in the hands of Jesus, he believed (vv. 27–28).

We need to take a lesson from Thomas. Even though we haven't seen any of the wonderful miracles, we believe. We trust (without sight) in Jesus and are therefore far more blessed than Thomas (v. 29). We walk by faith, and in so doing, we please the God who gave us life: "Without faith it is impossible to please Him, for he who comes to God must believe that He is, and that He is a rewarder of those who diligently seek Him" (Hebrews 11:6 NKJV).

Father, I long for the day that faith is done away with and we see you face-to-face.

With Me

Simon Peter said to them, "I am going fishing." They said, "And we are coming with you." So they went out and got into the boat; and that night they caught nothing.

John 21:3

When the sun rose, the apostles saw Jesus standing on the beach, but they didn't know it was him. The fact that he wasn't easily recognized is a common theme after his resurrection. He then called to them and asked if they had any fish. Jesus had told his disciples to follow him and he would make them fishers of men. He had also told them what they would do without him: "I am the vine, you are the branches. He who abides in Me, and I in him, bears much fruit; for without Me you can do nothing" (John 15:5 NKJV).

Tragically, much of modern fishing for men is done without Jesus, and those doing the fishing have caught nothing. They haven't listened to his Word, which says, "I would not have known sin except through the law" (Romans 7:7 NKJV). Charles Spurgeon warned, "I do not believe that any man can preach the gospel who does not preach the law. Lower the law and you dim the light by which man perceives his guilt."[8] We have to share the law when we share the gospel.

Father, help me to listen to the principles in your Word.

---

8 Charles Haddon Spurgeon, "Quotes," GoodReads, accessed February 13, 2025, https://www.goodreads.com/quotes/8804377-i-do-not-believe-that-any-man-can-preach-the.

The Right Side

They cast [the net], and then they were not able to haul it in because of the great catch of fish. Then that disciple (John) whom Jesus loved (esteemed) said to Peter, "It is the Lord!"

John 21:6–7

The resurrected Jesus appears to his disciples by the Sea of Galilee. The disciples, after a fruitless night of fishing, encounter a man on the shore (unrecognized as Jesus) who instructs them to cast their net on the right side of the boat. Obeying his command, they catch such a massive number of fish that they are unable to haul the net aboard.

This miraculous event opens the disciples' eyes to the identity of the man. John, often referred to as "the disciple whom Jesus loved," is the first to recognize that it is the Lord. His recognition reflects his spiritual insight and deep connection with Jesus. John immediately informs Peter, whose characteristic enthusiasm leads him to impulsively jump into the water to reach Jesus.

The scene mirrors a similar miracle when Jesus first called Peter and other disciples to follow him, symbolizing both a reaffirmation of their mission and the abundant provision found in Christ. It emphasizes the necessity of trusting and obeying Jesus, whose power transforms even the mundane into the miraculous. This encounter also reveals Jesus' continued presence and care, even after his resurrection.

Father, help me to fish for men the right way, knowing you are with me always.

First the Natural

When they had finished breakfast, Jesus said to Simon Peter, "Simon, son of John, do you love Me more than these [others do—with total commitment and devotion]?"

JOHN 21:15

It is interesting to note that Jesus waited until the apostles had eaten before he spoke of spiritual things to Peter. Many a hungry sinner has listened closely to the gospel because a Christian had the good sense and kindness to purchase them a burger first. First Corinthians 15:46 tells us, "The spiritual is not first, but the natural, and afterward the spiritual." I have witnessed to many strangers on planes, and on those long flights, I always wait until the passenger has finished eating so they won't be distracted by hunger.

In John 4, Jesus spoke to the woman at the well of natural water before he spoke of spiritual water. There is a good reason for this. She was unsaved, and Scripture says of the unsaved, "Their understanding [is] darkened, being alienated from the life of God, because of the ignorance that is in them, because of the blindness of their heart" (Ephesians 4:18). She needed spiritual light: "The natural man does not receive the things of the Spirit of God, for they are foolishness to him; nor can he know them, because they are spiritually discerned" (1 Corinthians 2:14 NKJV).

Father, help me to always be sensitive to the spiritual state and the needs of the lost.

The Reminder

Again He said to him a second time, "Simon, son of John, do you love Me [with total commitment and devotion]?" He said to Him, "Yes, Lord; You know that I love You [with a deep, personal affection, as for a close friend]." Jesus said to him, "Shepherd My sheep."

John 21:16

Life is a continual learning process. And there are many truths that we learn about this life that need to be fortified by repetition. Good parents don't tell their child to stay away from fire or water just the one time. We continually warn our children of the dangers that can hurt them.

Even when it comes to biblical truths, we need to be reminded again and again to prioritize God's Word by feeding on it daily, to be careful of sin, and to love righteousness. This is because the things we learn in this world are transient—nothing but a momentary vapor that appears and then vanishes away. But the things we learn in the spiritual realm are eternal. And so Jesus saw fit to tell Peter a second time that certain fruits should be evident if he truly loved Jesus.

Father, I need to be reminded daily of the importance of the principles in your Word.

Afar Off

He said to him the third time, "Simon, son of John, do you love Me [with a deep, personal affection for Me, as for a close friend]?" Peter was grieved that He asked him the third time, "Do you [really] love Me [with a deep, personal affection, as for a close friend]?"

John 21:17

Jesus didn't just use Peter's first name to remind him a third time of the importance of obedience. He used his full name to bring a sense of sobriety that this was personally for him. Most of us would be more than grieved if someone repeated something to us three times. We may become a little impatient. However, it may have been a powerful reminder that Peter had denied Jesus publicly three times, and it took the crowing of a rooster to awaken him to what he was doing.

God has graciously given each of us a rooster to awaken us when we are in peril of denying Jesus—whenever sin has its way in our lives. The problem with Peter was that he followed Jesus at a distance (Mathew 26:58). This speaks of more than a physical distance from Jesus. It speaks of our growing lukewarmness in our love for him. Never let that happen. Stay close to your Savior.

Father, help me to always cultivate a tender conscience and hear its awakening voice.

He Knows

He said to Him, "Lord, You know everything; You know that I love You [with a deep, personal affection, as for a close friend]." Jesus said to him, "Feed My sheep."

JOHN 21:17

God knows everything. It's an easy thing to say but an almost impossible truth to comprehend. The way I have expressed this in past years has been to say that God knows all about the secret love life of the fleas on the back of Napoleon's great-grandmother's black cat. He is thoroughly versed on the nature of the interior of the atom in the middle of the massive sun. The theological term for this is *omniscience.*

For the godly, the knowledge that God knows everything is a wonderful source of comfort. He knows our deepest thoughts and unspoken desires. Nothing takes him by surprise. But for the ungodly, it is a biblical truth that should make them shudder in terror. This is because God is holy, and he warns that he "will bring every work into judgment, including every secret thing, whether good or evil" (Ecclesiastes 12:14 NKJV). In his holy eyes lust is adultery (Matthew 5:27–28) and hatred is murder (1 John 3:15). That's why we need a Savior.

Father, help me to cultivate the fear of God in my life today.

December

Jesus rising from the dead (Luke 24:6–7)

Open Rebuke

Jesus said to him, "If I want him to stay alive until I come [again], what is that to you? You follow Me!"

JOHN

If we have cultivated a tender conscience, we will identify with Peter and all his failings. This is because as Christians, we have a constant battle with the world, the flesh, and the devil. Sinful thoughts will invade our minds and keep us aware of our own sinful hearts. As soldiers of Christ, we are constantly battling against selfishness, unbelief, lustful thoughts, impatience, envy, and jealousy. These are what the Bible calls "fiery darts" that come from the Enemy (Ephesians 6:16).

The Scriptures tell us that "open rebuke is better than secret love" (Proverbs 27:5 KJV), and in today's verse, Peter was once again the object of a rebuke from the Son of God. The fact that Jesus called Peter Satan at one point (Matthew 16:23) shows us Peter's resilience in that he didn't walk away from Jesus on that occasion. And here, when Jesus tells him to mind his own business, Scripture does not say that Peter was offended. This is because he knew that everything that Jesus said to him came from a motive of love.

Father, I know that you only chasten and rebuke those whom you love.

Wait for the Power

While being together and eating with them, He commanded them not to leave Jerusalem, but to wait for what the Father had promised, "Of which," He said, "you have heard Me speak."

Acts 1:4

Jesus told his disciples that they would, in the near future, be baptized with the Holy Spirit. This is what the Father had promised. It was the fulfillment of Old Testament prophecies (and Jesus' own predictions) about the coming of the Holy Spirit (John 14:16–17; Joel 2:28–29). He then made a comparison of John's baptism with water and the baptism with the Holy Spirit. This signifies a transition from the old covenant to the new covenant. John's baptism was a symbolic act of repentance, while the baptism with the Holy Spirit signifies an inward transformation and empowerment for believers.

Jesus then told the disciples to stay in Jerusalem and wait. The wait reminds us that God has his perfect timing. "Those who wait on the Lord shall renew their strength; they shall mount up with wings like eagles, they shall run and not be weary, they shall walk and not faint" (Isaiah 40:31 NKJV).

Father, I need your power daily.

The Times

He said to them, "It is not for you to know the times or epochs which the Father has fixed by His own authority."
ACTS 1:7-8

Many find it of great interest to listen to speculations about the days and times in which we live. It is fascinating to watch prophecy unfold before our eyes. Perhaps we are looking for the rise of the antichrist or the mark of the beast, or we are watching as nation rises against nation and events grow volatile in the Middle East. It's not only an interesting study, but it's biblical to try to understand the hour in which we live. Otherwise God wouldn't have included these signs in the Bible.

However, there is something that is infinitely more important than deciphering current events, and that's the proclamation of the gospel. Through the gospel, perishing sinners can find peace with God and consequently have everlasting life. Nothing else really matters. If you read the book of Acts, you won't find that the disciples were continually going to prophecy conferences. Instead, they were proclaiming the everlasting gospel at the peril of their own lives. God will unfold biblical prophecies in time, as he sees fit. Meanwhile, we must continue to obey the Great Commission and preach the gospel to every creature.

Father, help me to keep my priorities straight.

Grounded in Christ

He fell to the ground and heard a voice [from heaven] saying to him, "Saul, Saul, why are you persecuting and oppressing Me?"

Acts 9:4

If you hear a voice from heaven that sounds like thunder, mentioning you by name, it's wise to answer in the way Saul answered. He said, "Who are You, Lord?" (v. 5). Besides, when God speaks to us, the best and safest place for us to be is on the ground. We dare not even look up because we have sinned against the Lord of the universe. In doing so, we identify with the dirt from which we are made. We are nothing but dust.

And that's what Saul of Tarsus did. He was on the road to damnation when the Son of God stopped him in his sinful tracks. And he did the same thing for you and me. He spoke to us and then took us from darkness to light, from the kingdom of Satan to the kingdom of God. And as he had a special mission for the apostle Paul, so he has one for us: to preach the gospel to every creature.

Father, the day will come when time will be no more. Help me to make good use of what I have.

Sight Is Coming

Now in Damascus there was a disciple named Ananias; and the Lord said to him in a vision, "Ananias."

Acts 9:10

In the verses that follow today's Scripture quote, the Lord said to Ananias, "Arise and go to the street called Straight, and inquire at the house of Judas for one called Saul of Tarsus, for behold, he is praying" (v. 11 NKJV). How fascinating it would have been to be a fly on the wall listening to the prayers of Saul of Tarsus. He had held the clothes of those that stoned Stephen to death, and the Scriptures tell us that he consented to Stephen's death. This man had also been torturing Christians to death when suddenly the voice of Jesus spoke to him from heaven.

Whatever Saul prayed during that dark time, no doubt he prayed with fear and trembling. He had sinned against the Lord. And yet God, in his great mercy, sent his servant Ananias to open Paul's blind eyes. There are many Sauls out there, waiting in their blindness for you and me to share with them the gospel that will open their blind eyes.

Father, please prepare the soil for me to plant seeds today.

I Have Heard Many Things

Ananias answered, "Lord, I have heard from many people about this man, especially how much suffering and evil he has brought on Your saints (God's people) at Jerusalem."

Acts 9:13

Ananias had seen the headlines and heard the rumors. He knew that Saul of Tarsus had gained the authority to imprison Christians. This was clearly an evil man. And yet Jesus was telling Ananias that this tyrant was somehow a chosen vessel. And Ananias had to go to the house of someone called Judas (of all people) and ask for Saul, who had apparently gone blind. Ananias was to pray for Saul's sight to be restored.

It was entirely understandable that Ananias would bristle at what God was telling him to do. But he did it anyway because he trusted God. And there are times in our lives when we are tempted to think that somehow God doesn't possess all the facts. But no matter how seemingly bizarre our orders may be, God has his purposes. Listen to the apostle Paul: "For this reason I obtained mercy, that in me first Jesus Christ might show all longsuffering, as a pattern to those who are going to believe on Him for everlasting life" (1 Timothy 1:16).

Father, your ways are infinitely above my ways.

Overcoming My Fears

One night the Lord said to Paul in a vision, "Do not be afraid anymore, but go on speaking and do not be silent."

ACTS 18:9

The Lord told Paul the reason he need not be afraid: God was with him. He had already steadfastly reasoned in the synagogue every Sabbath, and he was able to persuade both Jews and Greeks concerning Jesus. However, when he testified that Jesus was the Christ to certain Jews, there was serious opposition. When they blasphemed, "he shook his garments and said to them, 'Your blood be upon your own heads; I am clean. From now on I will go to the Gentiles'" (Acts 18:6 NKJV).

It was then that God gave Paul this vision, telling him to not be afraid. Paul, like each of us, battled with fear, but the Lord told him to continue preaching the gospel. Fear may torment us, but it should never silence us from fulfilling the Great Commission (Mark 16:15). Listen to how Paul overcame his fears: "For I determined not to know anything among you except Jesus Christ and Him crucified. I was with you in weakness, in fear, and in much trembling" (1 Corinthians 2:2–3 NKJV).

Father, may my determination to share the gospel overcome all my fears.

The Power of a Testimony

"I fell to the ground and heard a voice saying to me, 'Saul, Saul, why are you persecuting Me?'"

Acts 22:7

Don't let the dramatic nature of Paul's testimony discourage you from sharing yours. This is because yours is just as special. The fact that he gave his testimony three times in the book of Acts should be an encouragement to regularly tell sinners your own experience. It's your unique testimony of God's power in your life. An unbelieving world can say that they think that you're deluded, and they can disagree with you, but all they can do is give their opinion. We are to speak the truth in love, and if they reject it, that's between them and God. They can't take your experience from you.

Also, never denigrate your testimony. It's easy to do that when we hear of Christians who have had road to Damascus experiences. They were in gangs or addicted to drugs and alcohol. But your testimony isn't what the devil did to you. It's what God did for you. It is Jesus on the cross, suffering for our sins so we could live forever. That's a powerful testimony.

Father, may my testimony be a boast of your goodness.

Make Haste

"I saw Him saying to me, 'Hurry and get out of Jerusalem quickly, because they will not accept your testimony about Me.'"

ACTS 22:18

Paul was speaking in Jerusalem, recalling his conversion experience on the road to Damascus and the vision that followed. The phrase "Hurry and get out of Jerusalem quickly" emphasizes the urgency and divine direction God gave to Paul. It underscores the immediacy with which he wanted Paul to leave Jerusalem, indicating that his mission lay elsewhere. The statement "they will not accept your testimony about Me" shows the hostility Paul would face in Jerusalem.

Despite Paul's previous standing as a Pharisee, his former peers were not going to accept the message he now carried about Jesus. This vision of the future speaks to what would happen in the book of Acts, where Paul was increasingly directed to minister to the gentiles. The rejection in Jerusalem contrasts with the acceptance Paul finds among gentiles, marking a significant shift in the mission of the early church. These things are a consolation when we, too, are rejected because of the name of Jesus. Men will always love the darkness and hate the light.

Father, help me to preach the gospel in season and out of season.

The Clear Command

"The Lord said to me, 'Go, I will send you far away to the Gentiles.'"

ACTS 22:21

How encouraging it must have been for the apostle Paul to have such a clear command from Jesus himself. This wasn't a directive from one of the disciples. It came from Jesus, and he said to "Go!" Paul wasn't to stay where he was or become involved in other legitimate godly practices. Jesus said that he would send Paul far away to the gentiles. And how encouraging it is for us as Christians to also have a clear command from Jesus himself. He also told us to "Go," and he gave us specifics of where we are to go: "Go *into all the world* and preach the gospel to every creature" (Mark 16:15 NKJV, emphasis added).

We are to go near and far away—into *all* of the world and preach the glorious gospel to every person on earth. That's our clear agenda: "And how shall they preach unless they are sent? As it is written: 'How beautiful are the feet of those who preach the gospel of peace, who bring glad tidings of good things!'" (Romans 10:15 NKJV).

Father, how honored we are to preach your gospel.

Courage Can Be Taken

On the following night the Lord stood near Paul and said, "Be brave; for as you have solemnly and faithfully witnessed about Me at Jerusalem, so you must also testify at Rome."

Acts 23:11

Courage is something that we take—just as we take a deep breath. Joshua took courage as he prepared the people to enter the promised land. David took courage as he stood before a blaspheming Goliath. Ruth took courage as she went with Naomi to a place she didn't know. If we don't take courage, fear will take its place and paralyze us into inaction. The Jews at Jerusalem were plotting to kill Paul. There was such anger from a crowd to whom he'd spoken that the Roman commander, "fearing lest Paul might be pulled to pieces by them," told his soldiers to go down and take him by force. They were to bring him into the barracks for safekeeping (Acts 23:10 NKJV). And during that dark night, Jesus stood at Paul's side and told him to take courage.

We live in dark times. This evil world hates us because we belong to Jesus and stand for righteousness. But we are to take courage because he stands by our side. We are not alone in this battle: "What then shall we say to these things? If God is for us, who can be against us" (Romans 8:31 NKJV).

Father, today I take courage because you are for me.

Do This in Remembrance

When He had given thanks, He broke it [the bread][9] and said, "This is (represents) My body, which is [offered as a sacrifice] for you. Do this in [affectionate] remembrance of Me."

1 Corinthians 11:24

Jesus told us why we partake in communion. We do it in remembrance of him. Also, Jesus often used metaphorical language in his teachings. He referred to himself as the "bread of life" (John 6:35) and the "door" (John 10:9). Metaphorically interpreting "This is My body" (Luke 22:19 NKJV) and "This cup is the new covenant in My blood" (v. 20 NKJV) aligns with this pattern.

Again, Jesus explicitly said, "Do this in remembrance of Me." The purpose of the act is commemorative, indicating that the bread and wine are symbols to remember his sacrifice. It's also obvious that it wasn't his literal flesh and literal blood because he was literally there with his disciples. He was speaking spiritually: "It is the Spirit who gives life; the flesh profits nothing. The words that I speak to you are spirit, and they are life" (John 6:63 NKJV).

Father, may communion always be a solemn time of self-reflection.

---

9 Words added for the sake of clarification.

Grace Is Sufficient

He has said to me, "My grace is sufficient for you [My lovingkindness and My mercy are more than enough—always available—regardless of the situation]; for [My] power is being perfected [and is completed and shows itself most effectively] in [your] weakness." Therefore, I will all the more gladly boast in my weaknesses, so that the power of Christ [may completely enfold me and] may dwell in me.

2 Corinthians 12:9

We may think that today's verse is giving us an answer to the dilemma of "unanswered prayer." But in reality, Paul's prayer *was* answered. It just wasn't answered in the way that he desired. It was rather answered in the way that God desired. We don't know what his prayer request was, but we do know that God left him with that weakness for a good reason.

For more than fifty years, I have battled fear when it comes to sharing my faith. It's always there. I've asked God many times to release me from fear, but he hasn't. This is because if I didn't fear before I approached a stranger, I wouldn't bother praying. So that fear continually keeps me humbled and trusting God rather than in my own fearless ability. My weakness has become my strength. Therefore, most gladly I will boast about my weaknesses, so that the power of Christ may dwell in me.

Father, your wisdom is awesome.

He Never Changes

"I am the Alpha and the Omega [the Beginning and the End]," says the Lord God, "Who is [existing forever] and Who was [continually existing in the past] and Who is to come, the Almighty [the Omnipotent, the Ruler of all]."

REVELATION 1:8

Alpha (A) and Omega (W) are the first and last letters of the Greek alphabet, indicating that God encompasses all of time and existence. This emphasizes his eternality and his authority over the beginning and the end of all things. There is, however, some controversy from Bible scholars as to who is saying, "I am the Alpha and the Omega [the Beginning and the End]" (v. 8). Some say that it is Jesus who was speaking, and others believe that it is the Father because it uses the title "Almighty" (v. 8). Whatever the case, there can be no argument as to Jesus being the beginning and the end. The Bible says, "Jesus Christ is the same yesterday, today, and forever" (Hebrews 13:8 NKJV).

The phrase "He who is and who was and who is to come" highlights his unchanging nature. It reassures believers that his character and promises remain constant throughout time. This continuity provides a foundation for faith, as God's nature and his plans are reliable and steadfast.

Father, because you never change, I can always trust you.

The Seven Churches

"Write on a scroll what you see [in this revelation], and send it to the seven churches—to Ephesus and to Smyrna and to Pergamum and to Thyatira and to Sardis and to Philadelphia and to Laodicea."

REVELATION 1:11

Jesus revealed the condition of each of the seven churches he addressed in the early chapters of the book of Revelation:

- Ephesus had abandoned their first love (Revelation 2:4).
- Smyrna was encouraged to remain faithful in the face of suffering and persecution (Revelation 2:10).
- Pergamum had tolerated those who taught false doctrines and engaged in idolatry and immorality (Revelation 2:14–15).
- Thyatira had tolerated a false prophetess who led members into sexual immorality and idolatry (Revelation 2:20).
- Sardis had a reputation for being alive but was spiritually dead, with incomplete works before God (Revelation 3:1–2).
- Philadelphia was commended for keeping God's Word and not denying his name (Revelation 3:8).
- And the people of the Laodicean church were lukewarm, neither hot nor cold, and were spiritually complacent and self-satisfied, failing to recognize their need for Christ (Revelation 3:15–17).

It would seem that we are in the Laodicean era, as many contemporary churches lack zeal for God. May we never be guilty of becoming lukewarm for our God.

Father, never let me lose my first love or become lukewarm in my Christian walk.

Do Not Be Afraid

"Do not be afraid; I am the First and the Last [absolute Deity, the Son of God], and the Ever-living One [living in and beyond all time and space]."

REVELATION 1:17–18

In the face of uncertainty and fears in life, the words of Jesus provide great comfort because we know who he is. His identity as "the First and the Last" underscores his sovereignty and control over all things, offering believers a sense of security. By declaring himself as "the Ever-living One," he asserts his divinity and eternal existence. This aligns with the Old Testament depiction of God, thus affirming his divine nature and his oneness with God the Father.

"Thus says the LORD, the King of Israel, and his Redeemer, the LORD of hosts: 'I am the First and I am the Last; besides Me there is no God'" (Isaiah 44:6 NKJV). It highlights his authority over time and existence and reinforces the belief in his supreme power. It also signifies that Jesus has conquered death and lives forever, which offers believers hope in their own resurrection and eternal life. His victory over death is a cornerstone of our faith, emphasizing that through him, believers can share in this triumph.

Father, I will not be afraid because you are faithful.

The Ultimate Keys

"I died, but see, I am alive forevermore, and I have the keys of [absolute control and victory over] death and of Hades (the realm of the dead)."

REVELATION 1:18

If we possess the keys to a safe or a house or a car, we have control and authority over that thing. In today's verse, Jesus affirmed that he has the ultimate keys—the keys to death. He unlocked death to set us free and locked it up so that it could never touch us again. God has given him both legal and absolute authority over the enemy of death. It's often said that if something seems too good to be true, it probably is. That is not the case with this. Death has no dominion over Jesus of Nazareth, and it has no dominion over those who belong to him.

Scripture teaches that Jesus' victory over death is our victory: "Now if we died with Christ, we believe that we shall also live with Him, knowing that Christ, having been raised from the dead, dies no more. Death no longer has dominion over Him" (Romans 6:8–9 NKJV). What a glorious gospel we have in Christ! What a glorious future we have because of his amazing love!

Father, thank you for the victory we have over death.

The Number Seven

"To the angel (divine messenger) of the church in Ephesus write: 'These are the words of the One who holds [firmly] the seven stars [which are the angels or messengers of the seven churches] in His right hand, the One who walks among the seven golden lampstands (the seven churches).'"

REVELATION 2:1

Scripture introduces the message to the church in Ephesus, delivered by Jesus himself. The verse emphasizes his authority and intimate relationship with the church. The "angel" or "divine messenger" refers to the spiritual representative or leader of the church, entrusted with its care and guidance. Jesus, described as the one who holds the "seven stars" in his right hand, demonstrates his sovereign control and protection over the messengers of the seven churches. His control symbolizes his ultimate authority.

The imagery of Jesus walking among the "seven golden lampstands" conveys his active presence within the churches. The lampstands, representing the seven churches, highlight believers' roles as bearers of light in a dark world. By walking among them, Jesus assures his continual oversight, care, and evaluation of his people. This vivid description reminds believers of Christ's closeness and his expectations for faithfulness, love, and obedience. It sets the tone for the subsequent messages in the book of Revelation, emphasizing accountability and the importance of remaining steadfast in devotion to him.

Father, thank you for caring intimately about each local church.

The Ministry of Angels

"To the angel (divine messenger) of the church in Smyrna write: 'These are the words of the First and the Last [absolute Deity, the Son of God] who died and came to life [again].'"

REVELATION 2:8

Angels often act as God's messengers, delivering important messages to human beings. For example, the angel Gabriel announced the birth of Jesus to Mary (Luke 1:26–38) and appeared to Zechariah to announce the birth of John the Baptist (vv. 11–20). Angels are also depicted as protectors of God's people. An angel protected Daniel in the lion's den (Daniel 6:22). Scripture depicts angels as mighty warriors in spiritual battles. Michael the archangel leads God's army against Satan and his forces. In Revelation 12:7–9 there is a description of a war in heaven where Michael and his angels fight against the dragon (Satan) and his angels. Angels can also provide guidance. An angel guided Philip to the Ethiopian eunuch to share the gospel with him (Acts 8:26–40), and angels led Lot and his family out of Sodom before its destruction (Genesis 19:15–17).

Look now at how angels can help us: "But to which of the angels has He ever said: 'Sit at My right hand, till I make Your enemies Your footstool'? Are they not all ministering spirits sent forth to minister for those who will inherit salvation?" (Hebrews 1:13–24). God often works through angels to serve his people, as the Scriptures reveal. You have likely benefited from their ministry and may not have even known it.

Father, may your angels go before me today.

Mine Eyes Have Seen

"To the angel (divine messenger) of the church in Pergamum write: 'These are the words of Him who has and wields the sharp two-edged sword [in judgment].'"

REVELATION 2:12

The same sharp, two-edged sword of the Word of God that brought creation into being on the first day will bring swift judgment on the last day. When God said, "Let there be light," there was light. And the day will come when the light of his perfect righteousness will seek out the darkness of every evil word and deed and bring swift retribution, as we sing in "The Battle Hymn of the Republic":

> Mine eyes have seen the glory of the coming of the Lord.
> He is trampling out the vintage where the grapes of wrath are stored.
> He hath loosed the fateful lightning of his terrible swift sword.[10]

Our agenda as Christians is to warn every human soul that God will have his day of judgment and that they desperately need a savior. The hymn writer captured the urgency of our message:

> He is sifting out the hearts of men before his judgment seat.
> Oh, be swift, my soul, to answer him! Be jubilant, my feet![11]

Father, stir me to faithfully warn this wicked world.

---

10 "Battle Hymn of the Republic," written by Julia Ward Howe, 1862, public domain.

11 "Battle Hymn of the Republic."

Fiery Indignation

"To the angel (divine messenger) of the church in Thyatira write: 'These are the words of the Son of God, who has eyes [that flash] like a flame of fire [in righteous judgment], and whose feet are like burnished [white-hot] bronze.'"

REVELATION 2:18

The eyes of the Son of God flash like a flame of fire. Behind them is a fiery indignation that is coming like livid lightning to this evil world. Scripture warns, "The Lord Jesus [will be] revealed from heaven with His mighty angels, in flaming fire taking vengeance on those who do not know God, and on those who do not obey the gospel of our Lord Jesus Christ" (2 Thessalonians 1:7–8 NKJV).

What a fearful day that will be, when sinful men cry out to the mountains and rocks, "Fall on us and hide us from the face of Him who sits on the throne and from the wrath of the Lamb! For the great day of His wrath has come, and who is able to stand?" (Revelation 6:16–17 NKJV). Although God is angry with the wicked every day, he takes no pleasure in their death. He is rich in mercy to all who call upon him.

Father, today fill my heart with empathy for the unsaved.

Rest in "Peace"

"To the angel (divine messenger) of the church in Sardis write: 'These are the words of Him who has the seven Spirits of God and the seven stars: I know your deeds; you have a name (reputation) that you are alive, but [in reality] you are dead.'"

REVELATION 3:1

There is no greater example of a parade of lies than that which is often heard at the funeral of an ungodly man. God knows his deeds. His sins still cling to him as fleas to a dog. He has a multitude of sins from a lifetime of lust, greed, envy, pride, jealousy, anger, and hatred that have built up like a massive dam that will burst on him on the day of wrath. And yet these wrongs are merely the sins of his mind. They don't include his lies, theft, fornication, and adultery.

Still, the world says he was a good man, and they believe that he will rest in peace. But Scripture warns of no such peace; rather, it says that he will be torn from his grave by the fierce justice of Almighty God to give an account over every idle word and sinful deed. On that day, no one will rest in peace unless they are trusting in the shed blood of the Prince of Peace.

Father, give me opportunity to warn a lost sinner today.

The Greatest of All Doors

"To the angel (divine messenger) of the church in Philadelphia write: 'These are the words of the Holy One, the True One, He who has the key [to the house] of David, He who opens and no one will [be able to] shut, and He who shuts and no one opens.'"

REVELATION 3:7

God opened many doors in Scripture. He opened doors for Peter as he awaited his fate in Herod's prison. He opened doors for Paul to preach the glorious gospel to the gentiles. He opened the doors of the Red Sea so that the children of Israel would escape the armies of Pharaoh. He wonderfully opened doors for Joseph to become a ruler in Egypt.

But the greatest of all doors that God has opened are the doors of heaven. In Jesus' dark and cold tomb, a warmth began to move through the flesh of the three-days-dead Son of God, and his heart miraculously began to beat. Those tiny beats of that heart signified the opening of the doors of immortality for a lost and dying human race. And the golden key that unlocked the doors was the key of the grace of God.

Father, I will be forever grateful for your amazing grace.

The Amen

"To the angel (divine messenger) of the church in Laodicea write: 'These are the words of the Amen, the trusted and faithful and true Witness, the Beginning and Origin of God's creation.'"

REVELATION 3:14

Laodicea was known for its wealth and self-sufficiency, yet the Lord criticized the church there for being lukewarm in its faith. The word *amen* signifies certainty, truth, and affirmation. In the context of today's Scripture verse, it refers to Jesus, highlighting his role as the one who brings ultimate truth and reliability. He is the "Amen" in the sense that he is the final word, the one who confirms and fulfills God's promises.

Then Jesus describes himself as being trustworthy, faithful, and true. This emphasizes his reliability and the accuracy of his testimony. As a "Witness," Jesus testifies to the truth of God's nature, plans, and wonderful promises. His words and actions reflect God's will perfectly. And the words "the Beginning" mean that Jesus is the source or origin, indicating that he's the divine agent through whom all things were made. He is not a created being but the originator of creation itself, emphasizing his divine nature and eternal existence.

Father, Jesus has proved himself to be trustworthy, faithful, and true.

Watch Like a Hawk

"Behold, I am coming like a thief."
REVELATION 16:15

This Christmas season, we celebrate the miraculous gift of Jesus Christ, who first came into the world as a humble baby and was laid in a manger. His arrival brought hope, peace, and salvation, fulfilling God's promise to redeem humanity. As we reflect on his first coming, we are reminded of his love, humility, and sacrifice. We are reminded of a Savior who stepped into our darkness to bring light to the world.

Yet the story of Jesus doesn't end with the manger or the cross. In Revelation 16:15, Jesus declares, "Behold, I am coming like a thief." Just as a thief in biblical times came unexpectedly, Christ's second coming will take the world by surprise. Unlike his first arrival in humility, his return will be in power and glory, bringing judgment and establishing his eternal kingdom.

This Christmas, let us not only remember the baby in the manger but also prepare our hearts for Jesus' promised return:

> He has sounded forth the trumpet that shall never call retreat;
> He is sifting out the hearts of men before His judgment seat;
> Oh, be swift, my soul, to answer Him; be jubilant, my feet!
> Our God is marching on.[12]

Blessed are those who watch and are ready to welcome him.

Father, remind me to continually be on my watch.

---

12 "Battle Hymn of the Republic."

The Shame of Our Nakedness

"Blessed is he who stays awake and who keeps his clothes [that is, stays spiritually ready for the Lord's return], so that he will not be naked—spiritually unprepared—and men will not see his shame."

REVELATION 16:15

When sin entered the garden of Eden, both Adam and Eve were suddenly ashamed of their nakedness. Therefore, God killed an animal to cover their shame. Likewise, Jesus was killed to cover our shame on judgment day, when every human being will stand exposed in their nakedness before a holy God. Scripture reveals their inward thoughts: "They slay the widow and the stranger, and murder the fatherless. Yet they say, 'The LORD does not see, nor does the God of Jacob understand'" (Psalm 94:6–7 NKJV).

How deluded we are before God opens our eyes! If he made our eyes, of course he can see everything we do and think. And Scripture warns that each of us is accountable: "Neither is there any creature that is not manifest in his sight: but all things are naked and opened unto the eyes of him with whom we have to do" (Hebrews 4:13 KJV).

Father, may I be always aware of your holy presence.

Faster than Lightning

"Behold, I am coming quickly."
REVELATION 22:7

When we read the five words Jesus said in today's Scripture quote, it should remind us that he is divine. Only God speaks in such a way. His "quickly" isn't our quickly. He spoke these words two thousand long years ago. It's hard to reconcile this until we realize that a day to the Lord is a thousand years to us. "Beloved, do not forget this one thing, that with the Lord one day is as a thousand years, and a thousand years as one day" (2 Peter 3:8 NKJV).

It's difficult for our finite minds to understand that the God who created lightning also created the snail. He can move faster than the speed of light, but when we wait on him to do something for us, he seems to move so very slowly. We pray for years to see the fulfillment of what we believe is urgent, and yet heaven remains silent. It's because of our human frailty that lions' dens put us in panic prayer mode. But the knowledge that God never panics—because he sees the outcome of all things—can give us peace and patience in every circumstance, no matter how seemingly dire.

Father, help me to always be patient in tribulation.

Take It to Heart

"Blessed (happy, prosperous, to be admired) is the one who heeds and takes to heart and remembers the words of the prophecy [that is, the predictions, consolations, and warnings] contained in this book (scroll)."

REVELATION 22:7

This truth certainly is a consolation that gives us great peace in the perilous times in which we live. What a blessing it is to know that God knows the beginning from the end. This unique book, the book of Revelation—fearful though it is in places as it speaks of deadly plagues, God's terrifying wrath against sin, and great battles in the future—tells us who wins in the end. Good triumphs over evil, God triumphs over the devil, and because of God's unfathomable grace, we triumph over our greatest enemy—death itself.

The Scriptures say that we are blessed if we remember the things that are written in this book. In these troubled times, it is easy to forget that God knows everything from the absolute beginning to the absolute end. That's why we must discipline ourselves to regularly call to remembrance the predictions, the many consolations, and the fearsome warnings contained in this sacred volume. Blessed is the one who heeds and takes to heart and remembers what is in the book of Revelation.

Father, help me to remember that nothing catches you off guard.

The Benevolence of God

"Behold, I (Jesus) am coming quickly, and My reward is with Me, to give to each one according to the merit of his deeds (earthly works, faithfulness)."

REVELATION 22:12–13

We just have to look around us to see the benevolence of God. He has lavished us with kindness by giving us a beautiful blue sky with big puffy white clouds, the sunrise and sunset, the birds singing in the morning, the gorgeous array of flowers, the magnificent trees, and the fascinating animals. Beyond this, God grants us the blessings of love and laughter, of friends and family. All these things reveal to us the generosity and benevolence of a God who is the lover of our souls.

But when we think of what he did through the cross and how he has granted us everlasting life, our mouths should stop at his goodness. And on top of all this, he has rewards waiting for those who love him, and these rewards are like nothing we've ever seen on this earth. The Bible says our eyes have not seen, neither has it even entered the imagination of any human being, the wonderful things that God has prepared for those that love him.

Father, I can hardly begin to comprehend your unending kindness.

The Root of Jesse

"I am the Root (the Source, the Life) and the Offspring of David, the radiant and bright Morning Star."
REVELATION 22:16

Jesus not only called himself the Source of all life, but he referred to himself as the offspring of David. When Scripture identifies Christ as the son of David, it shows that he fulfilled Old Testament prophecies such as those in Isaiah 11:1 and Jeremiah 23:5, which foretold that the Messiah would come from David's lineage. Also, this title emphasizes Jesus' legitimate claim to the throne of Israel, highlighting his royal heritage through David, the revered and beloved king of Israel.

Both Matthew and Luke trace Jesus' genealogy back to David (Matthew 1:1–16; Luke 3:23–38), reinforcing his identity as the promised descendant. And in Mark 10:47–48, the blind beggar Bartimaeus called Jesus "Son of David" because he recognized Jesus as the Messiah who could heal and save him. We also see that Jesus fulfilled the covenant God made with David, promising that his descendants would reign forever (2 Samuel 7:12–16). The eternal kingship of Jesus of Nazareth is the ultimate fulfillment of this promise.

Father, thank you for making the identity of Jesus so clear.

The Water of Life

"I, Jesus, have sent My angel to testify to you and to give you assurance of these things for the churches..." The [Holy] Spirit and the bride (the church, believers) say, "Come." And let the one who hears say, "Come." And let the one who is thirsty come; let the one who wishes take and drink the water of life without cost.

REVELATION 22:16–17

More than twenty-eight hundred years ago, the prophet Isaiah spoke of this universal offer to the whole of humanity, irrespective of fame or fortune, race or color—all are precious in God's sight.

> "Ho! Everyone who thirsts,
> Come to the waters;
> And you who have no money,
> Come, buy and eat.
> Yes, come, buy wine and milk
> Without money and without price." (Isaiah 55:1 NKJV)

Then eight hundred years later, Jesus stood amid the crowds in Jerusalem and cried out, "If anyone thirsts, let him come to Me and drink. He who believes in Me, as the Scripture has said, out of his heart will flow rivers of living water" (John 7:37–38 NKJV). Wonder of wonders, everlasting life is now the free gift of God for all who thirst for life.

Father, give me courage to follow the example of Jesus.

About the Author

Ray Comfort is the best-selling author of more than one hundred books. He is the cohost of an award-winning television program that airs in 190 countries and the producer of award-winning movies that have been viewed by millions (see www.FullyFreeFilms.com). He lives in Southern California with his wife, Sue, and has three grown children. For more information, visit LivingWaters.com.